International Mobility in the Military Orders
(Twelfth to Fifteenth Centuries)

International Mobility in the Military Orders (Twelfth to Fifteenth Centuries): Travelling on Christ's Business

Edited by

JOCHEN BURGTORF and HELEN NICHOLSON

THE UNIVERSITY OF ALABAMA PRESS
Tuscaloosa

The University of Alabama Press
Tuscaloosa, Alabama 35487-0380
Copyright © 2006 The University of Wales Press

First published as part of the Religion and Culture in the Middle Ages
series, edited by Denis Renevey (University of Lausanne) and Diane
Watt (University of Wales, Aberystwyth).

∞

The paper on which this book is printed meets the minimum
requirements of American National Standard for Information
Science—Permanence of Paper for Printed Library Materials,
ANSI Z39.48-1984.

Library of Congress Cataloging-in-Publication Data

International Mobility in the Military Orders (Twelfth to Fifteenth
Centuries) : Travelling on Christ's Business / Edited by Jochen Burgtorf
and Helen Nicholson.
        p. cm.
Includes bibliographical references and index.
ISBN-13: 978-0-8173-1512-2 (cloth : alk paper)
ISBN-10: 0-8173-1512-8 (alk paper)
1. Military religious orders I. Burgtorf, Jochen. II. Nicholson, Helen J.,
1960—

2005051413

Printed in Great Britain by Cromwell Press, Trowbridge, Wiltshire

CONTENTS

Figures

Notes on Contributors

Jean-Marie Allard works at the Bibliothèque municipale de Limoges. He is a member of the Centre des recherches historiques et archéologiques at the Université de Limoges, where he also received his doctorate degree. He recently published: 'Templiers et Hospitaliers en Limousin au Moyen Age', *Revue Mabillon* 14 (2003; with B. Barrière).

Elena Bellomo received her Ph.D. from the Università Cattolica del Sacro Cuore in Milan. She has published numerous articles on the crusades as well as the Templars in northern Italy and has recently completed a book on Caffaro of Genoa: *A servizio di Dio e del Santo Sepolcro: Caffaro e l'Oriente latino* (Padua, 2003).

Pierre Bonneaud received his doctorate degree from the École des Hautes Études en Sciences Sociales in Paris. His research concerning the Hospitaller priory of Catalonia has produced several articles as well as a new book: *Le prieuré de Catalogne, le couvent de Rhodes et la couronne d'Aragon, 1415–1447* (Millau, 2004).

Judith Bronstein teaches in the Department of Land of Israel Studies at the University of Haifa. She received her Ph.D. from the University of Cambridge and has published several articles on the Hospitallers as well as a book, *The Hospitallers and the Holy Land: Financing the Latin East, 1187–1274* (Woodbridge, 2005).

Jochen Burgtorf is Associate Professor of Medieval World History in the Department of History at California State University, Fullerton. He has published several articles on the Templars and Hospitallers in the Latin east and is currently working on a book concerning the leadership structures of these orders (twelfth to early fourteenth centuries).

Maria Cristina Cunha is Professor Auxiliar in the Department of History at the Universidade do Porto. Her research focuses on the military orders in Portugal as well as the archiepiscopal chancery of medieval Braga. She has published several articles on the orders of Avis and Calatrava.

ALAIN DEMURGER is Maître de conférences honoraire in Medieval History at the Université de Paris I. He has published extensively on the history of the crusades and the military orders. His books include: *Jacques de Molay* (Paris, 2002), *Chevaliers du Christ* (Paris, 2002) and *Vie et mort de l'ordre du Temple* (Paris, 1985).

AXEL EHLERS earned an M.Phil. from the University of Cambridge and a Ph.D. from the Georg-August-Universität Göttingen. He has published several articles on the Teutonic Knights as well as on Hartmann Grisar's 'unfinished' edition of papal documents and is currently working on a book concerning the indulgences for the Teutonic Knights.

ALAN FOREY has taught at the universities of Oxford, St Andrews and Durham. His extensive publications include: *The Fall of the Templars in the Crown of Aragon* (Aldershot, 2001), *The Military Orders from the Twelfth to the Early Fourteenth Centuries* (London, 1992) and *The Templars in the Corona de Aragón* (London, 1973).

ZSOLT HUNYADI is Assistant Lecturer in the Department of Medieval and Early Modern Hungarian History at the University of Szeged. He recently completed his Ph.D. dissertation on 'Hospitallers in the medieval kingdom of Hungary, c.1150–1387' at the Central European University, Budapest. His research has yielded numerous articles.

KAY PETER JANKRIFT is Privatdozent of Medieval History at the Westfälische Wilhelms-Universität Münster. His research focuses on the history of medicine and the urban response to famine, epidemics and natural disasters. His extensive publications include a history of the Order of Saint Lazarus: *Leprose als Streiter Gottes* (Münster, 1996).

DAVID MARCOMBE is Senior Lecturer in Local History and Director of the Centre for Local History at the University of Nottingham. His books include: *The Saint and the Swan: The Life and Times of St Hugh of Lincoln* (Lincoln, 2000) and *Leper Knights: The Order of St Lazarus of Jerusalem in England, c.1150–1544* (Woodbridge, 2003).

HELEN NICHOLSON is Reader in History at Cardiff University. Her books include: *Love, War and the Grail: Templars, Hospitallers and Teutonic Knights in Medieval Epic and Romance 1150–1500* (Leiden, 2000) and *Templars, Hospitallers and Teutonic Knights: Images of the Military Orders* (Leicester, 1993).

JÜRGEN SARNOWSKY is Professor of Medieval History at the Universität Hamburg. His extensive publications on the military orders include: *Macht und Herrschaft im Johanniterorden des 15. Jahrhunderts* (Münster, 2001) and *Die Wirtschaftsführung des Deutschen Ordens in Preussen (1382–1454)* (Cologne, 1993).

KLAUS VAN EICKELS is Professor of Medieval History at the Otto-Friedrich-Universität Bamberg. His recent research has focused on the Anglo-French relationship. His numerous publications on the Teutonic Knights include *Die Deutschordensballei Koblenz und ihre wirtschaftliche Entwicklung im Spätmittelalter* (Marburg 1995).

THERESA M. VANN is the Joseph S. Micallef curator at the Malta Study Centre of the Hill Monastic Manuscript Library at St John's University in Collegeville, Minnesota. Her research focuses on the military orders as well as medieval Spain. Her publications include numerous articles as well as the collection *Queens, Regents and Potentates* (Dallas, 1993).

CHRISTIAN VOGEL is a Ph.D. candidate at Heinrich-Heine-Universität Düsseldorf where he is working on a dissertation concerning the Templars' legal history. His MA thesis dealt with the bishops in the metropolitan province of Narbonne at the time of the Albigensian Wars, 1179–1229, and is currently being prepared for publication.

PREFACE

If you wish to be in the land on this side of the sea you will be sent to the other side.

French Rule of the Templars, § 661

The military religious orders developed out of the reform movement in the Latin Church which had started in the eleventh and continued into the twelfth century. Their members combined the three vows of the monastic orders (obedience, poverty and chastity) with a commitment to protect Latin Christendom. The primary area of operation for these orders was the cluster of four Latin Christian states set up in the Middle East in the wake of the First Crusade of 1095–9, but other orders were established in other fields of conflict, notably the Iberian peninsula and the Baltic region. Many began as hospital orders, caring for poor and sick Christian pilgrims, or in the case of the Order of St Lazarus for lepers, but some were set up with a purely military function, although these were also responsible for the upkeep of hospices which cared for pilgrims.

All military religious orders received donations of property from their supporters in regions far from their original areas of operation. The three largest orders, the Templars, the Hospitallers and the Teutonic Knights, began their military activities in the kingdom of Jerusalem in the twelfth century and held property throughout the area now called Europe. They recruited the bulk of their members and raised income for their military operations far from the frontier regions where their military activities took place. It was therefore necessary for them to develop systems for moving personnel and resources from the places of recruitment and production to the places of use. In addition, because their administrative centres were in the Middle East or, in the case of the Teutonic Order after 1309, in Prussia, they had to develop systems of communication to keep their members in the west informed of the needs of their headquarters and to ensure that those administering the orders' properties far from the centre of military operations remained focused on the orders' actual needs and did not become diverted into local needs and priorities. Provincial commanders and priors had to be summoned periodically to headquarters to report on events in their provinces and to give an account of their stewardship, while officials had to be sent out to the provinces on a regular basis as 'visitors' to ensure that all was operating as it should, that income was being collected efficiently and that the appropriate portion was remitted to headquarters. Thus, the mobility of personnel and resources was seldom voluntary; it required obedience and had to be enforced. Those joining the orders were warned that they would have no voice in whether or not they were sent overseas, as indicated in the extract from the Templars' reception ceremony quoted at the beginning of this preface. Members of the orders travelled under the compulsion of their religious vow of obedience, as part of their service for Christ: as indicated in the title of this volume, they were travelling on Christ's business.

Research into the military religious orders has always reflected the geographical diversity of the orders, yet until now there has been no in-depth assessment of how and to what extent the orders actually moved personnel and resources around Christendom. In 2002 the theme of the International Medieval Congress at the University of Leeds, England, was 'Exile'. We judged that this would be a suitable occasion to explore the problem of international mobility within the military religious orders more extensively than had hitherto been attempted. We organized four sessions on the theme, and the majority of the papers in this volume are based on those given in Leeds. We are delighted that it has been possible to include additional papers here to give a fuller picture: those by Jean-Marie Allard, Maria Cristina Cunha, Kay Peter Jankrift, David Marcombe and Christian Vogel. We are also very grateful to Alan Forey, whose contribution to the development of research on the military religious orders over the last three decades has been immense, for writing an introduction and contributing to the conclusion. Thus, this collection brings together seventeen scholars from different academic generations as well as residents of nine different countries (France, Germany, Great Britain, Hungary, Israel, Italy, Portugal, Spain and the United States of America).

In a period before the emergence of the nation state, the use of the term 'international' is anachronistic, but we have used it here because it has the virtue of familiarity to readers who are not specialists in medieval political structures but who are interested in the history of the military religious orders. Contributors have interpreted 'international mobility' in different ways, to mean movement of personnel, resources and even information in and out of a geographical region, such as north-western Italy or the British Isles, or an area under a single regnal authority, such as Hungary, or a region of linguistic or ethnic solidarity, such as Catalonia. The papers concentrate on 'horizontal' movement, which did not necessarily involve promotion within the order, rather than 'vertical' movement, movement up and down the scale of authority within the orders. Some of the contributors have referred to 'Europe': this is a term that was seldom used in the medieval period, but it is used here for convenience and clarity to mean the area that the brothers of the military religious orders in the Latin east would have called 'outremer' – overseas (while their counterparts in the west would have used the same term, that is 'outremer', to refer to the eastern Mediterranean).

Although much of the mobility in the military religious orders was prompted by military needs, the papers here do not offer detailed study of the military campaigns of the orders or of the wider crusading context. Both have been considered by many excellent specialist works and it is not our intention to duplicate these here.

In editing this volume we have endeavoured to reflect the changes within the organization of the military religious orders over a period of four centuries and reconcile the demands of various national identities without confusing our readers. So, for instance, the chief executive of the Hospital of St John is referred to as 'the master' for the period before 1300 and 'the grand master' after that date, when the latter title had come into common usage within the order. The names of members of the orders have usually been given in the vernacular form most familiar to English-speaking readers. Where this has not seemed appropriate, the alternative forms of the name have been given together at first reference. While scholars agree over the standard abbreviations for most of the archives used by historians of the military religious orders, in some cases they differ. Rather than cause an international dispute by insisting on one abbreviation or another, we have allowed contributors to use their own preferred abbreviations, and these are set out clearly in the notes to their papers.

We would like to thank the editors at University of Wales Press, past and present, for their help in the production of this volume: Duncan Campbell, Claire Powell, Sarah Lewis and Leah Jenkins. We would also like to thank Susan Edgington for her comments. We are especially grateful to Kelly Donovan of California State University, Fullerton, for producing the maps, as well as to Reyes Fidalgo, Heather Carter, Daniel McClure and Kenneth Shonk for their help with linguistic issues, procuring rare books and compiling the index. The original conference sessions were sponsored by the Society for the Study of the Crusades and the Latin East and the Central European University, Budapest, and we thank them for their support.

Jochen Burgtorf and Helen Nicholson
Fullerton and Cardiff, August 2005

ABBREVIATIONS

ACA	Barcelona, Archivio de la Corona de Aragón
ACA, AGP	Barcelona, Archivio de la Corona de Aragón, Archivio de Gran Priorado
ACA, CRD	Barcelona, Archivio de la Corona de Aragón, Cartas reales diplomaticás
ACA, RC	Barcelona, Archivio de la Corona de Aragón, Cancellería real
ADép.	Strasbourg, Archives départementales du Bas-Rhin
ADHG	Toulouse, Archives départementales de la Haute-Garonne
AN	Paris, Archives Nationales
AOM	Valletta, Malta, National Library (of Malta), Archives of (the Order of) Malta
ARiDO	Utrecht, Archieven van de Ridderlijke Duitsche Orde, Balije van Utrecht
ASV	Città del Vaticano, Archivio Segreto Vaticano
ASV, Reg. Lat.	Città del Vaticano, Archivio Segreto Vaticano, Codex Reginensis Latinus
BL	London, British Library
BN	Paris, Bibliothèque Nationale
BN, n.a.l.	Paris, Bibliothèque Nationale, nouvelles acquisitions latines
CCR	*Calendar of the Close Rolls Preserved in the Public Record Office, Prepared under the Superintendence of the Deputy Keeper of the Records* (London, 1892–1963)
CEPR	*Calendar of Entries in the Papal Registers Relating to Great Britain and Ireland: Papal Letters*, ed. William H. Bliss et al., 14 vols (London, 1893–1960)
CLR	*Calendar of the Liberate Rolls Preserved in the Public Record Office, Prepared under the Superintendence of the Deputy Keeper of the Records: Henry III* (London, 1914–64)

CPR	*Calendar of the Patent Rolls Preserved in the Public Record Office, Prepared under the Superintendence of the Deputy Keeper of the Records* (London, 1891–1939)
Df.	Hungary, National Archives, *Collectio Antamohacsiana*, Diplomatics Photocopy Collection
Dl.	Hungary, National Archives, *Collectio Antamohacsiana*, Diplomatics Archives
DOZA	Vienna, Zentralarchiv des Deutschen Ordens
DOZA, Urk.	Vienna, Zentralarchiv des Deutschen Ordens, Abteilung Urkunden
Finke, AA	Heinrich Finke, *Acta Aragonensia: Quellen zur deutschen, italienischen, französischen, spanischen, zur Kirchen- und Kulturgeschichte, aus der diplomatischen Korrespondenz Jaymes II. (1291–1327)*, 3 vols (Berlin, 1908–22)
GRO	Gloucestershire Record Office
GStA-PK	Berlin, Geheimes Staatsarchiv, Preußischer Kulturbesitz
HStA	Stuttgart, Hauptstaatsarchiv
MS Bod.	Oxford, Bodleian Library, MS Bodley
NLM	Valletta, Malta, National Library of Malta, Archives of the Order of St John/Archives of the Hospital
Rot. lit. claus.	*Rotuli litterarum clausarum in Turri Londinensi asservati*, ed. Thomas D. Hardy, 2 vols (London, 1833–44)
Rot. lit. pat.	*Rotuli litterarum patentium in Turri Londinensi asservati*, ed. Thomas D. Hardy (London, 1835)
StA	Marburg, Staatsarchiv
TNA: PRO	The National Archives of the UK: Public Record Office
TNA: PRO, SC	The National Archives of the UK: Public Record Office, Special Collections
T.T.	Lisbon, Instituto dos Arquivos Nacionais, Torre do Tombo

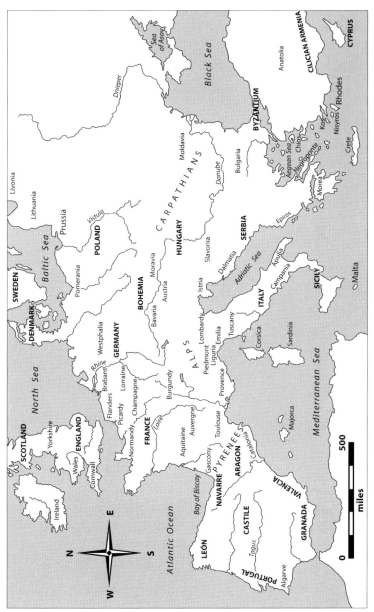

Figure 1 Map of Europe, showing locations mentioned in the text

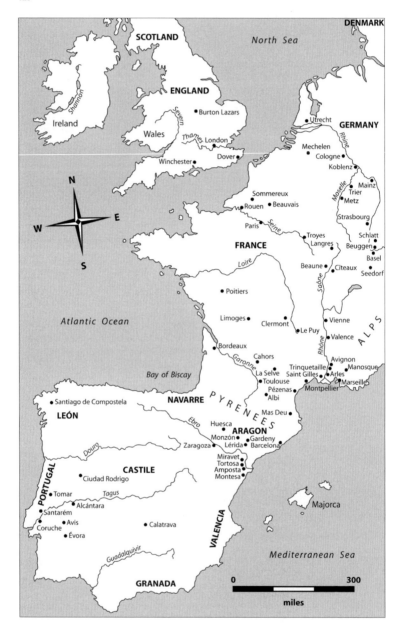

Figure 2 Map of western Europe, showing locations mentioned in the text

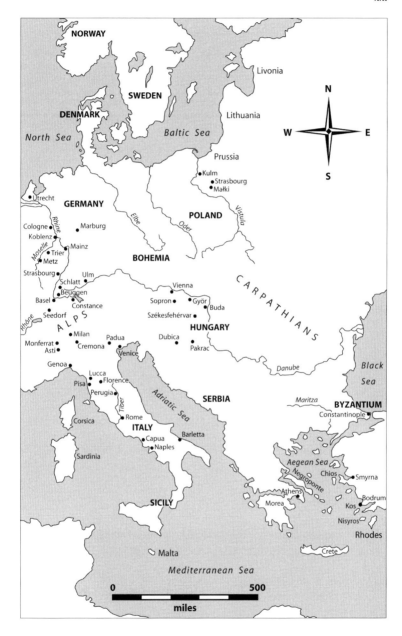

Figure 3 Map of central Europe, showing locations mentioned in the text

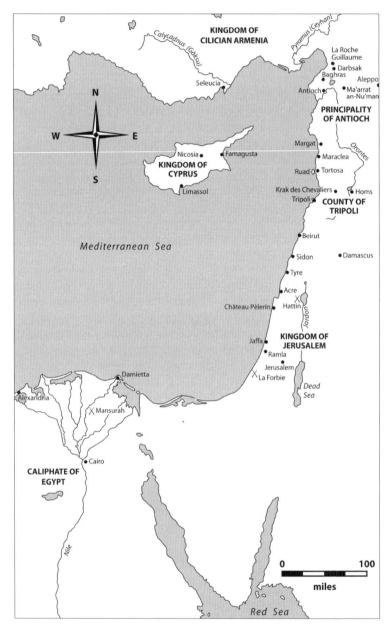

Figure 4 Map of the eastern Mediterranean, showing locations mentioned in the text

1

Introduction

ALAN FOREY

Most military orders were international in character, in the sense that they had rights and interests in more than one state. Those orders which in the twelfth and thirteenth centuries were based in the Holy Land and helped to defend the crusader states rapidly acquired properties in western Europe: these provided resources for the conflict with the infidel – aid was dispatched in the form of money, food supplies, weapons and horses – and prompted the creation of houses in areas where men could be recruited. This was true not only of the leading orders of the Temple, the Hospital of St John and the Teutonic Order, but also of lesser foundations such as St Thomas of Acre and St Lazarus. From the early thirteenth century the Teutonic Order was also active in Hungary and then the Baltic region, and for fulfilling its obligations in these areas it drew on recruits from states outside these districts. The Swordbrethren and the Order of Dobrin, which had a brief existence in north-eastern Europe before being swallowed up by the Teutonic Order, also obtained recruits from farther west.

The situation of military orders based in the Iberian peninsula was somewhat different. Although some had properties outside Spain, these were of little importance. Spanish orders depended essentially on manpower and resources obtained within the peninsular kingdoms, rather than from states remote from the frontiers of western Christendom. And whereas the Temple and the Hospital had members who participated in the Spanish *reconquista*, the Spanish orders were not militarily active to any extent outside the peninsula. Calatrava did establish a convent near the Prussian border, but it appears to have been short-lived, and although at times there were plans to extend Santiago's activities to the Holy Land and the Latin Empire of Constantinople, these were not realized. But Santiago and Calatrava had interests in most of the Spanish kingdoms, and even those orders which were based in one kingdom, such as Avis or Montesa, usually had ties and links in the peninsula outside that kingdom.

To mobilize resources and manpower, orders developed a centralized form of government. In the larger orders local houses were grouped into provinces or priories, which were in turn responsible to an order's headquarters, although there was not, of course, complete uniformity in organization: in some instances further intermediate officials were appointed. Various measures were adopted to ensure the maintenance of control within this hierarchical structure. A less elaborate administration characterized smaller foundations, but everywhere the trend was towards centralization, and this usually involved the movement of men as well as supplies, even if only within a limited area.

Although the phrase *stabilitas loci* is encountered in documents relating to military orders, the nature of these institutions tended to preclude a career spent entirely in one house: in the context of these orders, *stabilitas* signified lifelong adherence to an institution rather than to a particular house. There was much mobility, as in the orders of friars, and many brothers travelled long distances, leaving their native kingdoms for either short or longer periods of time.

As the leading orders recruited mainly in regions away from the frontiers of western Christendom, brothers were frequently sent to give military service for a period in areas of conflict. Judith Bronstein, Theresa Vann and Pierre Bonneaud suggest that in the Hospital newly recruited knights were commonly dispatched to the Holy Land and later to Cyprus and then to Rhodes, and evidence from the Templar trial indicates that a similar practice was followed in the Temple. Jürgen Sarnowsky shows, however, that the Hospitallers summoned to Rhodes in the fifteenth century were by no means all newcomers. Judith Bronstein also stresses that after severe reverses in the field, it was sometimes necessary to undertake hasty recruitment in the west to replace losses. But Templars and Hospitallers who had joined their respective orders in western Europe were normally dispatched only to the eastern Mediterranean to fight: their colleagues in Spain did not regularly receive manpower from other parts of western Europe. Nor were members of these orders routinely sent from other districts to fight in eastern Europe, which was not an important theatre of war for the

Temple and the Hospital. The situation of the Spanish orders was different, and military service tended to be on the frontier of the kingdom in which brothers were based. Yet this was not always the case: Maria Cristina Cunha reminds us that brothers of Avis were present at the siege of Seville in 1248.

Those who served in a frontier region, either at an order's headquarters or elsewhere, were, of course, not necessarily engaged in fighting or involved solely in warfare. Some brother sergeants fulfilled domestic and household tasks, while other brothers performed administrative duties, and held posts in central or more local administration in frontier regions. Jochen Burgtorf demonstrates that most central officials in the Temple and the Hospital in the twelfth and thirteenth centuries had their origins in the west, and discusses from which parts of western Europe they came.

Service in a frontier region and at an order's headquarters meant that a brother might spend years in an alien environment, hundreds or thousands of miles from his homeland: this aspect of mobility is discussed with reference to the Hospital by Jürgen Sarnowsky, who writes of life on Rhodes in the fifteenth century.

Service on the frontier or at an order's headquarters was undertaken primarily to meet the needs of the institution in question, although Klaus van Eickels makes the point that there were also benefits to be had if some brothers remained in their native localities where they had contacts and influence. He also stresses that not all brothers were anxious to move: there was a growing reluctance among Rhenish brothers of the Teutonic Order to go to Livonia, where they had little hope of advancement. But service in a frontier region and especially at an order's headquarters usually helped to further a brother's career and enhance his chances of obtaining posts of importance. Although there are earlier indications of this situation, most evidence comes from the later Middle Ages, and is illustrated by Pierre Bonneaud's and Jürgen Sarnowsky's comments on the Hospital in the fifteenth century.

Members of orders also made briefer visits to frontier regions or an order's headquarters. Heads of provinces or priories were expected to report on their terms of office and to attend general chapters; and at times they were summoned to give counsel on particular issues. This is true of the more important orders in the Iberian peninsula as well as of the Temple, the Hospital and the Teutonic Order, but in Spain mobility in this context was also necessitated by the dependence of some lesser orders – such as Avis and Alcántara – on Calatrava, for their masters were expected, as Maria Cristina Cunha explains, to attend the general chapter of Calatrava, just as the master of Calatrava might be present at the general chapter of Cîteaux. Some brothers, after lengthy journeys, also participated briefly in military activities against the infidel or other opponents of western Christendom in areas remote from the countries where they were based. Elena Bellomo reports that the Templar provincial master of Lombardy took part in the Fourth Crusade, and Alain Demurger suggests that Berenguer of Cardona, the Aragonese provincial master of the Templars, saw brief service on the island of Ruad off the Syrian coast in 1300. Others were involved in the transporting of money and goods to an order's headquarters or a frontier zone, although this was not always done by brothers, as Helen Nicholson shows. Brothers could further be dispatched to an order's headquarters for judgement if they were accused of offences which were of a serious nature or difficult to resolve. Some who were known personally to the master of an order were also given permission to visit an order's headquarters whenever they wished, presumably to further their own interests.

There was also movement from the centre and from frontier regions. Brothers who served for a term in a frontier district in the eastern Mediterranean could be sent back to provinces in western Europe: testimonies given during the Templar trial suggest that the military establishment of the Temple in the eastern Mediterranean was made up mainly of young knights, who served for only a limited period in the east. Those who had suffered injuries and were unfit for service were certainly quickly sent back to the west. Brothers who had served for a time at an order's headquarters were in addition often given administrative posts in western provinces. The practice of visitation also involved the dispatch of brothers to report on the situation in outlying areas, although those appointed by the leading orders to carry out visitations in western districts were sometimes individuals who were based in the west; but these – while not travelling from an order's headquarters – acted outside their own provinces and kingdoms. The master of Calatrava in the same way undertook the visitation of affiliated orders in the Iberian peninsula. And the interests of an order's headquarters were further maintained by brothers who were sent on particular missions to provinces as well as by those nominated as visitors. David Marcombe reports that the master of St Lazarus was himself in England in 1256, apparently on a recruiting drive, and some masters of other orders based in the Holy Land are similarly known to have made journeys to western Europe. Brothers were also dispatched to the papal and royal courts on embassies and missions. But representations at these courts were made not only by the central authorities of an order. Axel Ehlers examines the particular case of John Malkaw, commander of the Teutonic Order's house of Strasbourg, who may have travelled to Rome to obtain both particular and general concessions from the papacy.

There seems to have been less movement between provinces in regions away from the main frontier districts, although some did occur. Zsolt Hunyadi shows that many Hospitaller priors of Hungary originated in France or Italy, and Christian Vogel and Jean-Marie Allard demonstrate that there was some interchange of personnel at this level between Templar provinces in France and England, and it is apparent from Elena Bellomo's essay that the same happened to some extent in Italy. On the other hand, it can be shown that in some regions heads of provinces were almost always of local origin. Language differences would no doubt have often made the appointment of outsiders undesirable. And at a lower level there appears usually to have been little movement between provinces: Christian Vogel points out that Templar commanders were normally nominated by those exercising authority within a province, and outsiders were therefore unlikely to be appointed. Zsolt Hunyadi does, however, draw attention to the fact that heads of Hospitaller commanderies in Hungary, like the priors, were often of French or Italian origin.

The most common form of mobility was that which occurred within provinces or their equivalent. It was not only those who had charge of houses who did not usually remain in one place permanently. There was also frequent interchange of brothers without office between houses in a province. It was probably unusual for a brother to spend the whole of his career in the same convent. The boundaries of provinces were, of course, often influenced by political frontiers, and movement within a province often did not involve crossing 'national' boundaries. But some provinces did extend beyond a single kingdom: in the later thirteenth century, for example, the Templar province of 'Aragon and Catalonia' also included Templar houses in the kingdoms of Navarre and Majorca. Nor does there seem to have been any reluctance to transfer Templars to houses in the Aragonese province which lay in another kingdom. Movement within a province could sometimes therefore be categorized as 'international mobility'.

The movement of brothers in the interests of a military order inevitably at times conflicted with the concerns of secular rulers, and in some circumstances these sought to restrict travel by brothers of an order as well as the transmission of supplies. As Helen Nicholson shows, the English kings sought to impede some brothers from leaving the country. The evidence consists mainly of royal instructions to prevent the movement of personnel, but presumably these could not be completely ignored, as military orders – like other religious institutions – were considerably dependent on royal favour. But some rulers who placed general embargoes on the movement of goods and men in time of war were prepared to make an exception for the dispatch of men and supplies to the eastern Mediterranean.

Yet, while secular rulers were at times seeking to impede movement out of a kingdom or district, Elena Bellomo, Helen Nicholson and Pierre Bonneaud show that kings and popes commonly employed brothers of military orders in various capacities, and that this was a significant factor in increasing international mobility. Brothers of military orders were employed by rulers as envoys or were commissioned to transport moneys or other goods; and they were also given posts in papal or royal administration which might take them away from the regions where they had been based. Especially in the later Middle Ages military orders might also be expected to contribute troops to participate in secular wars outside the frontiers of a kingdom.

International mobility often involved lengthy journeys, by both land and sea, and although the conditions and consequences of travel tend to be considered only briefly in the essays presented here, the comments made do point to certain conclusions. Alain Demurger illustrates the time which a visit by a Templar provincial master from Spain to Cyprus might take: Berenguer of Cardona was away from his province for the greater part of a year. Some comment is made by Jürgen Sarnowsky and Pierre Bonneaud about the costs incurred by Hospitallers travelling to the east, while the arrangements made for journeys and for the dispatch of supplies are also discussed briefly by Alain Demurger.

Although most brothers of the military orders did not lead completely static lives, probably those engaging in long-distance travel constituted only a minority of an order's membership. As Helen Nicholson notes, many Templars interrogated in England in the early fourteenth century indicated that they had never been to the east; and Jean-Marie Allard similarly argues that few Templars from the diocese of Limoges had journeyed overseas. Kay Peter Jankrift further draws attention to the special case of St Lazarus, and questions whether leprous brothers were dispatched from the west to the Holy Land.

In a number of essays the lack of adequate evidence about mobility is stressed. It is clearly difficult to reach firm conclusions which are of general application from the materials relating to a particular order in a particular region. But the studies in the present volume show that international mobility within the military orders is a subject worthy of study, and they make a significant contribution to the understanding of various aspects of the topic. It is to be hoped that they will serve to inspire further research which eventually will provide as complete a picture of international mobility in the military orders as the surviving sources allow.

I

General Aspects
and Individual Cases

2

The Templars' and Hospitallers' High Dignitaries: Aspects of International Mobility

JOCHEN BURGTORF

The Templars' Catalan rule relates the story of Pons of Gusans who, in the later thirteenth century, left a Provençal Templar house to get married. After his wife's death, he asked to be readmitted, but was told that, since he had been a brother and should not have left in the first place, he would have to do penance. Pons replied that he had never taken vows. Rather, during a trip to the east he had become mortally ill, had asked to be admitted to the order and had received the Templars' habit without taking vows. After his recovery, he had continued to wear the habit, even held the office of *turcopolier* in the central convent, but remained convinced that he would not have to stay in the order. Thus, before he got married, he had returned the habit. The brothers debating the case ruled that Pons's spending over a year and a day in the order had to be interpreted as a pledge according to canon law and ordered him to do penance, after which he recovered his habit.[1]

Pons's story does not reflect the typical career of the Templars' or Hospitallers' high dignitaries, but strictly speaking there were no 'typical' careers anyway, at best certain tendencies.[2] However, his career – from Provence to the east and back – does illustrate the dignitaries' international mobility. The dignitaries referred to are those of the orders' central convents, that is the seneschals, commanders, marshals, drapers, treasurers, *turcopoliers*, hospitallers, priors and admirals (and their lieutenants) from the twelfth to the early fourteenth centuries. Both orders' masters have been studied extensively and will here only be considered in passing.[3] Over 40 per cent of these dignitaries travelled more than once between west and east, which makes them a worthy subject for anyone interested in medieval mobility. On the basis of charters, normative texts, trial records and various narrative sources, this chapter will address two aspects: the high dignitaries' geographical origin and their international mobility before, during and after their tenure of office in the east.

In 1309, King Philip IV of France complained to Pope Clement V that, while – according to custom – there should be twenty-six French brothers in the Hospitallers' central convent, there were only about twelve. Moreover, after a recent tour of the west the order's master had taken fifty knights with him to Cyprus, but only a few of them were French. Philip IV wanted the proper number of French brothers restored.[4] According to Alan Forey, most members of the military religious orders who spent parts of their careers in the Holy Land probably originated from France.[5] Nevertheless, in the early fourteenth century, the king of France did find grounds for complaint. What do we know about the dignitaries' geographical origin and how can we establish this geographical origin in a methodological fashion? For the time period until 1310, one can identify 226 high dignitaries (135 Hospitallers and 91 Templars, excluding masters but including lieutenants).[6] With regard to their geographical origin, I would like to suggest eight different case-types.

Type one: for eight of these 226 dignitaries (3.5 per cent) the sources inform us explicitly about their geographical origin.[7] For example, the Templars' trial records state that Matthew Sauvage, conventual commander in 1260, was *Picardus*,[8] and while the trial records are not the most reliable sources, in the case of mere geographical origin one might tend to give them the benefit of the doubt.

Type two: for fifteen of these 226 dignitaries (6.6 per cent) their cognomina are both geographical terms and genealogical information. For example, one of the Hospitallers' early fourteenth-century dignitaries was Albert of Schwarzburg, and Schwarzburg is a county in central Germany (Thuringia/Saxony) as well as the name of a comital family.[9]

Type three: for thirty-five of these 226 dignitaries (15.5 per cent) their names or cognomina point to certain regions and their careers indicate that they probably originated from these very regions. For example, Peter of Hagham, hospitaller in the central convent of the Hospital (1269), originated from England. His cognomen 'Hagham' points to various locations in Leicestershire (and probably elsewhere in England). He functioned as Pope Nicholas IV's envoy to King Edward I of England, later served as lieutenant of the Hospitallers' prior of England and eventually took office as prior of England himself.[10]

Type four: for fifty-nine of these 226 dignitaries (26 per cent) their cognomina are geographical terms. One example is Adam of Cromwell, the Templars' draper in 1300.[11] Whether he received the cognomen 'of Cromwell' because he was actually born in Cromwell (Nottingham-shire), because he was received into the order there or because he spent considerable time there, is unknown. While his geographical 'origin' cannot really be proven, he was more than likely 'English'.

Type five: for seventeen of these 226 dignitaries (7.5 per cent) their names are not sufficient to ascertain their geographical origin, but the events or contacts of their careers can serve as indicators. For example, in the case of the twelfth-century Templar dignitary Geoffrey *Fulcherii* the name itself is not enough, but his connection to King Louis VII of France – through personal visits, letters and references to him in the correspondence between the king and the master of the Temple – suffices to assume his French origin.[12]

Type six: for eleven of these 226 dignitaries (4.9 per cent) their names or patronymics are usually found within specific geographical boundaries. For example, *Craphus* (Kraft), hospitaller in his order's central convent (1260), was probably German because the name 'Kraft' was common in the county of Hohenlohe in south-western Germany at the time.[13]

Type seven: for nine of these 226 dignitaries (4 per cent) their geograph-ical origin is 'controversial'. One example is Gerard of Ridefort who, before he became master, served as the Templars' seneschal. He was probably Flemish, but alternatives have been suggested (including Irish, English and Anglo-Norman origin).[14]

Type eight: for seventy-two of these 226 dignitaries (31.9 per cent) their geographical origin is unknown. Next to those cases in which existing cognomina cannot be tied to certain places or dynasties, there are several dignitaries who remain completely unnamed, that is they appear under their titles but are – because of the career developments of their predecessors or successors – not identical with dignitaries whose names we already know. Finally, there are all those Bernards, Geoffreys, Henrys, Stephens and Williams. A study of the Hospitallers' charters issued in the Latin east between 1136 and 1184 reveals that there were at times four different Stephens in the central convent and, despite an occasional cog-nomen or title, their careers cannot be linked beyond reasonable doubt.[15]

With regard to the dignitaries' geographical origin, the dominance of
the French provinces is not as strong as one might expect. Only 1 of 7
pre-1191 Templar conventual commanders seems to have been French.
However, 7 of 20 Templar commanders between 1191 and 1291 were
French (a noticeable increase), and the 6 post-1291 Templar commanders came from Aragon, Italy, southern France and Burgundy.[16]
With regard to the Hospitallers' conventual commanders, France does
not dominate until after 1191, which may have to do with the Hospital's
Italian origins. Before 1191, only 3 of 12 Hospitaller commanders came
from France. Between 1191 and 1291, 10 of 25 Hospitaller commanders
originated from France. The Cypriot phase between 1291 and 1310 is,
however, most revealing: 3 of 5 conventual commanders came from
Provence.[17] This foreshadows a future development as, in the course of
the fourteenth century, the office of grand commander would begin to
be staffed exclusively by brothers from the *langue* (or tongue) of
Provence.[18] However, in the Hospitallers' pre-1310 history, the connection between a certain office and a certain *langue* can only be seen in
this case, that is for the office of grand commander, the highest-ranking
office below the master, and the *langue* of Provence, the order's oldest
and most highly regarded one.

Turning to the marshals, we find that 15 of the 20 Templar marshals
originated from France, but no Spaniard seems to have served as
marshal of the Temple.[19] Maybe Spanish Templars with military ambi-
tions were kept in the Iberian peninsula to take part in the *reconquista*.
Another explanation could be that the military command language in
the crusader states was French, and someone with this language as his
native tongue was probably the first choice for a high military office.
Thus, in the case of the Templar marshal, geographical origin seems to
have been a career-determining factor. Of 28 pre-1310 Hospitaller
marshals 13, that is almost half, were certainly French. There is a remarkable 'international' interlude in the mid-thirteenth century when 3
non-French marshals served consecutively, namely a Spaniard, a Sicilian
and a Castilian.[20] These appointments coincide with the years during
which Hugh Revel, one of the most famous Hospitaller masters, who
was probably French, rose to power, and it could be an example of his
attempt to reform or internationalize the order.[21] Under his mastership
the central convent saw German and Spanish grand commanders, as well
as German, Spanish and English hospitallers and an English treasurer.[22]

Two individual cases may serve to conclude these reflections on
geographical origin. The first Englishman who held a high office in the

central convent of a military order was probably Robert (*Anglicus*), the Hospitallers' treasurer of 1192.[23] This treasurer Robert (*Anglicus*) of 1192 is identical with Robert the Treasurer who served as the Hospitallers' prior of England between 1204 and 1214. In contrast to Joseph Delaville le Roulx's speculation that the English prior's cognomen 'the Treasurer' might refer to an earlier function as treasurer of Clerkenwell (for which there is no evidence), the prior's cognomen most likely refers to his earlier tenure as the Hospitallers' conventual treasurer. This means that in Acre Robert would have been known as Robert 'the Englishman' and back home in England he would become known as Robert 'the Treasurer', celebrating his past as the order's highest treasurer.[24]

Another case: in his lists of Hospitaller officials, Delaville presents an admiral by the name of 'Sanzoli de Grasse'.[25] The cognomen 'de Grasse' could point to a place of this name in southern France (northwest of Cannes). It pays, though, to give the document cited as evidence a close reading.[26] The admiral in question seems to appear at the end of a witness list which Delaville transcribed as follows: *presentibus . . . [several names follow in the ablative case] militibus; et frater Sanzoli, Grassie amirato ordinis Hospitalis predicti, testibus.* This is a misreading: there was never a Sanzoli de Grasse, nor an admiral by that name, nor an admiral of the city of Grasse. The correct reading has to be: *presentibus (. . .) militibus, et fratribus Sancti Anzoli, Grassie, et Amirati, ordinis Hospitalis predicti, testibus*, that is the brothers of St Andiol, Grasse and Amirat (all three places survive to this day) served as witnesses. Thus, prosopographical studies with their attention to individuals' geographical origin and international mobility sometimes 'eliminate' rather than 'generate' high dignitaries of the military orders.

We now turn to the second aspect, namely the high dignitaries' international mobility before, during and after their tenure of office in the east. Many who were received into the military orders in the west were probably sent to the east to serve there.[27] Candidates for reception were told that they had to expect to be moved around.[28] However, this was not to occur in an arbitrary fashion. The Templars' *Retrais* stipulate that when the master wanted to send brothers from the east to the west because of ill health or to conduct the order's business, he had to instruct several dignitaries (at a general chapter) to compile a list of those to be sent, and he was only allowed to alter this list after consultation with these same dignitaries.[29] The Hospitallers' statutes of 1204/06 decree that baillis and brothers should only be sent to the west or summoned to the east if a general chapter had passed a corresponding resolution. If the master saw a need to send or summon brothers after the closing of the general chapter, he had to consult with the council of the brothers.[30]

That the master and the brothers were supposed to cooperate on personnel decisions was common knowledge. In 1288, King Alfonso III of Aragon wrote to the Hospitallers' marshal and central convent and, in a separate letter, to the master. Two Aragonese Hospitallers had been 'relocated' unfavourably, one to Armenia which had a bad reputation because of its climate, the other to Aragon with a frivolous message to his own discredit. Alfonso III found it hard to believe that the master had made these decisions without consulting the brothers.[31] However, unilateral decisions must have occurred: in 1296, the Hospitallers' central convent complained that masters in the past had frequently sent brothers back and forth and made it clear that this was a grievance they expected their new master (William of Villaret) to address.[32]

As most of the military orders' high dignitaries originated from the west, they had to travel to the east eventually. However, to meet my standard for 'real' international mobility, a dignitary has to have made at least one more trip back to the west before returning to the east to take office there. This is the case with 4 of 12 Templar seneschals, 4 of 33 Templar commanders, 3 of 42 Hospitaller commanders, none of 8 Templar commanders of Acre, 2 of 20 Templar marshals, 1 of 28 Hospitaller marshals, 1 of 8 Templar drapers, 1 of 11 Hospitaller drapers, none of these orders' treasurers and none of the hospitallers and priors of the Hospital.[33] Hence, international mobility can hardly be seen as a precondition to gain any of the central convents' high offices. Nevertheless, 'experience' was a catalytic factor for a career in the military orders: most commanders and marshals in both orders had held high offices before they became commanders or marshals, and many later continued their careers on a high level in the east or the west.[34]

During their tenure of office in the east, very few of the dignitaries ever left the central convent or its environs. There are, however, a few noteworthy exceptions. The Templars' seneschal Robert Burgundio travelled in Europe between 1132 and 1133/4 and received several important donations for his order while his master stayed in the east.[35] In 1222–3, the Templars' conventual commander William Cadel travelled to the west as the official envoy of his master and as a member of a very prestigious delegation from the crusader states that included the king and the patriarch of Jerusalem.[36] In 1279, the Templars' conventual commander Theobald Gaudini toured France where he received new members into his order.[37] In 1306/7, one of his successors, Raimbald (II) of Caromb, accompanied his master James of Molay on their fateful last journey to France.[38] Only one of the Hospitallers' conventual commanders, namely Guy of Mahón, travelled to the west and, just like the Templar commander William Cadel, was a member of an official delegation from the crusader states (1169).[39]

Until the early fourteenth century, only one marshal of each order seems to have travelled to the west. In 1193, the Templar marshal Geoffrey took a trip to France that included a visit to Mary of Champagne, the mother of Henry, the regent of the kingdom of Jerusalem.[40] In 1255 and 1259, the Hospitaller marshal Raimbald travelled to Spain on his order's business.[41] We do know for 1193 and for 1255 that the crusader states had just concluded truce agreements with their Muslim neighbours, so maybe the orders' central convents considered it 'safe' to operate temporarily without their military experts.[42] Thus, the mobility of the dignitaries – while in office – could also depend on the order's foreign policy. There is one other Templar marshal who travelled to the west while in office, but his trip was one of 'defiance'. For reasons unknown, Pope Urban IV held a grudge against the Templar marshal Stephen of Cissey, and in the early 1260s he ordered the Templar master Thomas *Berardi* to depose Stephen and send him to the Curia. Stephen did go to see the pope, but he came as marshal, refused to surrender his seal, rebuked the pope in public and then went into hiding, whereupon Urban IV excommunicated him. The conflict was resolved under Clement IV, and Stephen was pardoned after he had done penance.[43] It seems that the master and the marshal tried to stop the pope from interfering with the order's personnel decisions and, in this case, deemed international mobility necessary to make that point.

In 1269, the Hospitallers' draper William of Villaret, who originated from Provence, travelled to southern France to oversee the vacant priory of St Gilles. This was probably intended as a *pro tempore* arrangement, but it soon turned into a permanent post. William surrendered the office of draper and took over the priory of St Gilles.[44] He remained prior until he was elected master in 1296. When he was still in St Gilles in 1299, the central convent forced him to relocate to the order's head-quarters in Cyprus and reminded him that in his thirty years as prior of St Gilles, he had only travelled to the east twice to render account, even though he had been expected to come six times, that is every five years.[45] Obviously, international travel was not everybody's 'thing', for William could not claim the impediment that some of his colleagues had to face in England or Aragon, where leaving the country was contingent upon royal permission, which, on occasion, was actually denied.[46]

There is one official in the Hospitallers' central convent that has yet to receive proper attention with regard to his international mobility, namely the prior, who – in addition to being responsible for his order's conventual church – seems to have been one of the Hospitallers' favourite foreign ambassadors. Apart from the questionable appearance of Prior Hubald in Italy in 1136, we find the Hospitallers' prior at the papal Curia in 1172; as one of the crusader states' envoys to the west after the battle of La Forbie (1244); again at the papal Curia in 1264; as one of the conventual envoys to the west to demand the aforementioned relocation of William of Villaret to Cyprus (1299); and, finally, as the master's lieutenant in southern France and Spain in 1308.[47] Taken together, the scattered cases of travelling commanders, marshals, drapers and priors show that, when the military orders' central convents felt the need to get directly involved on the provincial level of their respective orders, or when a matter of international dimensions called for particular attention, the conventual dignitaries had to be ready to travel.

Finally, what do we know about the high dignitaries' international mobility once they had completed their tenure of office? The evidence is best for marshals and commanders. Only 4 of 20 Templar marshals and only 6 of 28 Hospitaller marshals returned to the west. The picture changes when we turn to the office of commander. In both orders, at least one-third of all conventual commanders returned to the west. Commanders had to be administrators with very flexible skills, and the offices of commanders in both orders were constantly adapted to new circumstances. The skills of commanders were transferable, and their prestige as former conventual commanders equipped these individuals perfectly for high offices in the west. This was somewhat true of marshals as well; however, their expertise was needed in the east and that may have been reason enough to keep them there. The same seems to have been true of the hospitallers of the Hospital's central convent: of 19 hospitallers before 1310 we only have evidence for two who returned to the west. The expertise gained from supervising a major hospital was most useful in or near that very hospital. The high dignitaries of both orders did, however, have another reason to want to stay in the east, namely the chance to become the next master.

Templars and Hospitallers depended on intense west–east contacts for the exchange of personnel and resources. Thus, Joshua Prawer's thesis that the military orders were an 'instrument of social mobility'[48] can be augmented, as they were obviously also important instruments of international mobility. For the careers of these orders' dignitaries, their geographical origin seems to have become an increasingly determining factor; however, prior to 1310, this is certain only for the Hospitallers' grand commander. The dignitaries' international mobility during their tenure of office in the east deserves more attention, certainly that of the Hospitallers' conventual prior, as the central governments of both orders occasionally increased the prestige of a mission abroad by sending one of their highest dignitaries. Travelling was much more dangerous in the Middle Ages than it is today, and it is safe to assume that very few of the Templars' and Hospitallers' high dignitaries volunteered to travel. Thus, the Templar Geoffrey *Fulcherii*, who travelled at least five times from the east to the west,[49] was the exception, but may be one of the best examples of medieval 'Wanderlust'.

Notes

1   Joseph Delaville le Roulx (ed.), 'Un nouveau manuscrit de la règle du Temple', *Annuaire-Bulletin de la Société de l'histoire de France*, 26 (1889), 185–214, here 212. The new edition is Judi Upton-Ward (ed.), *The Catalan Rule of the Templars* (Woodbridge, 2003), pp. 86–9 no. 183.

2   Jochen Burgtorf, 'Führungsstrukturen und Funktionsträger in der Zentrale der Templer und Johanniter von den Anfängen bis zum frühen 14. Jahrhundert' (Ph.D. thesis, Heinrich-Heine-Universität Düsseldorf, 2001), 291–339.

3   Jonathan Riley-Smith, *The Knights of St. John in Jerusalem and Cyprus c.1050–1310* (London, 1967); Marie Luise Bulst-Thiele, *Sacrae domus militiae Templi Hierosolymitani magistri: Untersuchungen zur Geschichte des Templerordens 1118/19–1314* (Göttingen, 1974).

4   Joseph Delaville le Roulx (ed.), *Cartulaire général de l'ordre des Hospitaliers de Saint-Jean de Jérusalem (1100–1310)* (Paris, 1894–1905), vol. 4, no. 4831.

5   Alan Forey, 'Recruitment to the military orders (twelfth to mid-fourteenth centuries)', *Viator*, 17 (1986), 139–71, here 140.

6   For references see Burgtorf, 'Führungsstrukturen', 355–768. The distribution for the Hospitallers' high dignitaries is as follows: 42 commanders (plus 1 lieutenant commander), 3 commanders of Cyprus (1291–1310), 28 marshals (plus 1 lieutenant marshal), 19 hospitallers, 11 drapers (plus 1 lieutenant draper), 21 treasurers, 13 priors (plus 1 vice-prior), 2 admirals and

3 *turcopoliers*; for the Templars' high dignitaries: 12 seneschals, 33 commanders, 8 commanders of Acre (1191–1291), 20 marshals (plus 2 lieutenant marshals), 8 drapers (plus 1 lieutenant draper), 8 treasurers, 1 prior and 7 *turcopoliers*. These numbers add up to 246, however, the 'real' number is 226 because in both orders some individuals held more than one high office in the course of their careers.

7   Due to space constraints I only give the full references for these eight of the first case-type (T = Templar; H = Hospitaller). Anthony (T, *de Suria*): Jules Michelet (ed.), *Le procès des Templiers* (Paris, 1841–51), vol. 1, p. 646; Boniface of Calamandrana (H, *consanguineus* of King Alfonso III of Aragon): Delaville, *Cartulaire*, vol. 3, no. 4007; Matthew Sauvage (T, *Picardus*): Michelet, *Procès*, vol. 1, p. 645; Peter of Sevrey (T, *bourgognon*): *Les gestes des Chiprois*, ed. Gaston Raynaud (Geneva, 1887), p. 256; Pons of Gusans (T, *de Proença*): Upton-Ward, *Catalan Rule*, 86; Raymond of Ribells (H, *consanguineus* of King Alfonso III of Aragon): Delaville, *Cartulaire*, vol. 3, no. 4007; Walter of Liencourt (T, *Picardus*): Konrad Schottmüller (ed.), *Der Untergang des Templer-Ordens* (Berlin, 1887), vol. 2, p. 181; William of Villaret (H, *provensal*): *Gestes*, ed. Raynaud, p. 319.

8   Michelet, *Procès*, vol. 1, p. 645: *Matheus dictus le Sarmage.*

9   Detlev Schwennicke, *Europäische Stammtafeln*, Neue Folge (Marburg, 1980–99), vol. 1, part 3, tables 312–15; Karl Borchardt, 'Hospitallers, Bohemia and the Empire', in Jürgen Sarnowsky (ed.), *Mendicants, Military Orders and Regionalism in Medieval Europe* (Aldershot, 1997), pp. 201–31, here p. 221.

10 Hospitaller (1269): Delaville, *Cartulaire*, vol. 3, no. 3047; papal envoy to England (1289): Thomas Rymer (ed.), *Foedera, conventiones, literae, et cujuscunque generis acta publica*, third edition (The Hague, 1739–45), vol. 1, part 3, p. 49 and Delaville, *Cartulaire*, vol. 3, no. 4054; lieutenant prior of England (1290): ibid., vol. 3, p. 568 note 1; prior of England (1290–8): William Dugdale (ed.), *Monasticon Anglicanum*, new edition (London, 1830), vol. 6, part 2, p. 799; *Calendar of the Patent Rolls, Edward I* (London, 1893–1901), vol. 3, pp. 16, 75, 138, 194, 256; *Calendar of the Close Rolls, Edward I* (London, 1900–6), vol. 3, p. 378; Delaville, *Cartulaire*, vol. 3, nos 4216, 4217, 4272 and p. 620 note 1; Michael Gervers (ed.), *The Cartulary of the Knights of St. John of Jerusalem in England: secunda camera, Essex* (Oxford, 1982), p. 571 no. 961.

11 Alan Forey, *The Templars in the Corona de Aragón* (London, 1973), pp. 414–15 no. 44.

12 For references see Jochen Burgtorf, 'Die Ritterorden als Instanzen zur Friedenssicherung?', in Dieter Bauer, Klaus Herbers and Nikolas Jaspert (eds), *Jerusalem im Hoch- und Spätmittelalter* (Frankfurt, 2001), pp. 165–200, here pp. 191–2.

13 Hermann Grote, *Stammtafeln* (Leipzig, 1877), p. 86 no. 61; Joseph Delaville le Roulx, *Les Hospitaliers en Terre Sainte et à Chypre (1100–1310)* (Paris, 1904), p. 411.

[14] J. Horace Round, 'Some English crusaders of Richard I', *English Historical Review*, 18 (1903), 475–81, here 480 (English or Irish); Hans Eberhard Mayer, 'Zur Verfasserfrage des Itinerarium Peregrinorum', *Classica et Mediaevalia*, 26 (1965), 279–92, here 283–6 (English); Malcolm Barber, *The New Knighthood: A History of the Order of the Temple* (Cambridge, 1994), p. 109 (Flemish or Anglo-Norman); Steven Runciman, *A History of the Crusades* (Cambridge: 1951–4), vol. 2, p. 406 (Flemish); Marie Luise Bulst-Thiele, 'Templer in königlichen und päpstlichen Diensten', in Peter Classen and Peter Scheibert (eds), *Festschrift Percy Ernst Schramm* (Wiesbaden, 1964), vol. 1, pp. 289–308, here p. 294 (Flemish); Jean Richard, *Latin Kingdom of Jerusalem* (Amsterdam, 1979), vol. A, p. 119 (Flemish); Burgtorf, 'Führungsstrukturen', 481–2 (Flemish).

[15] Reinhold Röhricht (ed.), *Regesta Regni Hierosolymitani (MXCVII–MCCXCI)* (Osnabrück 1893–1904), nos 457, 201, 205, 204, 215, 226, 257, 274, 458, 434a, 502, 501, 516, 535, 547, 540, 558, 611, 603, 607, 640. For the chronology of these charters see Hans Eberhard Mayer, *Die Kanzlei der lateinischen Könige von Jerusalem* (Hanover, 1996), vol. 2, pp. 845–86.

[16] The geographical origins of the Templars' thirty-three central commanders and their years in office are as follows: Odo (1155, unknown); Geoffrey *Fulcherii* (1164, France); Walter of Beirut (1169, 1171, Latin east); Robert Fraisnel (1179/81, France/Antioch); Girbert Eral (1183, 1190–1, Aragon); O. of Vend. (1184, France/England); *Terricus* (1187–8, unknown); Irmengaud (1198, unknown); Peter of *Manaia/Mone(t)a* (1204–7, Latin east); William Cadel (1222–3, southern France); N.N. (1229, unknown); Bartholomew of Moret (1237–40, France); Peter of St Roman (1241, France); William of *Roc(c)aforte* (1244, Spain/Italy); Stephen of Ostricourt (1249–50, Flanders); Giles (1250, unknown); N.N. (1250, unknown); N.N. (1253/4, unknown); Guy of Bazainville (1256, France/Flanders); Matthew Sauvage (1260, France); Amalric of La Roche (1262, France); William of Montañana (1262, Aragon); Simon of La Tor (1271, unknown); William of Pontóns (1273, Aragon); Goufier (1273, unknown); Arnold of Castellnou (1277, Aragon); Theobald *Gaudini* (1279–91, France); Berenger of St Just (1292, Aragon); Baldwin of Andria (1293, Italy); Florentin of *Villa* (1299, unknown); Peter of Vares (1300, unknown); Raimbald (II) of Caromb (1300–13, southern France); James of Dammartin (1307–10, France). For references see Burgtorf, 'Führungsstrukturen', 355–768.

[17] The geographical origins of the Hospitallers' forty-two central commanders and their years in office are as follows: Berengar (1150–2, unknown); Gerald *Hugonis* (1155–6, unknown); Garin of *Melna* (1159, 1173–6, Flanders); *Rostagnus* (1162, southern France); Guy of Mahón (1163–70, Spain); Pons Blan (1170, unknown); O. (1170–2, unknown); Garnier of Nablus (1176–7, 1180–4, Latin east); Raymond of St Michael (1178, southern France); Archembald (1185, Italy); Borell (1187–8, southern France/Spain); *Ogerius* (1190–1, France); William of Villiers (1192, France/England); Martin Gonsalve (1193, Spain); Robert *Anglicus*/Treasurer (1194, England);

William *Lombardus* (1201, Italy); Peter of Mirmande (1203, southern France); Garin of Montaigu (1204–6, southern France); Isembard (1207, 1217–19, France); *Golferius* (1221, unknown); Raimund Motet (1222/5, southern France); William of *Tyneriis* (1231, France); Andrew Polin (1235, France); Peter (I) of Vieillebride (1237–9, southern France); William of Senlis (1240–2, France); N.N. (1244, unknown); John of Ronay (1245–50, France/Latin east); N.N. (1250, unknown); Hugh Revel (1251–8, southern France); Henry of Fürstenberg (1259–62, Germany); Stephen of *Meses* (1264–6, unknown); Boniface of Calamandrana (1268/9–71, 1279, Aragon); Nicholas Lorgne (1271, 1277, unknown); Stephen of Brosse (1273, France); Guy of La Guespa (1281, Spain); James of Tassi (1286, Italy); Matthew of Clermont (1289, France); N.N. (1299, unknown); Fulk of Villaret (1301, 1303–5, Provence); Raymond of Ribells (1303, Aragon); Joscelin (II) of Tournel (1306, Provence); Guy of Séverac (1307–10, Provence). For references see Burgtorf, 'Führungsstrukturen', 355–768.

18 See for example Jürgen Sarnowsky, 'Der Konvent auf Rhodos und die Zungen (lingue) im Johanniterorden (1421–1476)', in Zenon Nowak (ed.), *Ritterorden und Region: politische, soziale und wirtschaftliche Verbindungen im Mittelalter* (Toruń, 1995), 43–65, here 44–6, 59.

19 The geographical origins of the Templars' twenty marshals and their years in office are as follows: Hugh *Salomonis* of Quily (1153, France); Robert Fraisnel (1187, France/Antioch); Geoffrey Morin (1188–9, France); Adam Brion (1192, France); Geoffrey (1193, unknown); William of Arzillières (1204–5, France); N.N. (1219, unknown); Hugh of Montlaur (1242–4, Spain/southern France); Rainald of Vichiers (1249–50, France); Hugh of Jouy (1251/2, France); N.N. (1256, unknown); Stephen of Cissey (1260–1, France); William of *Malaio* (1262, France); Amblard of Vienne (1271, southern France); Guy of *Foresta* (1277, England/France); Geoffrey of Vendat (1289, southern France); Peter of Sevrey (1291, France); Baldwin of Andria (1292, Italy); Bartholomew of *Chinsi* (1300–2, unknown); Aimo of Oiselay (1303–16, France). For references see Burgtorf, 'Führungsstrukturen', 355–768.

20 The geographical origins of the Hospitallers' twenty-eight marshals and their years in office are as follows: Raymond of Tiberias (1165–70, Latin east); Lambert (1188, unknown); N.N. (1191, unknown); William Borell (1193, southern France); William of Marolh (1194, France); Albert *Romanus* (1204, Italy); Pons (1206, unknown); Garin of Montaigu (1206–7, southern France); Geoffrey (1210, unknown); Aymar of L'Ayron (1216–19, France); Ferrand of Barras (1221, southern France); Arnold of Montbrun (1232–3, southern France); William of Châteauneuf (1241, France); William of Courcelles (1248, France); Peter of Beaune (1254, France); Raimbald (1255–9, Spain); Guiscard of Lentini (1259, Italy); Rodrigo *Petri* (1259/61, 1271, Spain); Joscelin (I) of Tournel (1262, southern France); Henry (1267, unknown); Nicholas Lorgne (1269–71, 1273, unknown); N.N. (1272, unknown); N.N. (1288, unknown); Matthew of Clermont (1291, France); Simon Le Rat (1299, 1303, 1306–10, France); Raymond of Beaulieu (1301,

France); Gerard of Gragnana (1303, Italy); Albert of Schwarzburg (1306, Germany). For references see Burgtorf, 'Führungsstrukturen', 355–768.

21 Delaville, *Hospitaliers (1100–1310)*, p. 212. The attempt to prove that Hugh Revel was of Anglo-Norman origin has been made by Cecil Humphery-Smith, *Hugh Revel: Master of the Hospital of St John of Jerusalem, 1258–1277* (Chichester, 1994), pp. 1–8, 30–2, 67–8, 77; however this idea has been rejected in a review by Malcolm Barber, published in *Medieval Prosopography*, 16, 2 (1995), 135–7.

22 Grand commanders: Henry of Fürstenberg (1259–62, Germany) and Boniface of Calamandrana (1268/9–71, 1279, Aragon); hospitallers: *Craphus* (1260/1, Germany), Garcias Ximenes (1262, Spain), Peter of Hagham (1269), Rodrigo *Roderici* (1273, Spain); treasurer: Joseph of Cancy (1248–71). For references see Burgtorf, 'Führungsstrukturen', 355–768.

23 Delaville, *Cartulaire*, vol. 1, no. 919. See ibid., vol. 1, nos 617, 972.

24 Ibid., vol. 4, p. 355.

25 Delaville, *Hospitaliers (1100–1310)*, p. 413.

26 Delaville, *Cartulaire*, vol. 4, no. 4756.

27 Alan Forey, 'Novitiate and instruction in the military orders during the twelfth and thirteenth centuries', *Speculum*, 61 (1986), 1–17, here 9.

28 Hospitallers: Delaville, *Cartulaire*, vol. 2, no. 2213 usance 121; Templars: Henri de Curzon (ed.), *La règle du Temple* (Paris, 1886), pp. 338–9 no. 661.

29 Curzon, *Règle*, p. 83 no. 93.

30 Delaville, *Cartulaire*, vol. 2, no. 1193.

31 Ibid., vol. 3, no. 4007.

32 Ibid., vol. 3, no. 4310.

33 Burgtorf, 'Führungsstrukturen', 305–11.

34 Ibid., 314–30.

35 Marquis André d'Albon (ed.), *Cartulaire général de l'ordre du Temple 1119?–1150* (Paris, 1913), nos 47, 48, 52, 61.

36 *L'estoire de Eracles empereur et la conqueste de la terre d'Outremer*, in *Recueil des historiens des croisades, Historiens occidentaux*, vol. 2 (Paris, 1859), p. 355; Karl Rodenberg (ed.), *Epistolae saeculi XIII* (Berlin 1883), vol. 1, pp. 152–5 no. 225.

37 Michelet, *Procès*, vol. 2, p. 313.

38 Ibid., vol. 2, p. 374.

39 Jacques-P. Migne (ed.), *Alexandri III Romani pontificis opera omnia*, Patrologia Latina, vol. 200 (Paris, 1855), cols 599–601 no. 626.

40 Paris, Bibliothèque Nationale, nouvelles acquisitions latines (BN, n.a.l.), vol. 43, fols 73–5.

41 Santos Agustín García Larragueta (ed.), *El grand priorado de Navarra de la orden de San Juan de Jerusalén, siglos XII–XIII* (Pamplona, 1957), vol. 2, pp. 365–7 no. 363; Carlos de Ayala Martínez (ed.), *Libro de privilegios de la orden de San Juan de Jerusalén en Castilla y León, siglos XII–XV* (Madrid, 1995), pp. 550–3 no. 336.

42   Runciman, *History of the Crusades*, vol. 3, pp. 73, 281–2.

43   The most detailed account is Clement IV's bull *Sicut nimirum admirantes*: Édouard Jordan (ed.), *Les Registres de Clement IV (1265–1268)* (Paris, 1893–1945), no. 836.

44   Delaville, *Cartulaire*, vol. 3, nos 3376, 3384, 3387, 3394, 3416.

45   Ibid., vol. 3, no. 4462.

46   See for example Delaville (ed.), *Cartulaire*, vol. 3, no. 3728 and Helen Nicholson's paper in this volume.

47   1136: Johann Christian Lünig (ed.), *Codex Italiae diplomaticus* (Frankfurt, 1725–35), vol. 2, cols 1635–8 no. 1; 1172: Rudolf Hiestand (ed.), *Papsturkunden für Templer und Johanniter: Neue Folge* (Göttingen, 1984), pp. 227–30 no. 20; 1244: *The Chronicle of Melrose*, ed. Alan O. Anderson et al. (London, 1936), p. 95; 1264: Léon Porez and Jean Guiraud (eds), *Les Registres d'Urbain IV (1261–1264)* (Paris, 1901–58), no. 2064; 1299: Delaville, *Cartulaire*, vol. 3, nos 4468, 4469; 1308: ibid., vol. 4, nos 4797, 4829.

48   Joshua Prawer, *The Latin Kingdom of Jerusalem* (London, 1972), p. 278.

49   For references see Burgtorf, 'Ritterorden als Instanzen zur Friedenssicherung?', 191–2.

3

The Mobilization of Hospitaller Manpower from Europe to the Holy Land in the Thirteenth Century

JUDITH BRONSTEIN

One of the main difficulties scholars face when studying Hospitaller manpower and its mobilization is the lack of evidence. The sources provide little if any information about the losses the Hospitallers suffered on the battlefield and how the order restored and restrengthened its ranks in the east. The difficulty is compounded by the absence of lists giving the names and number of Hospitaller brothers who served in the order and by the inadequacy of information about the order's military strength.[1] Nonetheless, while studying aspects of the order's international deployment, I have been able to work with a rich body of materials concerning the Hospitallers in the Latin east and the 'French' priories (i.e. the priories of France, St Gilles and Auvergne).[2] These materials allowed me to compile lists of Hospitallers serving in these areas between 1187 and 1274, which I then subdivided according to their areas of service: those who were active in the Latin east and those who were active in the French priories.[3] This division has enabled me to shed some light on the issue of places of origin and service and on the transfer of manpower to the east.

From the lists of Hospitallers serving in the French priories and commanderies it is possible to conclude that these houses were manned by brothers serving close to their places of origin: Gerard of Paris was a brother in the houses of Corbeil and Paris in 1179–89.[4] Adam of Abbeville (Somme) was a simple brother in the commandery of Frasnoy (Flanders) in 1203.[5] Stephen of Cavaillon (Vaucluse) was a member of the commandery of Trinquetaille in the early thirteenth century,[6] and Bertrand of Caderousse and Bertrand of Gigondas (both

from Vaucluse) were simple brothers in the priory of St Gilles in 1199
and 1203.[7] It seems these commanderies were governed by locals. John
of Geneva commanded St Paul les Romans in 1245.[8] Pons of Cuers
(Var) was commander of Orange in 1270, and by May 1273 he was the
commander of Beaulieu.[9] He was replaced as commander of Orange by
another local, Raymond of Grasse (Alpes-Maritimes), in July 1272.[10] In
order to appoint commanders, brothers were promoted from within the
commanderies or transferred from other houses. William of Taulinan,
for example, was a simple brother in St Gilles in 1194, the commandery's *drapier* in 1198 and its vice-commander in 1202.[11] Jacob of
Bourg was transferred from St Gilles, where he had served as a simple
brother in 1192, to Trinquetaille, where he became commander in
1194.[12] The experience gained from running small commanderies was
probably a necessary springboard for posts in more important houses.
William of Mannas, who served as commander of Pernes (Vaucluse) in
1204, became the *drapier* of Trinquetaille in 1207.[13]

The tracing of changes that occurred in the order's leadership is an
important method for studying the order's institutional history. During
the thirteenth century commanders were appointed by their provincial
priors.[14] Previous experience and skills must have been important
prerequisites for new commanders, whose appointment allowed priors
to ensure competent management and, if necessary, skilful imple-
mentation of new policies. This was true at all levels of command.
William of Villiers, who, in 1192, was the grand commander of the
order in Acre (the master's second-in-command), became the grand
commander of 'outremer' in 1193. The conjoining of some of the
order's most important priories in Europe into one administrative unit
under the control of a highly experienced officer was probably intended
to ensure that the policies pursued by the priors overseas would match
the needs of the order in the east, especially following the disaster at
Hattin (1187).[15]

The reassignment of commanders, as has been shown above, was
normally done within the ambit of the provincial priories in Europe.
When comparing the list of brothers serving in the French priories and
commanderies against the list of brothers serving in the east, I did not
find examples of French commanders transferred to the east who then
served there as simple brothers or capitular bailiffs. Commanders in
Europe were administrators. With the exception of brothers serving in
the Iberian peninsula, who were involved in the military activities of the
reconquista, European commanders probably had little of the military

experience which was so necessary to command a town or a castle in the east.[16]

Hospitaller commanderies and priories in Europe served, nonetheless, as centres for the recruitment and transfer of forces to the east. Unfortunately there is no direct evidence for this process of recruitment and mobilization,[17] but a close examination of the lists of brothers can give us some useful indications.

Nearly all of the simple brothers who appear for the first time already serving in the east do not previously appear in documents relating to the order in Europe. Bearing in mind that information could be at times missing or fragmentary, one might conclude that many brothers destined for the Holy Land did not serve in European houses at all, or only for very short periods, before they crossed the Mediterranean. Moreover, in the lists of brothers who served in the French priories and commanderies, there is a significant number of brothers who appear only once or a very few times as witnesses to charters issued in their commanderies. To give just a few examples: Hugh of *Solillaris* was a simple brother in Trinquetaille and witnessed only two charters.[18] Hugh of Ascros, a simple brother in Manosque in 1235, and Adam of Cailly, a simple brother in Paris in 1189, appear only once as witnesses to charters issued in their commanderies.[19] These brothers could have been transferred from these houses after a short period, perhaps even to the Holy Land, where their names would not necessarily have been recorded in the surviving documents, especially if they only served there as simple brothers.

These brothers could have provided the core from which the order guaranteed a constant transfer of Hospitallers to the east, as well as additional shipments of manpower to restore depleted forces following military operations. I have tried to estimate the size of the order's forces in campaigns and its losses, but the lack of specific evidence makes this a difficult task. For example, during the siege of Damietta in 1218, the Order of the Hospital and the Order of the Temple each maintained approximately 2,000 men and 700 mounts. The sources are, however, not clear as to the total number of casualties suffered by the Hospitallers during this campaign. James of Vitry wrote to Pope Honorius III that the Hospitallers and the Templars had lost 200 brother-knights during the siege. After the conquest of Damietta the Christians raided the coastal town of Burlus, where the Hospitallers suffered more casualties, including their marshal, Aymar of L'Ayron.[20]

It seems that the military orders only maintained a limited number of brother-knights in the east. Severe casualties required immediate replacement. The losses at the siege of Darbsak in 1237, where the Templars lost 100 out of 120 knights as well as 300 crossbowmen,[21] caused both orders, the Templars and the Hospitallers, to mobilize their forces in Europe at once. A well-known passage in Matthew Paris's *Chronica majora* is highly illustrative of the Hospitallers' mobilization. The chronicler reports that, following the news of the Templars' defeat at Darbsak, thirty Hospitaller brother-knights left Clerkenwell, the headquarters of the order's English priory just outside London, and rode fully armed through London's streets on their way to aid their brothers in the Holy Land.[22]

The loss of one hundred brother-knights must have been a heavy blow to the Templars. One estimate of their total forces in the Latin east is around 600 knights.[23] With the deterioration of the situation in the Latin settlements in the thirteenth century, even a relatively small number of casualties was grave. During the siege of Tripoli in April 1289 the Hospitallers lost forty brother-knights and a large number of horses and arms – losses so severe that they had to be replaced immediately. Consequently, the master John of Villiers ordered each priory to send men, horses and money with the next August passage.[24]

The Hospitallers' contribution to the defence of the Latin settlements from the second half of the twelfth century onwards is unquestionable. Yet the sources have fewer allusions to their military activities than to those of the Templars. The correspondence sent to the west after the battle of Hattin describes the Templars' enormous losses at the hands of Saladin, but not those of the Hospitallers. Very soon after the battle, in late July or early August 1187, *Terricus*, the grand commander of the Templars, notified Pope Urban III, Count Philip of Alsace and all the Templar brothers that the order had lost 230 brother-knights in the battle itself and another sixty in the battle of the Spring of the Cresson on 1 May 1187.[25] Letters of appeal sent by the Hospitallers at about the same time describe the critical situation of the Christian settlers, but give no indication of the number of Hospitaller brother-knights killed at Hattin and after, when most of their castles fell into Saladin's hands.[26] This correspondence could give the erroneous impression that the Hospitallers' role at Hattin was negligible and their casualties insignificant. My study of the members of the order serving in the east before and after Hattin indicates that the Hospitallers' casualties must have been very heavy. Its leadership disappeared and had to be replaced by 'new' men, either those who were already in the east and could now be promoted to higher ranks or those transferred in from Europe.

Twenty-five brothers who served in the Latin east before Hattin have been identified by the toponyms found in their names. Some were castellans and commanders, leading to the expectation that they might have eventually attained a higher office. Yet their names disappear, to be replaced by those of simple brothers-at-arms promoted to their posts, such as Peter of Mirmande.[27] Peter, who survived Hattin, had joined the commandery of Alleyras (part of Le Puy en Velay) in 1163. Twenty years later he appeared as a simple brother in documents issued by the order in Acre and Jerusalem. In 1193, he was promoted to castellan of the Krak des Chevaliers, and he became the grand commander of the order (the master's second-in-command) in 1202.[28] After 1190, a new group of brothers appears for the first time in documents relating to the order in the east. Some of them already held offices, such as that of commander, in Tripoli or Tyre.[29] In this group there are brother-knights who would be leading figures of the order later on, including Geoffrey le Rat, who was commander of Antioch in 1198, castellan of the Krak des Chevaliers in 1204 and master in 1206.[30] There was also William of Villiers, who was commander of Acre in 1192, grand commander of 'outremer' in 1193, prior of England in 1199 and prior of France in 1207.[31] Heavy losses led to the rapid promotion of brothers in the east and the transfer of those from the west to Palestine and Syria to replace a leadership that had disappeared.

The battle of La Forbie in October 1244 has been compared to Hattin because of the huge Christian losses. In this case, unlike Hattin, the sources specify the number of casualties the Hospitallers suffered: 200 brother-knights were killed; the master and thirty brothers were captured.[32] The total number of Hospitallers in the kingdom of Jerusalem was about 300, so that for the order La Forbie constituted an almost complete annihilation of its eastern ranks, which a grand mobilization in the European provinces, as contemporary chronicles describe it, sought to remedy.[33]

Twenty-two brothers serving in the east during the period before La Forbie (1235–44) have been identified through the toponyms in their names. Some were castellans and commanders, so that, as was the case with Hattin, one might expect to find them later on occupying higher offices. However, only very few – such as John of Ronay, who was the commander of Tripoli in 1241 and lieutenant master in 1245, and William of Corcelles, a simple brother-knight in Acre in 1240 and marshal in 1248 – are named again in the sources immediately after La Forbie.[34] After the battle a new group of brothers appeared in the east for the first time. Some were simple brothers, suggesting that they may have been new recruits, among them Joscelin of Tournel, who is named as a simple brother in Acre in 1248, but was promoted to castellan of Mount Tabor in 1254 and marshal in 1262.[35] Others appear as officers from the outset, for example the commanders of Tyre, Tripoli, Antioch, Cyprus and the castellan of Margat. This could reflect a mobilization and promotion of brothers in Europe or the Latin east.[36] The restoration of Hospitaller manpower after La Forbie must have been extremely efficient, enabling the order to participate in the Egyptian crusade of Louis IX only four years later.[37]

To sum up: despite the lack of specific data, it is possible, by tracking down the members of the order and following their careers, to draw conclusions as to the regular shipment of brothers to the east and the restoring of the order's fighting forces after defeats on the battlefield. The ability to replenish depleted ranks over and over again is a sign of the order's ongoing vitality and its institutional capacity.

Notes

[1] The term 'brothers' is used in this study in its broader sense and refers to full members of the order. Although by the end of the twelfth century members of the Hospital were divided into several ranks, namely brother-priests and brothers-at-arms (the latter indicating both brother-knights and sergeants), it is often difficult to determine at which rank a specific brother served. Most sources mention the brothers under the general heading *fratres Hospitalis* and only occasionally specify their rank or office. For membership in the order of the Hospital see Jonathan Riley-Smith, *The Knights of St. John in Jerusalem and Cyprus c.1050–1310* (London, 1967), pp. 236–40.

[2] I am using the terms 'France' and 'French' for convenience. I have not restricted this research to the boundaries of the medieval kingdom of France, but, rather, follow those of the three French priories: France, St Gilles and Auvergne.

[3] See Judith Bronstein, *The Hospitallers and the Holy Land: Financing the Latin East, 1187–1274* (Woodbridge, 2005). These lists include only brothers for whom I have found a clear identification, namely a toponym, which – in many cases – has also allowed me to trace the places of origin of the brothers (for example Bertrand of Avignon). In those cases where the places of origin have been established, I have specified them next to the toponym. For French brothers this specification is in accordance with the departmental division of modern France, for example Bertrand of Mornans (Drôme).

Brothers whose first names only have survived or whose cognomina were not unique (such as *blancus, bravius* etc.) were not included, as first names or common nicknames do not allow the name to be used to follow a brother's career and places of service.

4   Joseph Delaville le Roulx (ed.), *Cartulaire général de l'ordre des Hospitaliers de Saint-Jean de Jérusalem (1100–1310)* (Paris, 1894–1905), vol. 1, nos 552, 842, 868.

5   Delaville, *Cartulaire*, vol. 2, no. 1172.

6   Paul A. Amargier (ed.), *Cartulaire de Trinquetaille* (Aix, 1972), no. 220.

7   Daniel Le Blévec and Alain Venturini (eds), *Cartulaire du Prieuré de Saint Gilles de l'Hôpital de Saint Jean de Jérusalem (1129–1210)* (Paris, 1997), nos 3, 312.

8   Claude Faure (ed.), *Inventaire sommaire des Archives départementales antérieurs à 1790, Rhône: Archives écclésiastiques, Série H*, vol. 3 (Lyon, 1945), pp. 97–8.

9   Delaville, *Cartulaire*, vol. 3, nos 3384, 3508.

10   Ibid., vol. 3, no. 3460. Raymond was commander of Orange until at least July 1273; see ibid., vol. 3, nos 3508, 3512.

11   Le Blévec and Venturini, *Cartulaire du Prieuré de Saint Gilles*, nos 79, 113, 118–19, 123, 269.

12   Ibid., nos 45, 69, 92; Amargier, *Cartulaire de Trinquetaille*, nos 52, 165.

13   Le Blévec and Venturini, *Cartulaire du Prieuré de Saint Gilles*, no. 4; Amargier, *Cartulaire de Trinquetaille*, no. 209.

14   Riley-Smith, *Knights of St. John*, p. 348.

15   William's career is not necessarily an example for that of other brothers. Jochen Burgtorf has pointed to the fact that in the twelfth and thirteenth centuries the careers of high dignitaries in the orders of the Hospital and the Temple did not follow a clear pattern. See Jochen Burgtorf, 'Leadership structures in the orders of the Hospital and the Temple (twelfth to early fourteenth century): select aspects', in Zsolt Hunyadi and József Laszlovsky (eds), *The Crusades and the Military Orders: Expanding the Frontiers of Medieval Latin Christianity* (Budapest, 2001), pp. 379–94. For the grand commandery of 'outremer' see Riley-Smith, *Knights of St. John*, pp. 366–9; Joseph Delaville le Roulx, *Les Hospitaliers en Terre Sainte et à Chypre (1100–1310)* (Paris, 1904), p. 414. For William of Villiers see Delaville, *Cartulaire*, vol. 1, nos 919, 945, 1056; vol. 2, nos 1243, 1330–2.

16   There are few examples of dignitaries who served in castellanies in the Iberian peninsula and were later transferred to the east: Aimery of Pax had been a commander in the castellany of Amposta in 1200, castellan of Margat in 1206, castellan of Seleucia in 1210 and grand commander of 'outremer' (i.e., the west) in 1215–16; see Delaville, *Cartulaire*, vol. 2, nos 1114, 1232, 1349, 1355, 1444, 1450, 1459–60, 1464, 1484.

17   These topics have been studied by Alan Forey and Malcolm Barber: Forey deals mainly with issues of places of recruitment and service as well as with personal motivations to enter the military orders. Barber has studied these

issues for the Order of the Temple. See Alan Forey, 'Recruitment to the military Orders (twelfth to mid-fourteenth centuries)', *Viator*, 17 (1986), 139–71; Malcolm Barber, *The New Knighthood: A History of the Order of the Temple* (Cambridge, 1994), pp. 214–19; Malcolm Barber, 'Supplying the crusader states: the role of the Templars', in Benjamin Z. Kedar (ed.), *The Horns of Hattin* (Jerusalem/London, 1992), pp. 317–21.

18 Amargier, *Cartulaire de Trinquetaille*, nos 216, 305.

19 Delaville, *Cartulaire*, vol. 1, no. 868; vol. 2, no. 2099.

20 Ibid., vol. 2, no. 1633; Robert B. C. Huygens (ed.), *Lettres de Jacques de Vitry, 1160/1170–1240, évêque de Saint-Jean d'Acre* (Leiden, 1960), p. 121 no. 5. For Burlus see 'Gesta crucigerorum Rhenanorum', in *Quinti belli sacri scriptores minores*, ed. Reinhold Röhricht (Geneva, 1879), pp. 51–2; 'Gesta obsidionis Damiate', ibid., p. 102. For Aymar of L'Ayron see Riley-Smith, *Knights of St. John*, p. 315. The military orders also employed a great number of mercenaries in this campaign. Marshall believes that many of the 2,500 crossbowmen who fought in the Fifth Crusade were employed by them: Christopher Marshall, *Warfare in the Latin East, 1192–1291* (Cambridge, 1992), p. 58.

21 The castle of Darbsak was located in the Amanus march. For the castle and the Templars' defeat see Barber, *The New Knighthood*, pp. 120, 232.

22 *Matthæi Parisiensis, monachi Sancti Albani, Chronica majora*, ed. Henry R. Luard, 7 vols, Rolls Series, 57 (London, 1872–83), vol. 3, pp. 404–6.

23 Barber, 'Supplying the crusader states', 318.

24 Delaville, *Cartulaire*, vol. 3, no. 4050.

25 For *Terricus*'s letter to the Templars see *Chronica magistri Rogeri de Houedene*, ed. William Stubbs, 4 vols, Rolls Series, 51 (London, 1868–71), vol. 2, pp. 324–5 (text); Reinhold Röhricht (ed.), *Regesta Regni Hierosolymitani (MXCVII–MCCXCI)* (Innsbruck, 1893–1904), no. 660 (regest); Barber, *The New Knighthood*, pp. 115–16. For the name and site of this battle, see Denys Pringle, 'The Spring of the Cresson in Crusading History', in *Dei gesta per Francos: Études sur les croisades dédiées à Jean Richard; Crusade Studies in Honour of Jean Richard*, ed. Michel Balard, Benjamin Z. Kedar and Jonathan Riley-Smith (Aldershot, 2001), pp. 231–40.

26 For Hospitaller correspondence see 'Magni presbyteri Annales Reicherspergenses', ed. Wilhelm Wattenbach, in *Monumenta Germaniae Historica, Scriptores*, vol. 17 (Hanover, 1861), pp. 508–9; Delaville, *Cartulaire*, vol. 1, nos 863, 945; Santos Agustín García Larragueta (ed.), *El gran priorado de Navarra de la orden de San Juan de Jerusalén (siglos XII–XIII)*, 2 vols (Pamplona, 1957), vol. 2, nos 85–7.

27 Castellans and commanders in the east must have been replaced by brothers-at-arms, as military experience was essential for these posts. After the mid-thirteenth century these posts were held by brother-knights only; see Riley-Smith, *Knights of St. John*, p. 320.

28 If the Peter mentioned in the sources is indeed one and the same man, he was

married and his charter of affiliation includes the consent of his wife and sons. See Augustin Chassaing (ed.), *Cartulaire des Hospitaliers (Ordre de Saint-Jean de Jérusalem) du Velay* (Paris, 1888), no. 16; Delaville, *Cartulaire*, vol. 1, nos 663, 754, 941, 1031, 1085, 1096; vol. 2, no. 1156.

[29] Delaville, *Cartulaire*, vol. 1, nos 932 (Trimond, commander of Tripoli), 972 (Ralph of Lodun, commander of Tyre).

[30] Delaville, *Cartulaire*, vol. 1, nos 1031, 1085, 1096; vol. 2, nos 1198, 1231, 1262.

[31] For William of Villiers see note 15 above.

[32] Letters sent to the west reported a much higher number of 325 knights. See, for example, a letter sent by the patriarch of Jerusalem to the Christian world in the aftermath of La Forbie in 'Cronica fratris Salimbene de Adam ordinis Minorum', ed. Oswald Holder-Egger, in *Monumenta Germaniae Historica, Scriptores*, vol. 32 (Hanover/Leipzig, 1905–13), p. 177. However, Riley-Smith, after comparing the different sources, has estimated that the order lost 'only' about 200 knights; see *Ayyubids, Mamelukes and Crusaders: Selections from the Tarikh al-Duwal wa'l-Muluk of Ibn al-Furat*, ed. and trans. Ursula Lyons and Malcolm C. Lyons, introduction and commentary by Jonathan Riley-Smith, 2 vols (Cambridge, 1971), vol. 2, p. 173 note 2; vol. 2, p. 174 note. 9.

[33] For the number of Hospitaller brother-knights serving in the east see Riley-Smith, *Knights of St. John*, pp. 124, 327. For a contemporary chronicle which describes the orders' mobilization see *Matthæi Parisiensis Chronica majora*, ed. Luard, vol. 4, p. 416.

[34] For John of Ronay see Delaville, *Cartulaire*, vol. 2, nos 2280, 2353, 2471, 2482, 2483. For William of Corcelles see ibid., vol. 2, nos 2245, 2482; Riley-Smith, *Knights of St. John*, p. 143.

[35] Delaville, *Cartulaire*, vol. 2, nos 2482, 2934; vol. 3, no. 3045.

[36] Many of these new brothers appeared for the first time as witnesses in a document issued in their headquarters in Acre in 1248: Delaville, *Cartulaire*, vol. 2, no. 2482.

[37] With regard to the military orders, this crusade is frequently mentioned because of the terrible losses suffered by the Templars at al-Mansurah. Although the Hospitallers did not suffer such heavy casualties, they did participate in this campaign and lost their lieutenant master, John of Ronay; see *Matthæi Parisiensis Chronica majora*, ed. Luard, vol. 6, pp. 191–7; Bronstein, *The Hospitallers and the Holy Land*.

4

The Exchange of Information and Money between the Hospitallers of Rhodes and their European Priories in the Fourteenth and Fifteenth Centuries

THERESA M. VANN

The institutionalized movement of men and materials from the European priories of the order of St John to the central convent on Rhodes played a vital role in the realization of the Hospitallers' mission during the fourteenth and fifteenth centuries. The responsions, an annual payment that the European priories contributed to the order's common treasury, were an important link between Rhodes and the west. The responsions paid the expenses of the infirmary on Rhodes, the sustenance of the main convent and for the military campaigns against the Muslims. Even in times of peace, however, this income was insufficient, while warfare created an additional burden. Moreover, wars and schism in Europe interrupted the payment of responsions, revealing an essential weakness in the order's international organization, one that remained the focus of papal attempts to reform the order and ensure its participation in crusades. To the order and the papacy, the payment of responsions was an important indicator of the order's well-being, and the central convent's apparent inability to collect the full amount of the responsions called the obedience of the western priories into question. At times the main convent faced considerable debt, due in part to arrears in responsions. Yet, except under extraordinary circumstances, the central convent continued to make up financial shortfalls and remained the order's administrative centre.

Although it appears that the priories could, by withholding responsions, flout the authority of the central convent, other mechanisms of discipline, authority and cooperation maintained ties between the central convent on Rhodes and the western priories. Papal oversight played a part in strengthening the central convent's ties with its western priories and preventing its enmeshment in the politics of the eastern Mediterranean. But direct magisterial appeals to the priories also had an important role in sustaining the Hospitaller network of personal contacts. The correspondence exchanged between the main convent and the western priories during emergencies, such as the Ottoman capture of Constantinople in 1453, provided justification for immediate collection of responsions and the imposition of additional levies, which were confirmed by the general chapter. Over the course of time, the letters evolved from simple demands to emotive invocations of the damage done to eastern Christendom by Turkish aggression. The correspondence became an important part of maintaining the relationship between the priories and the central convent, as they justified extraordinary exactions and provided texts for sermons or ambassadorial missions. The decision to seek more revenue from western Europe intensified the relationship that already existed between the central convent and the priories.

The central convent on Rhodes was the administrative headquarters of the order, the location of the master's residence and hospital. On Rhodes the master and the central convent met in councils to settle disputes among members in the western priories, award promotions and confirm commanderies. Most western Hospitaller knights would have some knowledge or experience of Rhodes. New members of the order, admitted through the western priories, served for a period of years at Rhodes before returning to their native priories. The general chapter, which met on an average of every two years in Rhodes (except when it was convened elsewhere, such as Rome), was the venue for priories to express criticism or to resolve differences with the master over policies and responsions. The western priors also served in the convent as the chief officials of the order, travelling to Rhodes and representing their priories at meetings of the general chapter.

Although the central convent maintained an infirmary on Rhodes and allocated a third of its revenue for its sustenance, it was the Hospitallers' military function that shaped its relationship with the west. Its mission to fight against the Muslims put considerable strain on the order's finances and occasionally raised questions about military expenditures. The western priories complained about the expenses of the conquest of Rhodes and the financial policies of Master Fulk de

Villaret (1305–17).[1] The resulting debts, estimated at about half a million florins by 1320, were offset by the eventual acquisition of Templar properties, including the estates on Cyprus, and contributions from the western priories.[2] The order did not pay off the debts incurred by Fulk de Villaret and the acquisition of the Templars' estates until 1334–5.[3] The convent had difficulties collecting responsions in Europe through the 1320s, especially in Denmark and Norway: King Haakon VII expelled the order from Norway in 1320, while King Eric VIII of Denmark had confiscated part of the order's property, which his successor Christopher II refused to return.[4] In addition, the order lost 360,000 florins in 1340 when its Florentine bankers went bankrupt.[5] In 1347 the master tried to collect the arrears of responsions from the priories of Denmark, Sweden and Norway by emphasizing obedience to the central convent in his letters to the priors.[6]

The Hospitallers' military strategy of the early fourteenth century reflected the financial strains on the order. The central convent formed leagues with the Venetians and focused on containing Mameluke fleets, a significant change in strategy that favoured trade in the eastern Mediterranean.[7] In the west, this strategy did not appear to advance recovery of the Holy Land. Pope Clement VI accused the Hospitallers of luxury and idleness, and, in 1344, ordered them to participate in the papal league with the Venetians and the kingdom of Cyprus that captured Smyrna.[8] During the campaign the Hospitallers received a papal subsidy to support four galleys, but the capture of Smyrna involved the order in a long-term commitment to subsidize the fortress at a cost of 3,000 florins a year. In 1374, the order was made responsible for its defence.[9]

The Ottoman capture of Gallipoli from the Byzantines in 1354 and the accension of a new pope, Innocent VI, in 1355 forced the Hospitallers to re-evaluate their mission and actions in the east. Previously, the order's financial situation caused it to make several accommodations with the Turks, the most recent in 1348.[10] But for Innocent VI, the order was most healthy and useful when it was pursuing an active agenda against the Turks. He, like many of the order's western critics, did not see how protecting eastern trade and reinforcing the fortifications of Rhodes extended the crusades against the Turks, and suspected that the central convent wallowed in eastern luxury. Innocent VI demanded several reforms of the order, including new campaigns against the Turks and the transfer of the convent to Turkish territory.[11] These reforms were not enacted, and the Hospitallers kept their convent on Rhodes.

Rhodes became a staging point for the crusade against Egypt in 1365. After the sack of Alexandria in October 1365, the master wrote a general appeal to the western priories for help. Unlike previous letters that were intended to collect outstanding responses by emphasizing obedience,[12] Master Raymond Berenguer wrote that he feared that the sultan would cut off Anatolian food sources for Rhodes in retaliation.[13] The letter may have brought results, for the accounts of the western receivers in 1365 show that the order was 'in the black', even though war and local politics blocked responses from Castile, Portugal and Aquitaine.[14]

The tenor of the master's letter revealed the extent of the central convent's dependence upon local sources of supply and the adverse effects this could have on the convent's ability to pursue papal policy. Responsions formed only a portion of the order's western revenue. The master collected the spoils of deceased knights and the revenues from vacant priories, as well as allocations from crusading tithes, the sale of indulgences and occasional donations from western rulers. The order's eastern sources of income included the responsions from its estates on Cyprus, leases and port fees from Rhodes, profits from its participation in the sugar trade and tribute from the Muslim mainland. The central convent collected port fees from the trading networks of Venetian, Genoese, Turkish and Rhodian merchants who used their harbour.[15] The master also made up deficits out of his own income.[16]

After the campaign against Egypt, subsequent reformers of the Hospitallers emphasized financial reform through the collection of western responsions, which would decrease the convent's reliance upon eastern sources of income and make it less vulnerable to local politics. This, however, assumed that European sources of revenue were steady, which was not always the case during the fourteenth century. The Hundred Years War and wars in Spain caused arrears of responsions, which were resolved by a meeting of the general chapter in Avignon in 1367.[17] The Black Death, which first appeared in Europe in 1347, also inflicted serious damage on the order, not only killing its personnel but also thereby reducing the income that could be raised from the commanderies.[18] By around 1370–3, the accounts of the western receivers showed deficits, and in 1373 Pope Gregory XI ordered an inquest into the order's western holdings as part of his plan to reform the order by improving the collection of responsions.[19] The inquest showed that the Hospitallers' French lands had suffered from the ravages of war, and that comparatively few members of the order resided in the western priories.[20] Gregory ordered the Hospitallers to collect 40,000 florins over the next three years for the expenses of the central convent, and an additional 80,000 florins to fight the Turks.[21] By 1377, Gregory XI permitted the Hospitallers to sell goods to finance a major campaign.[22] This campaign materialized as Master Juan Fernández de Heredia's expedition against Epiros but failed, leaving the Hospitallers in debt once more.[23]

The papal schism of 1378–1409 reduced the Hospitallers' western revenues. Although the central convent remained obedient to the Avignon pope, the western priories split in obedience between Rome and Avignon. In 1383, an anti-master, Richard Caracciolo, was elected, and the priories of Bohemia and Moravia stopped sending responsions to Rhodes.[24] To raise the money to fight the Turks, Heredia increased taxes in the west in 1390,[25] and in 1392 promulgated an assembly in Aragon to repair the arrears of responsions.[26] Already in 1390, the papacy had begun selling indulgences for the defence of Rhodes.[27] Heredia assured the western priories that the money would be used to fight the Turks, after the payment and administration of the responsions were adjusted. However, the new sultan, Bayazid I, proved a formidable adversary, defeating the Christian forces at Nicopolis in 1396. Although Hospitaller treaties with Muslim powers were always controversial in the west, and the order usually downplayed them, the order sought a treaty with Bayazid in 1403.[28] The treaty did not save Smyrna, which was lost to the Mongols in 1402.

Fifteenth-century Hospitaller records show the extent of the central convent's participation in the economy of the eastern Mediterranean. During periods of relative peace, the convent on Rhodes traded throughout the eastern Mediterranean. The central convent continued to collect revenues from its estates on Cyprus, leases and port fees from Rhodes, the sugar trade and tribute from the Muslim mainland. Smyrna had been an important source of corn, and its loss in 1402 required Rhodes to find new sources.[29] After the loss of Smyrna, the Hospitallers began construction of the castle of Bodrum on the coast of Anatolia.[30] The Hospitaller presence on the Turkish mainland attracted donations from the west, which helped offset its expenses, and helped secure a potential Turkish naval base against Rhodes. The mid-fifteenth-century records in the *Liber conciliorum* show that the order acquired grain from Sicily, and, under licence from the pope, wood and victuals from Egypt and Syria.[31] A sudden change in the political structure of the east would bring economic as well as military retaliation upon the Hospitallers.

This change occurred during the fifteenth century, when the Ottomans emerged as a significant threat at the same time that the Mongols were aggressive in the east and the Mamelukes remained a formidable enemy. The Mamelukes' ships threatened Rhodes, and Pope Martin V pledged the priories of Catalonia and Amposta against the sultan's fleet in 1427.[32] After 1440, direct attacks upon the central convent generated magisterial and papal appeals for help. The general chapter increased responses when the Mamelukes attacked the Rhodian fleet in 1440 and again in 1445, 1446 and 1450.[33] The papacy also appropriated crusade revenues for the Hospitallers, arguing that they fought the enemies of Christ.[34] After 1440, the pope relieved the Hospitallers' western priories of the crusading tithe, solicited additional revenues from the priories for Rhodes and granted indulgences to those who contributed to galleys for Rhodes in the order's European churches.[35]

Despite this activity, the fifteenth-century Hospitallers did not collect enough responses to cover their expenses. This problem is graphically illustrated in an estimate of the income and expenses of the Hospitallers of Rhodes that Brother Pierre Lamand, the proctor general of the order, presented to the pope in 1432 (see Figures 5 and 6).[36] The figures survive in a report of the proctor general of the Teutonic Knights to his master, and he appears to have entered some categories of expenditure twice. However, the figures may provide a rough idea of the proportion of income that the order received from various sources and the percentage of its income that was allocated to different aspects of its mission. Lamand reported that in 1432 the central convent received 46,550 ducats into its treasury and spent 65,500 ducats, creating a deficit of 18,950 ducats. More than half of the order's income came from western sources. The European priories paid 24,000 ducats in responses, representing 51 per cent of the income, with an additional 16 per cent from spoils, *passagium* and vacant priories. The priories each paid different amounts of responses: France paid 10,000 ducats, England 7,000, Germany 3,000 and Italy and Spain both paid 2,000. Pope Eugenius IV may have sought to make up these deficits by personally requesting the Holy Roman Emperor, the king of Castile-León and the king of England to ensure the payment of responses.[37] The order's eastern properties contributed 34 per cent of its income. This included the revenues from commerce and property in Rhodes (5,000 ducats) and the responses from Cyprus (6,900 ducats). The following year Master Antoni de Fluvià combined the commanderies of Cyprus and Lango with the island of Nisyros, and adjusted their contribution to the common treasury.[38] The largest single expenditure was food: grain for the brothers and horses (17,000 ducats) as well as meat and conventual living expenses (23,000 ducats). The budget allocated 4,000 ducats for the infirmary and 2,000 ducats to pay physicians and surgeons. The custodian of Bodrum received 10,000 ducats, representing 15 per cent of the order's costs. In 1450, the priories reached an agreement with the convent that it would reduce its maintenance costs to 54,000 florins a year and that of this sum, 20,000 would come from the west, 18,000 from the order's eastern holdings and 12,000 from the master.[39]

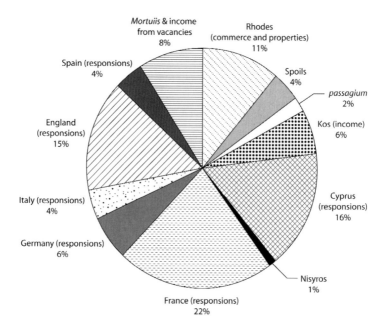

Figure 5 Sources of Hospitaller income, 1432 (according to Brother Pierre Lamand)

The Ottoman conquest of Constantinople in 1453 caused Pope Nicholas V to begin planning a new crusade. This, and the possible Ottoman threat to Rhodes, increased the correspondence between the central convent and the priories. The master, Jean de Lastic, immediately wrote to several western priories in July 1453, describing the fall of Constantinople and asking for revenues in addition to the usual responsions to spend on artillery and for a levy of able-bodied men and

their servants to be sent to Rhodes.[40] Lastic wrote additional letters
to collect outstanding responsions in January and February 1454.[41]
Magisterial appeals following the fall of Constantinople were sub-
stantively different from the appeal following the sack of Alexandria in
1365. The letters detail Turkish atrocities against Christians, and
indicate that the order had committed its resources to fight Mehmet the
Conqueror and required the full participation of the priories to defend
Rhodes. The letters offered justification for the extraordinary exactions
that were later confirmed in meetings of the general chapter of the
order. The letters also helped raise funds by their inclusion in sermons
selling indulgences in aid of Rhodes.[42]

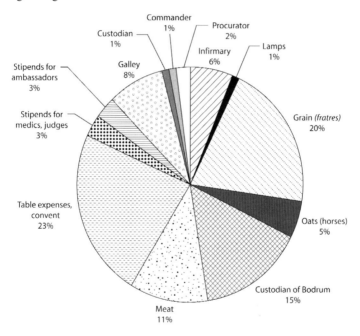

Figure 6 Hospitallers' expenditures, 1432, Rhodes
(according to Brother Pierre Lamand)

Despite these efforts, the convent's deficit increased after the fall of
Constantinople in 1453. When the new master, Jacques de Milly, was
elected in 1454, he held a general chapter to secure the payment of
50,000 florins still owed to the common treasury.[43] The recorded proceedings of this general chapter show that Nicholas V wanted the order to

reform its finances so that it could better perform its Hospitaller functions
for the sick and poor in the coming struggle against Mehmet II, not to
pursue a military function.[44] At the same time, an important change
occurred in the order's relationship with the western priories. Relations
with the Hospitallers' Muslim trading partners, such as the emir of
Menteshe,[45] were detrimentally affected by the predominance of the
Ottoman state, so that the central convent became more dependent
upon the west for survival.

The Hospitallers sent ambassadors to the courts of Europe to raise
money. Jean de Lastic pledged the order's Catalan properties in 1454 to
raise 30,000 florins for the expenses of the order.[46] Alfonso V, who
wanted to safeguard Catalan trade in the Aegean, facilitated the
transfer of funds.[47] But the death of Nicholas V in 1455 caused the
planned crusade to fall apart. His successor, Calixtus III, intended to
keep Rhodes supplied as an outpost against the Turks, basing the papal
fleet there.[48] Like Gregory XI, Calixtus argued that the Hospitallers
should receive western financing because they fought the enemies of
Christ, and he exempted the order in Europe from paying the ecclesiastical tithe to fight the Turks.[49] A gift from King Charles VII of
France, solicited by a Hospitaller ambassador, Pierre d'Aubusson, became the basis for funding the papal fleet.[50] The fleet arrived in 1457,
but accomplished little after the death of Calixtus III in 1458 other than
increasing hostility between the Hospitallers and the Ottomans. In
1460, Pope Pius II transferred treasure to Rhodes to fight Mehmet.[51]

Despite the threat posed by the Ottomans, internal rivalry between
the Spanish and French *langues* threatened the payment of responsions
in the 1460s. When the Spanish grand master, Raymond Zacosta, discussed renewing hostilities against the Ottomans with Pius II in 1462
after Mehmet captured the Hospitaller settlements of Mytilene and
Lesbos, the indebtedness of the common treasury was a major impediment.[52] The Hospitallers sent out ambassadors from Rhodes to appeal
for help, but also agreed to pay tribute to the Ottomans.[53] In 1465
Zacosta began a reorganization of the defences of Rhodes and raised
12,000 ducats from Philip of Burgundy to build the Tower of St
Nicholas, an important part of the harbour fortifications.[54] The French
priories, which had paid the largest share of responsions in 1432,
complained to Pope Paul II about Zacosta's policies and his demands
for responsions to fight Mehmet.[55] The kings of Aragon and France
supported this complaint. To restore discipline in the order, Paul II
insisted that the Hospitallers hold a meeting of the general chapter in

Rome in 1466. At the general chapter, the Hospitallers were found to be 250,000 ducats in debt because the responsions were in arrears.[56] Zacosta had to present a description of all the Hospitaller campaigns against the Turks between 1457 and 1462 to justify the cost of defence and the payment of tribute. Paul ordered the brothers to pay off the debts in ten years.[57] Zacosta relinquished the Iberian priory he still held, the castellany of Amposta, to pay for the remainder of the construction of the Tower of St Nicholas.

After the fall of the Venetian island of Euboea (Negroponte) to Mehmet II's fleet in 1470, the central convent expected Mehmet to besiege Rhodes next, and, with the papacy, put into operation the fund-raising apparatus that had developed since the fall of Constantinople, collecting money and materials from the European priories. The prior of Capua was sent to the pope and the king of Naples to seek aid against the Turks.[58] The new master, Ursini, wrote to the priories describing the battle for Euboea and held meetings of the general chapter in 1471 and 1477.[59]

Pope Sixtus IV, Paul's successor, issued a series of bulls in 1472 that assigned revenues to the order and permitted the Hospitallers to collect the income from vacant priories for the defence of Rhodes.[60] Like Gregory and Calixtus before him, Sixtus justified these acts because an invasion was expected, and it was incumbent upon all to support those who fought the enemies of the Cross of Christ. In addition, between 1478 and 1481 Sixtus authorized the sale of indulgences for the defence of Rhodes against the Turks.[61] In 1480 King Edward IV of England also permitted the sale of indulgences by John Kendall, the English prior, to finance the construction of fortifications on Rhodes and at the castle of Bodrum.[62] Fund-raising on behalf of Rhodes continued even after the conclusion of the Turkish siege, through the sale of indulgences and the circulation of the official account of the siege, printed in several editions in Venice, Ulm and Barcelona.[63]

This survey of Hospitaller interaction between the central convent and the western priories during the fourteenth and fifteenth centuries helps answer one very important question of how an order that frequently ran up huge amounts of debt was still able to mount effective military campaigns against the Mamelukes and the Ottomans. The answer lies in the maintenance of the central convent's ties with the western priories, aided by papal authority. The central convent was part of the rich economy of the eastern Mediterranean, but reliance upon local income involved treaties with schismatics and Muslims, which could impair the order's ability or willingness to fight and leave it open to criticism. Western sources of income were important for maintaining the Hospitallers of Rhodes within the ambit of papal policy and preventing them from becoming an independent state, enmeshed in the politics of the eastern Mediterranean. Papal attempts to reform the order focused on the payment of responsions, using them as a means to determine the strength of the institutional ties between the western priories and the central convent on Rhodes. The papacy helped make up deficits by identifying the defence of Rhodes as part of the crusades, making the Hospitallers eligible for crusade revenues. Unsuccessful or abortive campaigns against the Muslims left the convent on Rhodes open to retaliation, making the fortification of Rhodes a key part of any crusade strategy.

The fall of Constantinople in 1453 stimulated the strengthening of ties between the central convent and the western priories. The Ottoman advance through the eastern Mediterranean cut off the Hospitallers from their eastern sources of income. The master's written appeals to the priories for men, supplies and responsions aimed to compensate for the loss and acknowledged the role of the western priories in maintaining the central convent. These appeals leave an impression that the priories enjoyed considerable autonomy and might refuse to pay responsions with impunity. While paying the responsions was a matter of obedience to the order, it remained the master's responsibility to spend them wisely and prove the need for extraordinary exactions. The letters to the western priories served this purpose by describing battles and the political situation, keeping western Christendom informed of the convent's role in fighting the Muslims and facilitating fund-raising among the laity. The dramatic written appeals ensured that the general chapter remained the venue for exacting revenue from the priories. The letters presented the master's case for imposing extraordinary income. Western priories used the letters to raise money through preaching and sales of indulgences to pay the responsions levied by the order's general chapter. The exchange of information for money paid the convent's debts and involved western Europeans in the crusading movement.

Notes

[1] L'abbé René Aubert de Vertot d'Aubeuf, *The History of the Knights Hospitallers*, translation of *Histoire des Chevaliers Hospitaliers de St-Jean de*

Jérusalem (Edinburgh, 1757; reprinted New York, 1981), book 5 (Fulk de Villaret), vol. 2, pp. 99–100, 103; Joseph Delaville le Roulx, *Les Hospitaliers à Rhodes, 1310–1421* (Paris, 1913), pp. 12–13, 22–33; Norman Housley, *The Avignon Papacy and the Crusades, 1305–1378* (Oxford, 1986), pp. 283–6; Anthony Luttrell, 'Notes on Foulques de Villaret, master of the Hospital 1305–1319', in Anthony Luttrell, *The Hospitallers of Rhodes and Their Mediterranean World* (Aldershot, 1992), no. IV.

2   Norman Housley, *The Later Crusades, 1274–1580* (Oxford, 1992), p. 217; Delaville, *Hospitaliers à Rhodes*, p. 70.

3   Luttrell, 'Notes on Foulques de Villaret', p. 76.

4   Housley, *Later Crusades*, p. 217; Delaville, *Hospitaliers à Rhodes*, p. 70.

5   Anthony Luttrell, 'The Hospitallers of Rhodes confront the Turks: 1306–1421', in Luttrell, *Hospitallers of Rhodes*, no. II, p. 90; Housley, *Later Crusades*, p. 217.

6   Delaville, *Hospitaliers à Rhodes*, pp. 113–14; Sebastiano Pauli (ed.), *Codice diplomatico del sacro militare Ordine Gerosolimitano, oggi di Malta*, 2 vols (Lucca, 1733–7), vol. 2, p. 90 no. 62.

7   Peter W. Edbury, *The Kingdom of Cyprus and the Crusades, 1191–1374* (Cambridge, 1991), p. 157; Housley, *Avignon Papacy*, p. 25.

8   Luttrell, 'Hospitallers of Rhodes', p. 90; Kenneth Setton, *The Papacy and the Levant, 1204–1571*, 4 vols (Philadelphia, 1976), vol. 1, p. 218; Edbury, *Kingdom of Cyprus*, p. 158.

9   Anthony Luttrell, 'Gregory XI and the Turks: 1370–1378', in Anthony Luttrell, *Latin Greece, the Hospitallers, and the Crusades 1291–1440* (London, 1982), no. XV, p. 405; for the Hospitallers on Smyrna, see Jürgen Sarnowsky, 'Die Johanniter und Smyrna 1344–1402', *Römische Quartalschrift*, 86 (1991), 215–51.

10   Setton, *Papacy and the Levant*, vol. 1, p. 217.

11   Ibid., vol. 1, p. 230; Pauli, *Codice diplomatico*, vol. 2, pp. 91–2 no. 73.

12   Pauli, *Codice diplomatico*, vol. 2, pp. 90–1 no. 72.

13   Setton, *Papacy and the Levant*, vol. 1, p. 275; Comte Paul Riant, 'Six lettres relatives aux croisades', *Archives de l'Orient Latin*, 1 (1881), 383–92, here 391, from National Library of Malta, Archives of the Order of Malta (AOM) 48, fols 63v, 64, 223v–224. Also see letter to the proctor general of the order, in Pauli, *Codice diplomatico*, vol. 2, p. 95 no. 76; AOM 319, p. 42.

14   Anthony Luttrell, 'Papauté et hôpital: L'enquête de 1373', in Jean Glénisson (ed.), *L'enquête pontificale de 1373 sur l'ordre des Hospitaliers de Saint-Jean de Jérusalem*, vol. 1, *L'enquête dans le prieuré de France*, ed. Anne-Marie Legras, Robert Favreau and Anthony Luttrell (Paris, 1987), p. 14.

15   Luttrell, 'Hospitallers of Rhodes', pp. 91, 95.

16   Jürgen Sarnowsky, ' "The rights of the treasury": the financial administration of the Hospitallers on fifteenth-century Rhodes, 1421–1522', in Helen Nicholson (ed.), *The Military Orders*, vol. 2, *Welfare and Warfare* (Aldershot, 1998), pp. 270–1.

17   Luttrell, 'Papauté et hôpital', p. 14.

46 THERESA M. VANN

[18] Helen Nicholson, *The Knights Hospitaller* (Woodbridge, 2001), pp. 51–2 and note.

[19] Luttrell, 'Papauté et hôpital' p. 16; Luttrell, 'Gregory XI and the Turks', p. 404; and Jean Glénisson, 'L'enquête pontificale de 1373 sur les possessions des Hospitaliers de Saint-Jean-de-Jérusalem', *Bibliothèque de l'École des Chartes*, 129 (1971), 83–111.

[20] Glénisson, 'L'enquête pontificale', 94.

[21] Luttrell, 'Gregory XI and the Turks', p. 404.

[22] Pauli, *Codice diplomatico*, vol. 2, p. 99 no. 80.

[23] Housley, *Later Crusades*, p. 222.

[24] Pauli, *Codice diplomatico*, vol. 2, p. 408 no. 16.

[25] Luttrell, 'Hospitallers of Rhodes', p. 96; Housley, *Later Crusades*, p. 220.

[26] Delaville, *Hospitaliers à Rhodes*, pp. 381–3.

[27] Luttrell, 'Hospitallers of Rhodes', p. 96; Housley, *Later Crusades*, p. 220.

[28] Pauli, *Codice diplomatico*, vol. 2, p. 108 no. 86.

[29] Elizabeth A. Zacharidou, *Trade and Crusade: Venetian Crete and the Emirates of Menteshe and Aydin (1300–1415)* (Venice, 1983), pp. 163–4.

[30] Luttrell, 'Hospitallers of Rhodes', pp. 102–3; Anthony Luttrell, 'The building of the castle of the Hospitallers at Bodrum', in Anthony Luttrell, *The Hospitaller State on Rhodes and its Western Provinces, 1306–1462* (Aldershot, 1999), no. VI, pp. 143–61.

[31] AOM 76, fols 37, 164, 212.

[32] Pauli, *Codice diplomatico*, vol. 2, p. 117 no. 96.

[33] Sarnowsky, 'Rights of the treasury', p. 271.

[34] Pauli, *Codice diplomatico*, vol. 2, p. 123 no. 103; Jürgen Sarnowsky, *Macht und Herrschaft im Johanniterorden des 15. Jahrhunderts: Verfassung und Verwaltung der Johanniter auf Rhodos (1421–1522)* (Münster, 2001), pp. 527–30.

[35] Pauli, *Codice diplomatico*, vol. 2, pp. 120–5 nos 101–5; Léopold Devillers, *Inventaire analytique des commanderies belges de l'Ordre de Saint-Jean de Jérusalem ou de Malte* (Mons, 1876), p. 143 no. 742.

[36] Jan-Erik Beuttel, *Der Generalprokurator des Deutschen Ordens an der Römischen Kurie* (Marburg, 1999), pp. 614–16.

[37] Sarnowsky, 'Rights of the treasury', p. 271; Pauli, *Codice diplomatico*, vol. 2, pp. 118–19 nos 97–8.

[38] Louis de Mas Latrie, *Histoire de l'île de Chypre sous le règne des princes de la maison de Lusignan*, 3 vols (Paris, 1852–61), vol. 3, p. 15.

[39] Sarnowsky, 'Rights of the treasury', p. 272.

[40] R. Valentini, 'L'Egeo dopo la caduta di Constantinopoli nelle relazioni dei gran maestri di Rodi', *Bullettino dell'Istituto Storico Italiano per il Medio Evo e Archivio Muratoriano*, 51 (1936), 137–68, here 159–61 no. 1.

[41] Ibid., 161–4 nos 2–3.

[42] See Vienna, Österreichische Nationalbibliothek 3520, fols 30a–31b, for a copy of this letter in a collection of sermons for selling indulgences.

[43] Giacomo Bosio, Pierre de Boissat and Jean Baudoin, *Histoire des Chevaliers*

de l'Ordre de S. Jean de Hierusalem, 2 vols (Paris, 1659), vol. 1, p. 92.

44 AOM 282, fol. 8r.

45 Zacharidou, *Trade and Crusade*, pp. 31, 81–2. Menteshe was an important trading partner, continuing trade with Rhodes even during the Smyrna crusade and the sack of Alexandria.

46 Constantin Marinescu, 'L'île de Rhodes au XVe siècle et l'Ordre de Saint-Jean de Jérusalem d'après des documents inédits', in *Miscellanea Giovanni Mercati*, vol. 5, *Studi e Testi*, no. 125 (Città del Vaticano, 1946), 382–401, here 397.

47 Alan Ryder, *Alfonso the Magnanimous: King of Aragon, Naples, and Sicily, 1396–1458* (Oxford, 1990), p. 296.

48 AOM 1126, fols 385–386v; Setton, *Papacy and the Levant*, vol. 2, p. 189.

49 Devillers, *Inventaire analytique*, p. 14 no. 59.

50 Marinescu, 'L'île de Rhodes', 400.

51 Pauli, *Codice diplomatico*, vol. 2, pp. 138–9 nos 117–18.

52 Valentini, 'L'Egeo dopo la caduta di Constantinopoli', 147.

53 Housley, *Later Crusades*, p. 226.

54 Albert Gabriel, *La cité de Rhodes, MCCCX–MDXXII: Topographie, architecture militaire* (Paris, 1921), pp. 144–5; AOM 73, fol. 160.

55 Setton, *Papacy and the Levant*, vol. 2, p. 239 note 29.

56 Ibid., vol. 2, p. 281; *Le vite di Paolo II di Gaspare da Verona e Michele Canensi*, ed. Giuseppe Zippel, *Rerum Italicarum Scriptores*, new revised edition, vol. 3, part 16 (Città di Castello, 1904), pp. 185–8. Sarnowsky, *Macht und Herrschaft*, p. 540, finds the amount to be 346,000 écus, which included 98,000 écus that the master had provided for operating costs. There was an additional 40,000 écus owed to Catalonian annuities.

57 Valentini, 'L'Egeo dopo la caduta di Constantinopoli', 164–8.

58 AOM 74, fol. 48r–v.

59 Pauli, *Codice diplomatico*, vol. 2, p. 143 no. 122.

60 AOM 1126, fol. 408.

61 AOM 1126, fol. 410 (*Ad dilectorum filiorum*).

62 Pauli, *Codice diplomatico*, vol. 2, pp. 146–7 no. 123.

63 Theresa M. Vann, 'Guillaume Caoursin's *Descriptio obsidione Rhodiae* and the Archives of the Knights of Malta', in Zsolt Hunyadi and József Laszlovsky (eds), *The Crusades and the Military Orders: Expanding the Frontiers of Medieval Latin Christianity* (Budapest, 2001), pp. 109–20.

5

Hospitaller Brothers in Fifteenth-Century Rhodes

JÜRGEN SARNOWSKY

The Hospitallers conquered Rhodes between 1306 and 1310, and soon thereafter they transferred their convent, their headquarters and their main hospital to Rhodes town.[1] From then on, until the loss of Rhodes to the Ottomans in January 1523, 200, 300, and sometimes even more than 500 Hospitaller brothers lived together in the convent on Rhodes at the same time, coming from the priories in France, Spain, Italy, England and Germany.[2] This intensive international mobility required that the brothers who came to Rhodes as foreigners – as they had previously come to the Holy Land and Cyprus – had to accommodate themselves to an environment more or less different from their home countries. The aim of this paper is not to discuss the mobility itself, which is well known and beyond doubt, but to give an outline of its preconditions and consequences: of the life in the convent and of the situation the brothers had to face.[3] Therefore, some central aspects of the Hospitaller brothers' sojourns on Rhodes will be reviewed, but only for the well-documented second century of the order on Rhodes.

Every career within the order began, of course, with the reception. This was regulated by different statutes. From the thirteenth century, brother-knights had to be of noble origin and born in legal matrimony, and they had to be at least fourteen or even eighteen years old.[4] Reception was, at least in theory, strictly controlled by the order's leading officials. The permission to receive a limited number of brothers depended on a special permit issued by grand master and council and it was mostly given to high-ranking brothers in the west, to priors and commanders. In the registers, these permits appear in an abridged version. Their recipients were authorized 'to choose apt men and to decorate them with the girdle of the knighthood of Jerusalem'.[5] In fact, candidates had to appear before local or regional assemblies to prove that they fulfilled the necessary conditions to be received.[6]

Since the number of brothers on Rhodes was closely related to the economic and military situation of the order, a special permission from grand master and council was also necessary to travel to the convent. In the fifteenth century, most brothers coming to Rhodes would have been summoned by name, often expressly mentioned in circular letters to the priors. For example, when Negroponte fell to the Ottomans in the summer of 1470, 12 brothers from northern France, 19 from Auvergne, 10 from Germany and 3 from England were called to Rhodes; however, at least some of these were experienced and were no longer newcomers.[7] The brothers had to be sufficiently armed and equipped with horses, or they had to pay their *passagium*. In 1441, this was fixed at 100 ducats for brother-knights and 70 ducats for sergeants, but the value of the horses was still to be deducted from these sums.[8] From 1493, the *passagium*, now 68 or 44 French *écus*, had to be paid in advance even before making their profession.[9] Thus, the journey to Rhodes was very expensive, and brothers who lost their money in certain circumstances were sometimes forced to return to the west to be able to pay the necessary expenses.[10]

After their arrival on Rhodes, the brothers had to be received by one of the *langues* (or tongues). In most cases this was not a problem, but sometimes the divisions between the priories and therefore that between the tongues on Rhodes were not clear. Thus, for example, before 1450 Brother Charles de Valori was received as a brother-knight by the prior of St Gilles, but when he came to Rhodes, the tongue of Provence refused to take him in and he was only provisionally accepted by the French tongue. It was only after the decision of an internal court, the *esguardium fratrum*, that he became a member of the tongue of Provence.[11] The brothers were also to be assigned to one of the three status groups (knights, priests or sergeants), depending on their birth. Their status determined their rank within the order, because many offices were given only to brother-knights. Even in the priories a division of offices developed between the different status groups.[12]

In the same context, family relationships were obviously also very important. It was no accident that many high-ranking officials of the order came from a limited group of noble families. From northern Italy, for example, the counts of Piossasco and their affiliates, Brother

Giorgio di Piossasco, Brother Merlo di Piossasco, Brother Ludovico de Scalenghe and Brother Bernardino Piossasco di Ayrasca, served, from the 1470s to 1522, either as admiral or as prior of Lombardy.[13] Sometimes brothers even resigned their offices in favour of their relatives, as did Brother Guy de Domagnac in 1435, or Brother Giovanni Aloysio de *Garzonibus* in 1511, both in connection with certain commanderies which were designed as sources of income for their family members.[14]

Even though – as a consequence of their vow of poverty – the brothers formally depended on the decisions of their superiors over how to spend the money and incomes which they had brought into the order, in many respects they had control over their possessions during their lifetimes.[15] Formal wills or testaments were not permitted, only *despropriamenta* (literally: disappropriations, or surrenderings of property), but some brothers were allowed to give money to their relatives, as did Grand Master Antoni de Fluvià,[16] or to make donations for masses and even chapels, as did the bailiff of Negroponte, Brother Ramon Jou, who wanted to found a chapel in the *borgo* and to institute masses for the soul of Grand Master Fluvià.[17] Others lent considerable sums of money to the order, as did the prior of Auvergne, Brother Ademar du Puy, who gave 1,000 ducats in 1459.[18] Therefore, it is not surprising that brothers acquired property on Rhodes. One interesting example is that of Brother Nicole de Giresme, prior of *Francia* since 1447, who bought the garden and vineyard of *Calamona* in the castellany of Rhodes in 1441.[19] This property became in a sense hereditary in the Giresme family since it was managed by one of its members until the death of Brother Louis de Giresme sometime before 1510; even after 1510 the family's entitlement remained in place: should any brother-knight of this family come to Rhodes, *Calamona* was to be handed over to him.[20]

Some brothers even had resources to engage in (minor forms of) trade; however, this was only allowed by the statutes if it was aimed at financing the brothers' tasks within the order, and any kind of usury was strictly forbidden.[21] Nevertheless, as discussed after the general chapter of 1475, there were brothers who owned vineyards and sold their wine in smaller quantities or to taverns. This was tolerated, but the brothers had to pay the usual duties.[22] It seems that this remained a problem throughout the fifteenth century, since the lessees of the *commercium* and *gabella* (the customs at the harbour of Rhodes town) periodically complained that the brothers refused to pay, not only for wine which they imported to Rhodes, but also for other goods – even slaves – gained as booty from their piratical attacks on Muslim ships.[23] The brothers' involvement in trade obviously even took place at the order's outposts. Thus, in October 1511, the captain of St Peter (Bodrum), Brother Antoni de San Martí, was reminded by the grand master that brothers were selling goods at the local market (*bazar*) of the castle without the licence of the captain or his lieutenant.[24]

Other brothers participated in the *corso* (the aforementioned piratical activities directed against Muslim trade) with their own ships. Discussions in the council concerning the problem of sales reveal that brothers owned ships (or at least parts of ships). When a brother such as Brother Jacques August of the tongue of Provence wished to sell his ship completely, he was allowed to sell it only to another brother: sometime before July 1510, Brother Jacques August sold his ship to Brother Rembault de Olandiers for 110 ducats. If brothers wanted to sell their ships to seculars, they could only sell 'parts' of the rights of ownership and had to retain control of at least half the ship.[25] Around 1500, there were at least some brothers who agreed to certain terms for their piratical activities in the eastern Mediterranean and who probably at least partly owned the ships they were leading into combat. In 1507, Brother Gabriele de Solier promised not to attack any Christians, especially any Venetians, and to restrict his actions to an area from Chios to Kastellorizzo, while in 1518 Brother Onofrio Solanes *navigans ad damna infidelium* (sailing to damage the 'infidel') took an oath not to attack any Christians and to keep away from the Turkish coast close to Rhodes.[26] The profits from the *corso* were certainly an important factor in the brothers' involvement.

The brothers depended on the *auberges* (or 'inns') of their *langues* for their basic needs. These *auberges* were governed by the conventual bailliffs who received approximately two-thirds of their incomes of about 300 florins to support the *auberges*.[27] According to regulations of 1450, brothers with incomes of less than 100 or 90 florins received additional financial support, but this was soon reduced to (less than) 60 florins and limited to brothers who were not holding an office.[28] The payment was also granted to brothers doing military service on the order's ships.[29]

In any case, at least the brother-knights probably maintained a certain lifestyle. It is more than likely that they celebrated the ecclesiastical feast days not only in a liturgical fashion, but also in a secular manner. Thus, the evening before the day of St John the Baptist (24 June) was traditionally celebrated at the grand master's palace: bailiffs, brothers and others took part in festivities with fires and cannons.[30] The brothers were accompanied by servants whom they had to feed and clothe – since the treasury was not responsible for their support and they were not allowed to take over offices[31] – and this sometimes caused severe problems, as in the case of a young brother who was robbed by his servant.[32]

These *famuli* stayed with the brothers even on their *caravana*, that is when they had to do service on the order's ships, on Kos or in the castle of St Peter (Bodrum). The servants of the English brothers on *caravana* in St Peter seem to have lived from the pittances of the English tongue and they stayed together with their superiors in the tower of St Catherine, built by the English.[33] The *caravana* became one of the preconditions for a career within the order, and all brothers – even the priests – had to serve for a year, according to their *ancianitas*, that is a brother's 'age' within the order, which was calculated from the time he had paid for the *passagium*.[34]

Only a few brothers were selected as the *familiares* of the grand master (to act as his associates or representatives), which was also a potential stepping stone for a career within the order. One example is the Catalan Brother Francesch Bossolx who was retained by Grand Master Orsini in December 1472 – when he had already served the first of his five terms of office as captain of St Peter – and afterwards became bailiff of Majorca and then, finally, prior of Catalonia.[35] Even if their careers were not so spectacular, *familiares* were rewarded for their services with commanderies in the west or with properties on Rhodes itself. Thus, in January 1511, a brother from the priory of Navarre, Brother Martin Pasquera, a *familiaris* of Grand Master Émery d'Amboise and member of his household, received a garden in the castellany of Rhodes in exchange for a merely formal and very low rent.[36]

Some brothers obviously decided on a career in the Aegean. Although they also received commanderies in the west as their basic sources of income, they advanced their careers on Rhodes, for example by becoming captains of the towers in the harbour and the town walls or of the order's ships or by representing their tongues at the internal courts and committees, and later they were promoted to the more important offices in Rhodes town, such as castellan of Rhodes or bailiff of the *commercium*, eventually to become captain of St Peter, commander of Kos or Nisyros or grand commander of Cyprus.[37]

In these offices, they apparently had to deal with a number of disciplinary problems. Around 1451, the grand master and council were informed about disobedient brothers on Kos who stayed there without serving in the *caravana* or in any kind of office. Several did not live in the brothers' common area, the *collachium* of the castle of Narangia (today the castle of Kos), had their property and armour elsewhere and even neglected their duties concerning the defence of the castle.[38] Similar was the situation, at least according to a letter addressed to Grand Master Émery d'Amboise in 1511, at the castle of St Peter where brothers lived outside the *collachium* in the houses of seculars, and some mocked the captain or even insulted him with their offensive and scandalous speech.[39] As early as 1470, the captain and the brothers at St Peter's were quarrelling about the division of booty, cattle, goods and captives, gained during an expedition from the castle.[40]

Sometimes the order's officials had to deal with cases of sexual misbehaviour. Acts of fornication, violations of the vow of chastity, were rarely documented, and it is probably only to be explained by the general moral standards of the order, that, in 1494, the prostitutes in the *castellum* of Rhodes, close to the *collachium*, were moved to the town.[41] But there were also a few cases of homosexuality – 'sodomy' in medieval terms – which were recorded as severe crimes. In 1502, Brother Francesco Diascosi confessed to have committed, together with two boys, 'many sins against nature'. He was expelled from the order and probably faced the death penalty.[42] The same fate would have awaited Brother Joan de Villazan who, in 1494, faced with the instruments of torture, accused himself and Brother Niccolò Debaro, prior of St Catherine's, of having sinned 'against nature'. Both were imprisoned to await further judgement.[43]

Heavy punishments were also inflicted for other offences. In 1496, some brothers of St Peter's quarrelled, fought against each other and sustained injuries. They had to face imprisonment and other punishments.[44] Even high-ranking brothers were not protected from the order's judicial procedures. Thus, around 1445, the grand commander Jean de Cavaillon was accused of theft and sacrilege. He was imprisoned and exposed to torture several times. After he had confessed his guilt – and, in his distress, also accused other brothers (such as the treasurer Brother Roger Client and the conventual prior Brother Jean Morelli) – he lost his offices and was expelled from the order. It was only when Pope Eugenius IV took up the case during the general chapter at Rome in 1446 that Brother Cavaillon was rehabilitated and restored to his offices.[45] Another high-ranking official, Brother Fantino Quirini, former admiral and commander of Kos, was executed in 1454, even against the

protests of the republic of Venice.[46] In the last decades before the loss of
Rhodes to the Ottomans, if not earlier, the order had its dungeons at
Lindos. Thus, four brothers who had fought against each other were
sent *ad carceres Lindi* in 1501 and five others followed in 1512.[47]
According to the statutes of the general chapter of 1501, the dungeons
of Lindos were also the punishment for the blasphemous use of the
names of God, Mary and the saints (at least if a brother had relapsed
and offended the respective statute three times).[48]

Just as the brothers were officially summoned to Rhodes, they were
not allowed to leave the island without permission. Those trying to
'escape' from the convent had to face heavy punishment. Thus, in May
1493, a brother from the priory of Portugal tried to sail away secretly,
but his ship was driven back to Rhodes by a storm and he was
imprisoned. Others were expelled from the order.[49] It seems that in
most cases when brothers asked for permission to return to the west to
govern their commanderies, their requests were granted without any
further demands. However, there were some exceptions. In June 1461,
Brother Joan Ladron from the castellany of Amposta was ordered to
return within two years; otherwise he would face exclusion from the
order.[50] Others were only allowed to travel to certain priories.[51] Of
those who left Rhodes, most would have stayed in the west and only a
few came back to Rhodes to advance their careers.

In sum, the structures of the convent which had developed until the
fifteenth century guaranteed that most of the brothers could continue
their way of living while facing the challenges of the order's exposed
situation in the east. When they arrived at Rhodes, they were integrated
into the order's community in the convent, received financial support
and lived together in the *auberges* of their tongues, accompanied by
their own servants. They were offered several opportunities to advance
their standing within the order, went on *caravana*, served in different
offices and may have obtained support from their families or their
superiors, perhaps even from the grand master himself. Some were very
successful and rose to higher positions in the order's hierarchy, some
engaged in military or economic activities, others were confronted with
personal consequences from the austere regulations of the order's
statutes – even with imprisonment or death. However, by the time they
returned to the west to govern their commanderies or to occupy high-
ranking offices, most of them had earned a reputation which allowed
them to continue quite an aristocratic life. Even though the Hospitaller
brothers came as foreigners, Rhodes was far from being a place of exile

for them; rather, it offered all the structures and support which facilitated intense international mobility.

Notes

1   For the history of the Hospitallers on Rhodes see Anthony Luttrell, *The Hospitallers in Cyprus, Rhodes, Greece and the West, 1291–1440* (London 1978); Anthony Luttrell, *Latin Greece, the Hospitallers and the Crusades, 1291–1440* (London, 1982); Anthony Luttrell, *The Hospitallers of Rhodes and their Mediterranean World* (Aldershot, 1992); Anthony Luttrell, *The Hospitaller State on Rhodes and its Western Provinces, 1306–1462* (Aldershot 1999); Zacharias N. Tsirpanles, *He Rodos kai hoi Noties Sporades sta chronia ton Ioanniton Ippoton, 14os–16os ai.: sylloge historikon meleton* (Rhodes and the south-east Aegean islands under the knights of St John, fourteenth to sixteenth centuries: collected studies) (Rhodes, 1991); Nicolas Vatin, *L'Ordre de Saint-Jean-de-Jérusalem, l'empire ottoman et la Méditerranée entre les deux sièges de Rhodes, 1480–1522* (Paris, 1994); Helen Nicholson, *The Knights Hospitaller* (Woodbridge, 2001); Jürgen Sarnowsky, *Macht und Herrschaft im Johanniterorden des 15. Jahrhunderts: Verfassung und Verwaltung der Johanniter auf Rhodos (1421–1522)* (Münster, 2001).

2   We have some exact figures in the reports on the elections of masters: 286 (1461), 259 (1476), 377 (1503) and 551 (1513); see Sarnowsky, *Macht und Herrschaft*, p. 511.

3   See the works in note 1 (above), especially Anthony Luttrell, 'Rhodes: base militaire, colonie, métropole de 1306 à 1440', in Luttrell, *Hospitaller State on Rhodes*, no. VII, pp. 238–40; Nicholson, *Knights Hospitaller*, pp. 50–1; Sarnowsky, *Macht und Herrschaft*, pp. 508–9.

4   According to a statute of 1428 (French version of the statutes, Paris, Bibliothèque Nationale (BN), (fonds) français 17255, fol. 100r), *nul ne face frere chevalier de la religion se non quil soit gentil homme de non et darmes, et de leal mariage*, and while in the time of Brother Deodat de Gozon the age of reception was eighteen (ibid., fol. 62v), as confirmed by an *ordinatio* of 1504 (Valletta, National Library of Malta, Archives of the Order of St John (NLM) Arch. 284, fol. 77v), in 1448 a permission to receive brothers introduces a minimum age of fourteen (NLM Arch. 360, fol. 12v).

5   *Viros idoneos eligendi et eos milicie Hierosolymitane cingulo decorandi*; document of 10 October 1510: NLM Arch. 400, fol. 2r. The officials should receive only as many brothers as they were permitted: BN français 17255, fol. 111r–v.

6   See Sarnowsky, *Macht und Herrschaft*, pp. 72, 199.

7   See the letter to Brother Bertrand de Cluix, prior of *Francia*, dated 25 August 1470, NLM Arch. 379, fols 1v–3r, and the following entries, ibid., fols 3r–5v, concerning the letters to the other priors.

[8] According to a decision of the complete council, 22 August 1441, NLM Arch. 355, fols 228v–229r (now 226v–227r).

[9] See the addition to the statutes of 1489, NLM Library 244, fol. 122r.

[10] As in the case of Brother Étienne de Haluy who was robbed by his servant and who was allowed to return to the west to collect money from his parents, 26 July 1459, NLM Arch. 369, fol. 21r (now 31r).

[11] According to NLM Arch. 361, fol. 23v (7 September 1448) and ibid., fols 15v–16r (now 16v–17r) (28 July and 17 September 1450).

[12] See Sarnowsky, *Macht und Herrschaft*, pp. 200–5.

[13] Ibid., pp. 656, 682.

[14] The commandery of *Thoreac* for Brother Jean de Domagnac, NLM Arch. 351, fol. 14r (5 March 1435), and several houses in the priory of Venice for Brother Gabriele de Garzonibus, NLM Arch. 400, fol. 111r (26 April 1511); in the latter case, this concerned a resignation made before the pope.

[15] On 17 March 1512, for example, Brother Cristofero de Melo from Portugal received permission from Grand Master Émery d'Amboise to dispose of his inherited properties to finance his stay on Rhodes, NLM Arch. 400, fol. 142r.

[16] He not only took over the debts of another Brother Antoni Fluvià, commander of *Gibutti*, but also gave 1,000 florins of Aragón to his niece Beatrice, NLM Arch. 353, fols 81v, 158r (now 157r) (5 and 11 December 1437).

[17] According to the charter in NLM Arch. 379, fol. 223r–v (21 May 1471), the conventual prior Brother Joan Pugialt and a relative, Brother Guillèm Jou, acted as executors for his last will.

[18] According to the document of 8 November 1459, the money was lent for only three months and had to be paid back in February 1460, NLM Arch. 369, fols 182v–183r (now 214v–215r).

[19] The permission to sell *Calamona* to Brother Giresme was given to Brother Bertrand Javieron on 31 December 1441, NLM Arch. 355, fol. 233r (now 231r).

[20] According to the charter for the vice-chancellor Bartolomeo Policiano, who received *Calamona* to recultivate the garden on 8 October 1510, NLM Arch. 400, fol. 205r–v.

[21] According to a statute of the second general chapter of Grand Master Antoni de Fluvià (1433), BN français 17255, fol. 104r, repeated in the statutes of 1489/93, NLM Arch. 244, fol. 96r–v. For the order's trade and banking activities see Jürgen Sarnowsky, 'Handel und Geldwirtschaft der Johanniter', in Roman Czaja and Jürgen Sarnowsky (eds), *Die Ritterorden in der europäischen Wirtschaft des Mittelalters*, Ordines militares, Colloquia Torunensia Historica, vol. 12 (Toruń, 2003), pp. 19–34.

[22] For the discussion of the complete council see NLM Arch. 283, fol. 126r (11 January 1476).

[23] Such complaints were discussed in the council; see for example 25 October 1503, 27 April 1504 and 3 February 1508, NLM Arch. 80, fols 58r–v (now

71r–v) and 75r–v (now 88r–v), and NLM Arch. 81, fols 77v–78r (now 90v–91r). For the different customs see Sarnowsky, *Macht und Herrschaft*, pp. 450–4, 489–93.

[24] NLM Arch. 400, fols 15v–16r (letter dated 8 October 1511).

[25] For this decision of the complete council see NLM Arch. 282, fol. 167r (16 February 1467). For the case of Brother Jacques August and Brother Rembault de Olandiers (who failed to pay for the ship) see NLM Arch. 400, fol. 25v (19 July 1510).

[26] See NLM Arch. 81, fols 48r (now 61r), 62r (now 75r) (Brother Solier, 2 November 1506, 31 July 1507); NLM Arch. 407, fol. 212r (now 210r) (Brother Solanes, 27 September 1507).

[27] See the later versions of the statutes, for example BN français 17255, fol. 127v, and (the Caoursin version) NLM Library 244, fols 77v–78r.

[28] For the decision of 3 December 1450, see NLM Arch. 362, fol. 185v (now 186v). For the revised statute (from the time of Brother Pere Ramon Racosta) see NLM Library 244, fol. 52v.

[29] According to the supplication of Brother Janotto Argensola, NLM Arch. 80, fol. 15r (now 64r) (22 September 1503), with reference to the chapter *de fratribus* in the Caoursin version of the statutes, NLM Library 244, fol. 97v.

[30] As reported in an entry about the illness and death of Brother Pierre d'Aubusson: though ill, *interfuit recreationi que sit in ant[er]io palatii, bavilivis, fratribus, ac ceteris as[sis]tentibus secundum veterem consuetudinem cum leticia ignium et bombardarum*, NLM Arch. 80, fol. 14r (now 37r) (23 June 1503).

[31] According to a statute from the time of Brother Philibert de Naillac, NLM Library 244, fol. 50r.

[32] See above, note 10.

[33] At least in about 1437, see NLM Arch. 352, fol. 133v (now 131v), edited (and referred to) by Anthony Luttrell, 'English contributions to the Hospitaller tower at Bodrum in Turkey, 1407–1437', in Helen Nicholson (ed.), *The Military Orders*, vol. 2, *Welfare and Warfare* (Aldershot, 1998), pp. 163–72, here pp. 167–9, 172.

[34] Sarnowsky, *Macht und Herrschaft*, pp. 220–2.

[35] Brother Bossolx wanted to leave Rhodes to manage his commandery, but the master kept him on Rhodes, NLM Arch. 74, fol. 142r (now 154r) (dated 24 December 1472).

[36] Brother Pasquera had to pay one florin for a garden *in regione Chippurie*, NLM Arch. 400, fol. 211r (21 January 1511).

[37] For the careers see Sarnowsky, *Macht und Herrschaft*, pp. 222–3.

[38] According to the instructions for an unnamed brother going to Kos, NLM Arch. 362, fols 215r–216r (now 216r–217r), printed in Zacharias N. Tsirpanles (ed.), *Anekdota engrapha gia te Rodo kai tis Noties Sporades apo to archeio to Ioanniton Ippoton* (Unpublished documents concerning Rhodes and the south-east Aegean islands from the archives of the order of St John), vol. 1: 1421–1453 (Rhodes, 1995), pp. 605–9 no. 244.

[39] See the report in NLM Arch. 400, fols 15v–16r (dated 8 October 1511).

[40] NLM Arch. 379, fol. 222r–v (27 July 1470); the case had to be decided by an *esguardium fratrum*, NLM Arch. 74, fol. 18v (now 30v) (18 July 1470).

[41] According to the note in NLM Arch. 77, fol. 112r (now 127r) (26 May 1494).

[42] The boys were at first detained in the dungeon of the castellany, see NLM Arch. 79, fol. 73r (now 80r) (13 July 1502), but will also have been severely punished. According to the (later) *Pragmaticae Rhodiae*, all boys older than ten and all men committing sodomy were to be burnt, NLM Arch. 153, fols 106v–107r.

[43] See the discussion of the council, NLM Arch. 77, fols 118v–119v (now 133v–134v) (11, 20 October 1494); Brother Joan also named an Augustinian friar, but against him no measures were taken since he had already left the island.

[44] As the council decided, see NLM Arch. 78, fol. 49r (now 64r) (30 August 1496).

[45] For the pope's first reaction see NLM Arch. 8, no. 12 (22 April 1445); Brother Cavaillon's letter of conduct to Rome, ibid., no. 15 (19 August 1445); the rehabilitation of Brother Cavaillon, Brother Client and Brother Morelli in NLM Arch. 358, fols 19r–20r (28 April 1446).

[46] See Freddy Thiriet (ed.), *Régestes des délibérations du Sénat de Venise concernant la Romanie*, 3 vols (Paris, 1958–61), here vol. 3, pp. 180–1, 197 nos 2907, 2963. A lieutenant of the treasurer, Brother Jean Perrini, who had been accused of theft, was sentenced to death in 1443, but was able to escape and was supported by Pope Eugenius IV, Città del Vaticano, Archivio Segreto Vaticano, Reg. Vat. 361, fols 183v–184v and 185r–v (31 May 1443).

[47] See the decisions of the council, NLM Arch. 78, fol. 132v (now 147v) (28 January 1501), NLM Arch. 82, fol. 40r (now 53r) (22 December 1512).

[48] For the first offence, brothers were sentenced to the *quarantaine*, fasting for forty days; for the second they were imprisoned in a tower for two months, NLM Arch. 284, fols 28v–29r.

[49] For the case of the Portuguese brother see NLM Arch. 77, fol. 92r (now 107r) (24 May 1493). For brothers expelled from the order see ibid., fol. 8v (now 23v); NLM Arch. 80, fols 108v–109r (now 121v–122r); Arch. 83, fols 41v–42v (now 50v–51v) (17, 22 March 1522).

[50] A decision of master and council, NLM Arch. 73, fol. 87v (now 100v).

[51] As in the case of Brother Lluis de Caramyn from Catalonia who was only allowed to travel to Sicily, NLM Arch. 359, fol. 86v (now 84v) (15 June 1447).

6

International Mobility in the Order of
St Lazarus (Twelfth to
Early Fourteenth Centuries)

KAY PETER JANKRIFT

In 1256, King Henry III of England ordered his barons and bailiffs to exempt Brother Milo, grand master of the military Order of St Lazarus, and William of Hereford, commander of Burton Lazars, transporting their brothers, men, horses and equipment, from all tolls in the port of Dover.[1] This royal privilege is probably the most important piece of evidence for international mobility in the Order of St Lazarus during the second half of the thirteenth century. Such mobility was as necessary for the order's survival in the east as it was for the Hospitallers and Templars. However, considering the extraordinary composition of the order's community of both leprous and healthy brothers, one has to wonder whether these special conditions had any impact on the organization of international mobility in the Order of St Lazarus.[2] Did the patterns of international mobility in the Order of St Lazarus differ from those that can be observed in other military orders? Did leprous brothers move at all? Due to the extreme paucity of relevant documents for the medieval centuries of the order's history, it seems impossible to give definitive answers to these and other related questions. Yet the sources allow at least a cautious approach to these questions and do shed a little light on the theory and practice of international mobility in the order. The first hint, the starting-point of the following study, can be found in the order's normative texts.

Unfortunately, only a single manuscript of the order's medieval statutes has survived. Discovered in the Swiss commandery of Seedorf, it is called *Statutenbuch von Seedorf*.[3] Next to a version of the rule of St Augustine, the *Statutenbuch* contains the oldest known and obviously

already modified statutes of the Order of St Lazarus, their supplements
from the middle of the thirteenth century, as well as the statutes for the
order's houses in Seedorf, Gfenn and Schlatt written at the beginning of
the fourteenth century by Sifrid of Slatte, who was commander of Schlatt
in the Black Forest region and, by 1310, commander of the three houses
named above. While the oldest statutes are mostly concerned with the
internal government of the order's headquarters in the Holy Land, the
thirteenth-century supplements are the first to refer to questions of
mobility in the order. However, compared to the very detailed rule of
the Templars these statutes of St Lazarus still lack precise stipulations
with regard to military matters.[4] They merely describe the different
cloaks – such as the one for the knights – all embroidered with a green
cross, the distinctive symbol of the order.[5] Moreover, according to the
thirteenth-century statutes of the Order of St Lazarus, every brother
had to obey the order of his (grand) master to go to 'outremer'; there
and in all other places he was expected to protect his order's possessions
from the enemies of the Holy Cross.[6] The normative texts do not
specify whether this obligation applied to all or was restricted to the
healthy brothers of the order. Can this lack of specification be taken for
granted? Just how mobile was a medieval leper?

   First of all, it is important to note that the various forms of the
disease called *lepra, elephantiasis* or *mal ladre* in the medieval sources
are not identical with the disease defined as leprosy by modern
medicine.[7] Patients suffering from any other kind of a cutaneous
disease, which for some reason might have been diagnosed as leprosy,
could very well move hundreds or even thousands of kilometres
without any major difficulty.[8] Probably they served as an example to
show that even some of those who were afflicted with 'leprosy' could
still travel, survive for a longer period and be useful in battle. However,
even if infected with leprosy in the modern sense, the unfortunate
victim of the disease could survive for years. Certainly he was still able
to travel and even to fulfil administrative duties as is evidenced by the
well-known case of the leprous King Baldwin IV of Jerusalem (1174–85)
who had been suffering from leprosy since his childhood.[9] The Arabic
historiographer Kamāl ad-Dīn ibn al-ʿAdīm (1192–1262) reports that in
1119 – to the horror of the Muslims – the 'leprous' Count Robert of
Zerdana fought against the Muslims, was defeated, captured and
killed.[10] Nobody dared to touch him, because of his disease.[11] However,
as early as the sixth century, lepers – or those supposed by contemporary
eye-witnesses to be afflicted with leprosy – hoping for relief had not

shrunk back from a pilgrimage to the Holy Land. Gregory of Tours, for example, reports the case of a certain John travelling from Gaul to the River Jordan, desperately hoping that a bath near the place where Christ himself had entered the water would cure him.[12] Since a leper does not feel pain in the affected parts of his body, the highest risk in the early stages of the disease is a sepsis.[13] Even little injuries can be fatal. However, without any doubt, lepers could travel long distances and even fight: in 1253, the order asked Pope Innocent IV to grant them permission to elect a healthy grand master, because all leprous brothers had been killed in battle.[14] Still, the question remains whether it was in the order's interest to transport leprous brothers from Europe to the Holy Land.

In contrast to other military orders, the Order of St Lazarus – by the end of the twelfth century – was able to rely on a unique form of recruitment in the crusader states themselves. The forty-second chapter of the so-called *Livre au Roi* guaranteed a consistent supply of brothers: it stipulated that a free man who had contracted leprosy had to join the Order of St Lazarus.[15] Even before the middle of the thirteenth century, the rule of the Templars encouraged leprous Templars to become brothers of the Order of St Lazarus, thus reinforcing the latter's 'automatic' recruitment of leprous members.[16] It is beyond any doubt that this statute influenced the further development of the Order of St Lazarus into a military order.[17] Brothers of the order did participate in combat, even though their small contingent was probably more symbolic than effective. John of Joinville, who accompanied King Louis IX of France on his crusade in the middle of the thirteenth century, clearly states that the grand master of the Order of St Lazarus had no rank within the camp of the combatants.[18] He relates that most of the order's knights, undertaking a raid led by their grand master against a rather small contingent of Muslims, were killed in a battle near Ramla in 1252. Thus, the normative texts of the crusader states, the rule of the Templars and the contemporary chroniclers suggest that there was certainly no need to ship leprous brothers of the Order of St Lazarus from the west to 'outremer'. They would have been of little use. Healthy brothers, however, were apparently welcome – especially to ensure the daily hospital service in the order's houses in the Holy Land.

However, charters like the one issued by Henry III in 1256 underline that the demand to fight for the faith was more than theoretical in the Order of St Lazarus. According to René Pétiet, the order had already obtained similar privileges from St Louis in the port of Acre in 1253.[19]

On the basis of an archaeological survey, Rafaël Hyacinthe has recently claimed that the Order of St Lazarus might have used its commandery in Barletta (Italy) as one of its logistic centres to transport men and goods to the Holy Land.[20] So far no one has tried to answer the question of how the order transported its supply to 'outremer'. There is no evidence for Pétiet's statement that the order possessed its own ships.[21] However, it does not seem likely that members of the Order of St Lazarus could travel on board vessels other than their own. The oldest preserved passenger list of a crusader ship dating from the middle of the thirteenth century names Templars and Hospitallers, but no brothers of the Order of St Lazarus.[22] These knights with their green cross would certainly have evoked fear. Nobody could know whether they were healthy or already infected by the terrible disease that would cause long suffering and lead to a terrible death. Unfortunately, there is no source reporting the reaction of common crusaders when they encountered a knight of the Order of St Lazarus.

To sum up: the medieval sources alluding to international mobility in the Order of St Lazarus originate from the middle of the thirteenth century. The internal development of the order – the founding of houses in the west and the eventual establishment of a hierarchy as well as an institutional network – cannot completely explain the growing need for international mobility in a community that differed considerably from other military orders. By the middle of the thirteenth century the militarization of the order required an increase of mobility.[23] Furthermore, it seems that the first crusade of King Louis IX of France had a certain influence on the order's increasing mobility towards the east.[24] It is striking that all medieval documents referring to international mobility in the Order of St Lazarus – normative texts and charters – were written down within a few years around the middle of the thirteenth century. Yet, the scarcity of sources leaves many questions unanswered.

Notes

[1] 'Mandatum est baronibus et ballavis regis Dovor' quod fratrem Milonem, magistrum generalem milicie Sancti Lazari Jerusalem, et magistrum Willelmum de Hereford cum fratribus, hominibus, equis et hernesio suo, in portu Dovor' libere transfretare permittant', *Close Rolls of the Reign of Henry III Preserved in the Public Record Office, Printed under the*

Superintendence of the Deputy Keeper of the Records (London, 1902–38), *1254–1256*, p. 419.

[2] Kay Peter Jankrift, *Leprose als Streiter Gottes: Institutionalisierung und Organisation des Ordens vom Heiligen Lazarus von seinen Anfängen bis zum Jahr 1350* (Münster, 1996); Malcolm Barber, 'The Order of St Lazarus and the crusades', *The Catholic Historical Review*, 80 (1994), 439–56. With excellent maps and illustrations now also Rafaël Hyacinthe, *L'ordre de Saint-Lazare de Jérusalem au Moyen Âge* (Millau, 2003).

[3] For an edition of the text see P. Gall Morel, 'Die ältesten Statuten für die Lazariterklöster Seedorf, im Gfenn und in Slatte', *Der Geschichtsfreund: Mittheilungen des historischen Vereins der fünf Orte Lucern, Uri, Schwyz, Unterwalden und Zug*, 12 (1856), 1–51. The statutes were analysed by Elisabeth Sauer, *Der Lazariter-Orden und das Statutenbuch von Seedorf* (Freiburg/Schweiz, 1930) and Jankrift, *Leprose als Streiter Gottes*, pp. 121–50.

[4] Jankrift, *Leprose als Streiter Gottes*, p. 146.

[5] Morel, 'Die ältesten Statuten', 138.

[6] Morel, 'Die ältesten Statuten', 144: 'Aber denne de er var vber mer der es in heisset, vnd de er beschirme des ordens gvot da vnd anderswa vor den vigenden des heiligen cruces.' See also Sauer, *Der Lazariter-Orden und das Statutenbuch von Seedorf*, p. 34, and John Walker, 'The motives for patrons of the Order of St Lazarus in England in the twelfth and thirteenth centuries', in Judith Loades (ed.), *Monastic Studies: The Continuity of Tradition* (Bangor, 1990), pp. 171–81, here p. 172.

[7] Karl-Heinz Leven, 'Krankheiten: Historische Deutung versus retrospektive Diagnose', in Norbert Paul and Thomas Schlich (eds), *Medizingeschichte: Aufgaben, Probleme, Perspektiven* (Frankfurt am Main/New York, 1998), pp. 153–85; Jean-Charles Sournia, 'Discipline du diagnostic rétrospectif', in Neithard Bulst and Robert Delort (eds), *Maladies et société, XIIe–XVIIIe siècles: actes du colloque de Bielefeld, novembre 1986* (Paris, 1989), pp. 57–64.

[8] Kay Peter Jankrift, 'Leprakranke im Spiegel spätmittelalterlich-früh-neuzeitlicher Schauprotokolle und Selbstzeugnisse/Trędowaci w świetle późnośredniowiecznych i wczesnonowożytnych dokumenttów i w świadectwach własnych', *Polskie Towarzystwo Historii Medycyny i Farmacji: Archiwum Historii i Filozofii Medycyny*, 65, 2/3 (2002), 209–17; Kay Peter Jankrift, 'Jost Heerde: Das Schicksal eines Lepraverdächtigen in Münster', *Die Klapper: Mitteilungen der Gesellschaft für Leprakunde*, 6 (1998), 3–5.

[9] Piers D. Mitchell, 'An evaluation of the leprosy of King Baldwin IV of Jerusalem in the context of the medieval world', in Bernard Hamilton, *The Leper King and his Heirs: Baldwin IV and the Crusader Kingdom of Jerusalem* (Cambridge, 2000), pp. 245–58; Piers D. Mitchell, 'Leprosy and the case of King Baldwin IV of Jerusalem: mycobacterial disease in the crusader states of the 12th and 13th centuries', *Journal of Leprosy*, 61 (1993), 283–91; Mark Gregory Pegg, 'Le corps et l'autorité: la lèpre de Baudouin IV', *Annales: Économies – Sociétés – Civilisations*, 45 (1990), 265–87.

10   Kamāl ad-Dīn ibn al-ʿAdīm, 'Extraits de la Chronique d'Alep', in *Recueil des Historiens des Croisades, Historiens Orientaux*, vol. 3 (Paris, 1884), pp. 620–2.
11   'Galterii Cancellarii Antiocheni Bella Antiochena', in *Recueil des Historiens des Croisades, Historiens Occidentaux*, vol. 5 (Paris, 1895), p. 125; and see the translation by Thomas S. Asbridge and Susan B. Edgington, *Walter the Chancellor's The Antiochene War: A Translation and Commentary* (Aldershot, 1999), p. 160, with n. 241.
12   Gregory of Tours, *Liber in Gloria Martyrum*, in *Monumenta Germaniae Historica, Scriptores Rerum Merovingicarum*, vol. 1 (Hanover, 1885), p. 498.
13   Robert H. Gelber, 'Leprosy (Hansen's Disease)', in Gerald L. Mandell et al. (eds), *Principles and Practice of Infectious Diseases*, fourth edition (New York, 1995), pp. 2243–50.
14   Élie Berger (ed.), *Les Registres d'Innocent IV*, vol. 3 (Paris, 1897), no. 6204.
15   Comte de Beugnot (ed.), 'Assises de Jérusalem: Assises de la Haute Cour', in *Recueil des Historiens des Croisades, Lois*, vol. 1 (Paris, 1841), p. 636: 'S'il avaient que par la volonté de nostre Seignor un home lige devient mesel, si que mais ne puisse garir de sele meselerie qui fort s'est prise sur luy, le droit juge et comande que il deit estre rendue en l'ordre de saint Lasre, là où est estably que les gens de tel maladie deveint estre.' See now Myriam Greilsammer (ed.), *Le livre au roi* (Paris, 1995), pp. 256–7.
16   Henri de Curzon (ed.), *La règle du Temple* (Paris, 1886), pp. 239–40 nos 443–4: 'Quand il avient a aucun frere que par la volonté de nostre Seignor il chiet en meselerie et la chose est provée, il prodome frere de la maison le doivent amonester et prier que il demande congié de la maison et que il se rendre a saint Ladre, et que il preigne l'abit de frere de saint Ladre . . . Mais toutes fois sachiés que se le frere qui en tele maniere sera devenus meseaus fust si durs que il ne vousist demander le congié devant dit ne partir soi de la maison, l'on ne li doit ni puet jeter l'abit ni oster, ni jeter fors de la maison, mais, ensi comme dessus est dit des autres qui ont laides maladies, le doit l'on metre a une part fors de la compaignie des freres, et en cele place doner li sa soustenance.'
17   Jankrift, *Leprose als Streiter Gottes*, pp. 77–9.
18   Jean Joinville, *Histoire de Saint Louis*, ed. Natalis de Wailly (Paris, 1868), pp. 193–4.
19   René Pétiet, *Contributions à l'histoire de l'ordre de Saint-Lazare de Jérusalem* (Paris, 1914), p. 95.
20   Hyacinthe, *L'ordre de Saint-Lazare*, pp. 80–2.
21   Pétiet, *Contributions à l'histoire de l'ordre de Saint-Lazare*, p. 95.
22   Benjamin Z. Kedar, 'The passenger list of a crusader ship, 1250: towards the history of the popular element of the seventh crusade', *Studi Medievali*, 13 (1972), 267–79.
23   Jankrift, *Leprose als Streiter Gottes*, pp. 182–7.
24   *Matthæi Parisiensis, monachi Sancti Albani, Chronica majora*, ed. Henry R. Luard, 7 vols, Rolls Series 57 (London, 1872–83), vol. 5, p. 196.

7

Between Barcelona and Cyprus:
The Travels of Berenguer of Cardona,
Templar Master of Aragon and Catalonia
(1300–1)

ALAIN DEMURGER

The sending of news, decisions or orders, the transferring of goods, moneys, weapons and horses and the journeys of brothers played a major role in the life of the military orders. Without the exchange and communication between the centre and the periphery it would have been impossible for these orders to carry out their mission in the eastern Mediterranean. It was this mobility that set the military orders apart from other religious orders such as the traditional Benedictine orders that had little need for these matters. After the fall of Acre (1291), Templars and Hospitallers set up their headquarters on Cyprus. From this new centre, they established a network across the Mediterranean connecting them with the great Italian ports as well as Marseille and Barcelona. At Marseille, a *maître du passage* (master of the passage) supervised all the maritime activities of the Order of the Temple in the western Mediterranean.[1]

The documents preserved in the Archivo de la Corona de Aragón at Barcelona (and those in the Archivo Histórico Nacional of Madrid) are particularly important for the study of this mobility.[2] They reveal the intensity and the manifold aspects of the interaction between Cyprus and the Templar province of Aragon and Catalonia. On the basis of the itinerary established by Alan Forey, this case study will reconsider the journey to Cyprus which Berenguer of Cardona, the Templars' provincial master of Aragon and Catalonia, undertook in 1300–1.[3] The term 'case study' is, of course, somewhat misleading. Berenguer of

Cardona was not an ordinary Templar travelling to the east to perform his military service. He served as an important dignitary of the order, namely as master of the province of Aragon and as visitor in the 'five kingdoms' of Spain (i.e. the representative of his order's master in these territories).

The Cardona family was one of the major noble families of Catalonia. Berenguer became master of the province before 1292 and exercised this function until his death in July 1307. The Templar master James of Molay appointed him visitor before 1297. Berenguer travelled to the east at least three times. His first journey took place in 1286, when King Alfonso III of Aragon gave him permission to export six horses to the Holy Land.[4] The second journey (1300–1) and the third journey (1306–7) brought him to Cyprus. Evidence for the journey of 1300–1 comes – directly or indirectly – from letters written by Berenguer of Cardona and other Templars (unfortunately most of these letters are undated) and from some of the acts of Lamberto di Sambuceto, a Genoese notary working in Famagusta at the time.[5] For his absence of at least six months, Berenguer of Cardona appointed a lieutenant whose letters provide some chronological indications. This chapter will attempt to define the chronology of Berenguer's journey before examining its conditions and objectives.

Chronology

On 15 January 1300, Berenguer of Cardona summoned Peter of St Just, who was then commander of Corbins, to a provincial chapter which would be held at Monzón on the second Sunday of May (8 May). He asked him to come with the *responsiones* of his commandery and with the description (*albara*) of his commandery's condition (*estament*).[6] Nothing was said, at this time, of a journey to Cyprus. Three months after these summons (19 April), in another letter to the same addressee, Berenguer of Cardona wrote that he had received a letter from the order's master James of Molay asking him to come to Cyprus and help the 'convent' of the Templars to fight alongside the Tartars; the Ilkhan Ghazan (i.e. the khan of the Mongols of Persia) had been victorious over the Mamelukes at the battle of Homs on 24 December 1299 and had promised to return to Syria at the end of the year 1300 to conquer the Holy Land and Egypt.[7] Berenguer announced to Peter of St Just that he was ready to help this enterprise 'with all his power' and he asked him to bring supplies and money.[8] He repeated this request on 1 May; however, in the meantime – if the year 1300 for this repeated request is correct – Peter of St Just had been transferred from Corbins to Majorca.[9]

It is likely that Berenguer of Cardona held the chapter at Monzón on 8 May. According to Alan Forey, there was only one passage between Catalonia and Cyprus each year; while the spring was spent with preparations, the journey itself could not begin until July or August.[10] This was certainly the case for Berenguer of Cardona's third journey: in 1306, he left Spain in August.[11] However, it is possible that, in 1300, he left Catalonia earlier in the year. In his letter of 1 May, he asked Peter of St Just to get meats, bacons (*carnsalada*) and cheeses ready in Majorca as soon as possible. These supplies had to be loaded on to a ship coming from the Catalonian port of Tortosa.[12]

Berenguer of Cardona appears to have been ready to begin his journey at this moment. Another piece of evidence would be that, in June, Berenguer of St Just is mentioned as lieutenant of the provincial master,[13] but he appears as lieutenant only once. A lieutenant of the provincial master is mentioned again (unfortunately no name is given) on 17 August: on that day, King James II of Aragon wrote to this lieutenant and asked him for the military support of the Templars of this province against Castile.[14] Therefore, it is possible that Berenguer of Cardona began his journey in June or early July, but it is not certain; July and even August are also possible. At any rate, he could have arrived in Cyprus between August and October 1300. It seems certain that he participated in his order's general chapter on All Saints' Day of 1300 (the customary date for the general chapter): according to the master's letter of 10 November he was then confirmed as visitor of Spain.[15] What did he do during the winter? This question will be examined shortly.

Berenguer of Cardona left Cyprus in March or early April 1301. On 9 February, Bernard Marquet from Barcelona let the ship *Sanctus Nicolaus* to Berenguer Guamir, a Catalan Templar who was acting for himself and on behalf of Berenguer of Cardona. As captain or patron of the ship, Bernard Marquet committed himself to travel to Majorca and Barcelona with the two Templars, four knights and twenty-eight others who were accompanying them.[16] On 1 March, the ship was ready to leave Famagusta for Limassol, where the Templars were to go on board.[17] James of Molay wrote to Peter of St Just that he would soon receive 'good news from these parts' (i.e. Cyprus and the Holy Land) 'by Brother Berenguer, commander of Aragon, who is sailing to you presently'.[18] Unfortunately, the manuscript's condition makes the end of the letter, including the date, impossible to read, although it is reasonable to assume that it was written in March. Berenguer of Cardona arrived in Catalonia in June. He did not arrive before June because his lieutenant Peter of Thous was still in office in that month.[19] However, he must have arrived no later than 10 July as, on this day, *Romeus Burgueti*, the commander of Barcelona, and Bernardone Marquet, Bernard's son, concluded an agreement concerning the payment of the travel expenses incurred by Berenguer Guamir and Berenguer of Cardona.[20]

Travel conditions

Berenguer of Cardona used merchant ships, not Templar vessels, for his travel to and from Cyprus.[21] For the outward journey we know neither the ship's name nor its owner, but we do know that Berenguer returned to Catalonia on the *Sanctus Nicolaus* whose captain or patron (that remains to be determined) was Bernard Marquet of Barcelona. The ship was recorded in the port of Famagusta on 13 December 1300, but it had arrived there earlier: the document of 13 December mentions 'Bernard Marquet, patron of the ship called *Sanctus Nicolaus* which is in the port of Famagusta'. Coming to Cyprus from Catalonia, the *Sanctus Nicolaus* had carried 8,000 *muids* of corn for *Sance Peires*, a Catalan merchant who was acting on behalf of Count Bernard William of *Empressa* (Enteça). This corn was to be sold in Cyprus as collateral for a sum of 16,350 French silver *tournois* which Bernard William had borrowed from the Templars.[22] On 3 January, Bernard Marquet received the sum of 15,384 silver *tournois* from Bernard William; for 1,000 pounds of Barcelona, according to the receipt, 'the said noble count was obliged to us for the *nolis* (i.e. the chartering contract) by which we have conveyed the said count with the said vessel to Cyprus'.[23]

All contracts notarized by the Genoese notary Lamberto di Sambuceto between this date and 1 March 1301 name Bernard Marquet as the ship's patron. However, when the *Sanctus Nicolaus* had been in Famagusta in May and June 1299, Raymond Marquet of Barcelona (a father, uncle or brother of Bernard?) had appeared as the owner of the ship.[24] Was Bernard an 'active' owner? During the winter of 1300–1,

Bernard Marquet prepared his return journey. He sought to let out (*nolis*) parts (*loca*) of his ship: William of Serra, a merchant of Barcelona, rented a part of the ship to transport a load of cotton bought in Armenia,[25] and, as has been mentioned previously, Bernard negotiated with Berenguer Guamir, who was acting for himself and on behalf of Berenguer of Cardona, the conditions of the Templars' return journey to Catalonia.

There are two contracts concerning this return journey. According to the first contract (of 9 February), Bernard Marquet let his ship to Berenguer Guamir and the men accompanying him, namely one knight and sixteen other people, as well as to Berenguer of Cardona and the men accompanying him, namely three knights and twelve squires. The ship was supposed to be ready (crew, goods, ropes, sails etc.) by the beginning of March and the passengers would embark at Limassol. The contract was concluded for 270 pounds of Barcelona. Should Berenguer of Cardona be unable to be present for any reason or should he be delayed, the sum to be paid by Guamir would be reduced to 130 pounds on 1 March.[26] On 1 March, Bernard Marquet and his ship were ready to leave Famagusta for Limassol. Prior to leaving, Bernard Marquet presented himself before the notary Lamberto di Sambuceto and the Templar commander of Famagusta, Julian of St George; he certified that the ship was ready and he declined any responsibility for any delay.[27]

Two facts need to be emphasized here. First of all, Berenguer Guamir and Berenguer of Cardona had to travel together, but they were independent parties. Secondly, they were accompanied by four knights and twenty-eight other people, some of them squires; these persons appear to be Templars, but it is not certain that they were. Thus Berenguer of Cardona's journey (like that of Berenguer Guamir) does not seem to have been merely the journey of one of the order's dignitaries summoned by his superior for a consultation. The objectives of Berenguer of Cardona's journey must be seen in the larger context of what I call the 'Mongol alliance strategy'.[28]

Objectives

In October 1299, the Mongol khan of Persia, the Ilkhan Ghazan, left his capital Tabriz for Syria. He entered Aleppo on 12 December, and on 24 December he was victorious over the Mamelukes at the second battle of Homs. He then occupied Damascus (30 December), all of inner Syria and, allegedly, Jerusalem (this last part of the account seems to be legendary). One month after the beginning of the offensive (in November 1299), Ghazan had called on the military forces of the kingdom of Cyprus and, of course, on the military orders for help. The Cilician Armenians allied themselves with the Mongols right away. However, according to the chronicle of Amadi (or ascribed to Amadi), the Christians of Cyprus failed to help Ghazan and the chronicler points to the traditional rivalry between the Templars and the Hospitallers to explain the failure.[29] I believe that Amadi is wrong. We know from the Armenian historian Hayton of Korykos, whose chronology has been misinterpreted, that the military orders (including the Templars led by James of Molay) were in Armenia in 1298–9.[30] Their presence there stands in the context of a Mameluke attack on the kingdom of Armenia. The last Templar stronghold in the country (a Roche Guillaume) fell at this time. The Armenians called on the Mongols for help and Ghazan's offensive was a response to this call. The king of the Armenians, Hetoum, and the Armenian army were on the battlefield at Homs and participated in the conquest of Syria.[31] It is likely that the military orders' brothers of the province of Armenia were there as well.

We also have some 'western' letters about the events of the autumn and winter of 1299–1300 (including letters written by westerners who were in Cyprus at the time). First of all, it seems that these events were known in the west (at least at Venice) as early as the middle of March 1300.[32] A letter from Cyprus dated 24 March also gives the news of Ghazan's victory at Homs.[33] We know from Berenguer of Cardona (i.e. from his aforementioned letter dated 19 April) that James of Molay wrote to the west with the news. Finally, two letters published by Heinrich Finke prove an active interest in these events on the part of the Catalan Templars and the king of Aragon. The first letter, unfortunately undated, was sent by Raymond of Guardia, the commander of Mas-Deu in Roussillon, to James II of Aragon: twice, according to this letter, a messenger of the 'Tartars' had come to Cyprus and asked the king, the Templars, the Hospitallers and all other 'good people' of the country to cross over to Syria to fight with Ghazan and to recover the Holy Land from the Saracens, and it was decided to give the khan a positive answer. Ghazan, according to Raymond of Guardia, had defeated the Mamelukes at La Chamelle (Homs) and then occupied Damascus. The people of Cyprus – the king, the military orders and others – were making preparations to help the Tartars.[34] On 18 May, the king of Aragon sent a letter and a messenger to Ghazan promising him help to keep the Holy Land (at this time westerners thought that Jerusalem had been recovered by Christians).[35] Nothing in these letters supports Amadi's statement about quarrels among the Christian forces.

During the year 1300, the Templars, the Hospitallers, the king of Cyprus and his nobility made serious preparations to fight alongside Ghazan. A coastal raid against Alexandria, Acre and Tortosa was launched on 20 July. When Ghazan invaded Syria again in the second half of 1300, the Christian forces were ready to support him. In November, in order to facilitate the joining of forces with the Mongols in northern Syria, the island of Ruad (opposite Tortosa) was occupied by a significant Christian force including a substantial number of Templars and Hospitallers. The two masters, James of Molay and William of Villaret, were present. From this small base, a three-week raid was launched on to the coast and into the country around Tortosa. News of these events comes from a letter written from Cyprus by a Catalan, namely the aforementioned Bernard William of Enteça.[36] However, Ghazan postponed his offensive against Egypt once again and sent only a vanguard to northern Syria (January 1301). The major part of the Christian army left Ruad in February 1301; only a Templar contingent remained stationed on the island under the command of the Templar marshal. The Templars had, of course, no intention of establishing their headquarters on so small an island. Ruad was not their Rhodes! It was a useful base for the Christians should the Tartars come back to Syria – no more, no less. When, during the year 1301, Ghazan announced his intention to come to Syria once again at the end of 1301, James of Molay wrote to Edward I of England (on 8 April) and told him that he was ready to land on Ruad with 'all his convent' (the whole of the order's fighting force).[37]

It seems to me that Berenguer of Cardona's journey was closely linked to these events. He was called – with food, money and men – to assist the Templars on Cyprus in their joint actions with the Tartars that were planned for the end of 1300. Berenguer most likely landed on Ruad in November 1300 (after the Templars' general chapter) and the whole of the Christian army followed James of Molay and his Templars. Berenguer did not stay on the island more than a few days or weeks (as did the master) and probably returned to Cyprus in December or early January. When Ghazan's non-arrival was confirmed in February, Berenguer was free to return 'to his country' – those are the words we find in the permits issued by the master to those leaving Cyprus; unfortunately, the permit that Berenguer of Cardona (most likely) received has not come down to us.[38] His presence (and that of the small Catalan contingent) was no longer necessary. The Templars of Cyprus (like the Hospitallers) could not maintain a large number of people 'ready for war' for a long period of time. Thus, Berenguer of Cardona negotiated his return journey with Bernard Marquet in February and left Cyprus in March or early April. He was back in Catalonia in June 1301.

During his stay on Cyprus, Berenguer, of course, exercised his function as the Templars' provincial master of Aragon and visitor of Spain. He participated in the general chapter, offered counsel and supplied information about his province. The connection between the centre and the periphery could be maintained under all circumstances, even when the main activity was war. However, Berenguer of Cardona served the Order of the Temple mainly on the periphery, in Spain. He could not stay at the centre for too long, he could not be a permanent soldier on Cyprus – only an occasional one.

Berenguer of Cardona's journey in 1300–1 reveals the importance accorded by the Order of the Temple to the 'Mongol alliance strategy'. It was more than the travel of a dignitary: it represented his province's mobilization for the cause of the Holy Land.

Notes

[1]   Jules Michelet (ed.), *Le procès des Templiers* (Paris, 1841–51), vol. 1, pp. 458, 564–6; Archivo de la Corona de Aragón, Barcelona (ACA), Cartas reales diplomáticas (CRD), Jaime II, 139, no. 374: a letter of Peter of *Castillon* to J. *de Molimer*, the *maître du passage* at Marseille (14 June 1306).

[2]   Alan Forey, 'Sources for the history of the Templars in Aragón, Catalonia and Valencia', *Archives*, 21 (1994), 16–24.

[3]   Alan Forey, *The Templars in the Corona de Aragón* (London, 1973); Alan Forey, 'Letters of the last two Templar masters', *Nottingham Medieval Studies*, 45 (2001), 145–62; see also Pierre-Vincent Claverie, 'La contribution des templiers de Catalogne à la défense de la Syrie franque (1290–1310)', in Urbain Vermeulen and Jo van Steenbergen (eds), *Egypt and Syria in the Fatimid, Ayyubid and Mamluk Eras*, vol. 3 (Leuven, 2001), pp. 171–92.

[4]   ACA, registros (reg.), Jaime II, 66, fol. 62; see Forey, *Templars in the Corona de Aragón*, pp. 309 and 402 no. XXX (edition).

[5]   Cornelio Desimoni (ed.), 'Actes passés à Famagouste de 1299 à 1301 par devant le notaire génois Lamberto di Sambuceto', *Archives de l'Orient Latin*, 2 (1884), documents, 3–120; Michel Balard (ed.), *Notai genovesi in Oltremare: Atti rogati a Cipro da Lamberto di Sambuceto, 11 ottobre 1296 – 23*

giugno 1299 (Genoa, 1983); Valeria Polonio (ed.), *Notai genovesi in Oltremare: Atti rogati a Cipro da Lamberto di Sambuceto, 3 luglio 1300 – 3 agosto 1301* (Genoa, 1982); Romeo Pavoni (ed.), *Notai genovesi in Oltremare: Atti rogati a Cipro da Lamberto di Sambuceto, 6 luglio – 27 ottobre 1302* (Genoa, 1982); Romeo Pavoni (ed.), *Notai genovesi in Oltremare: Atti rogati a Cipro da Lamberto di Sambuceto, gennaio–agosto 1302* (Genoa, 1987).

[6] ACA, CRD, Jaime II, 139, no. 249.

[7] The term 'convent' here has the common meaning of 'the whole of the order's fighting force'.

[8] ACA, CRD, Jaime II, 9, no. 1177; Heinrich Finke, *Acta Aragonensia: Quellen zur deutschen, italienischen, französischen, spanischen, zur Kirchen- und Kulturgeschichte, aus der diplomatischen Korrespondenz Jaymes II. (1291–1327)*, 3 vols (Berlin, 1908–22) (AA), vol. 1, p. 79 no. 58.

[9] ACA, CRD, Jaime II, 137, no. 68; Claverie, 'La contribution des templiers', p. 180.

[10] Forey, *Templars in the Corona de Aragón*, pp. 326–7 with some references to the matter.

[11] ACA, CRD, Jaime II, Templarios, 138, no. 247; 139, no. 377.

[12] See above, note 9.

[13] Forey, *Templars in the Corona de Aragón*, p. 422 (table).

[14] ACA, reg. 332, fol. 75; Forey, *Templars in the Corona de Aragón*, p. 412 no. XLI (edition).

[15] Forey, *Templars in the Corona de Aragón*, pp. 414–15 no. XLIV.

[16] Polonio, *Notai genovesi, 3 luglio 1300 – 3 agosto 1301*, pp. 256–8 no. 219.

[17] Ibid., pp. 305–6 no. 255.

[18] ACA, CRD, Jaime II, 141, no. 489; Forey, 'Letters of the last two Templar masters', p. 163.

[19] Forey, *Templars in the Corona de Aragón*, p. 422. According to Forey, ibid., pp. 318–19 with p. 338 note 105, the lieutenant did not summon the provincial chapter in that year but, rather, ordered the commanders of the province to bring their *responsiones* to Gardeny (in May). Granted, Peter of Thous wrote to Peter of St Just on 1 February, gave him some news about Majorca and the war in the kingdom of Murcia and asked him to gather money and *responsiones*, but he did not mention any forthcoming chapter (ACA, CRD, Jaime II, 137, no. 106). However, in another letter to the same Peter of St Just – not dated but probably written during the same period – Peter of Thous summoned a chapter for the second Sunday of May 'on the master's orders' (ACA, CRD, Jaime II, 141, no. 566). The only possible year is 1301, in which the Sunday in question was 14 May and when the master was Berenguer of Cardona, who must have written to Peter of Thous some time earlier – but when? If however the chapter that was supposed to have convened in May 1301 did not convene (as Forey has suggested) we would be able to explain why, in December 1301, Berenguer of Cardona summoned a chapter to be held in February 1302, an unusual date (ACA, CRD, Jaime II, 137, no. 67; 138, no. 185; 140, nos 447 and 457).

20 ACA, pergaminos, Jaime II, 161, no. 1665. Bernard Marquet was absent; perhaps he was engaged in a new passage.

21 Lamberto di Sambuceto's notary acts indicate that several Templar vessels were in Cyprus during the years 1299–1302; the well-known *Faucon* was still in service in 1300 but Roger de Flor was no longer its captain: Polonio, *Notai genovesi, 3 luglio 1300 – 3 agosto 1301*, pp. 292–3 no. 246. Another Templar ship, the *St Anna*, was at Famagusta during the winter of 1302: Pavoni, *Notai genovesi, gennaio–agosto 1302*, pp. 132–3 no. 104 and pp. 179–80 no. 150.

22 Polonio, *Notai genovesi, 3 luglio 1300 – 3 agosto 1301*, pp. 170–1 no. 148.

23 Ibid., pp. 193–5 no. 166 and pp. 199–200 no. 171; also in Desimoni, 'Actes passés à Famagouste de 1299 à 1301', pp. 345–6 no. CDLXXVIII and pp. 348–9 no. CDLXXXII (the same act, dated 4 January).

24 Balard, *Notai genovesi, 11 ottobre 1296 – 23 giugno 1299*, pp. 174–81 nos 149–51. The captain of the ship was William of *Carato*.

25 Polonio, *Notai genovesi, 3 luglio 1300 – 3 agosto 1301*, pp. 304 – 5 no. 257.

26 Ibid., pp. 256 – 8 no. 219.

27 Ibid., pp. 305 – 6 no. 258.

28 Alain Demurger, *The Last Templar: The Tragedy of Jacques de Molay* (London, 2004), pp. 98–110.

29 *Chroniques d'Amadi et de Strambaldi*, ed. René de Mas-Latrie, 2 vols (Paris, 1891–3), vol. 1, pp. 234–5; see Demurger, *Last Templar*, pp. 96–8.

30 Hayton, 'La Flor des estoires de la Terre d'Orient', in *Recueil des historiens des croisades, documents arméniens*, 2 vols (Paris, 1869–1906), vol. 2, pp. 327–30; see Demurger, *Last Templar*, pp. 76–7 and 95–7.

31 Anthony Luttrell, 'The Hospitallers' interventions in Cilician Armenia, 1291–1373', in Thomas S. R. Boase (ed.), *The Cilician Kingdom of Armenia* (Edinburgh, 1978), pp. 116–44, here 122.

32 *Andreae Danduli ducis Venetiarum Chronica per extensum descripta: aa 46–1280 d.C.*, ed. Ester Pastorello, *Rerum Italicarum scriptores*, new revised edition, vol. 12, part 1 (Bologna, 1938–58), pp. 396–8; see Claverie, 'La contribution des templiers', p. 179.

33 Finke, AA, vol. 3, p. 90 no. 41 (1).

34 Ibid., pp. 90–1 no. 41 (2).

35 Ibid., pp. 91–2 no. 42; Sylvia Schein, 'Gesta Dei per Mongolos 1300: the genesis of a non-event', *English Historical Review*, 94 (1979), 805–19.

36 Heinrich Finke, *Papsttum und Untergang des Templerordens*, 2 vols (Münster, 1907), vol. 2, pp. 4–5 no. 4 (edition).

37 London, The National Archives of the UK: Public Record Office, Ancient Correspondence, SC 1/55, fol. 22; Marie Luise Bulst-Thiele, *Sacrae domus militiae Templi Hierosolymitani magistri: Untersuchungen zur Geschichte des Templerordens 1118/19–1314* (Göttingen, 1974), p. 366.

38 For examples of these permits see Forey, 'Letters of the last two Templar masters', pp. 160–1, 166.

8

John Malkaw of Prussia: A Case of Individual Mobility in the Teutonic Order, *c*.1400

AXEL EHLERS

For the German historian Aloys Schulte he was – in 1892 – 'one of the most peculiar persons of the later Middle Ages'.[1] Nevertheless it took more than one hundred years, until 1995, for the first monograph to appear on John Malkaw of Prussia, written by Michael Tönsing at the University of Constance.[2] John Malkaw was born sometime before 1360 in Strasbourg in Prussia (now Brodnica, Poland: see Figure 3, p. xxi). His father Nicholas came from a nearby village named Mahlkau (see Figure 3: now Małki).[3] Therefore the spelling 'Malkaw' is most appropriate, although some sources spell 'Malkow'. Much about John Malkaw's earlier life is known from an autobiographical pamphlet he wrote in 1391 while he was held prisoner by the Inquisition. In 1884 Herman Haupt edited the greater part of this text and thereby laid the foundation for subsequent studies.[4] However only a few marginal references in books and articles on the Inquisition and – in 1928 – one short essay by Josef Beckmann followed.[5] Michael Tönsing has recently uncovered new sources and edited all the relevant material, old and new, in his dissertation. As he has produced the authoritative account of Malkaw's life, much of the following is based on Tönsing's work. Historians of the Teutonic Order have hardly concerned themselves with Malkaw, even though he obtained important papal privileges for the benefit of the order, as we shall see. In addition, Malkaw's life is an example of social and individual mobility in the Teutonic Order.

John Malkaw began his career as a priest in the Prussian diocese of Kulm (see Figure 3). Some time before 1388 he left Prussia against the will of his parents and against the will of the administrator of the bishopric, who refused to certify Malkaw's priestly status and to issue a *dimissoriale* (a letter recommending him to another diocese). Malkaw wanted to enter the Carthusian Order, but his physical constitution was not suited for the rigorous monastic life.[6] The self-imposed exile from his homeland initiated a life of unrest, including some notable years as a brother-priest of the Teutonic Order. In 1388 Malkaw appeared at Cologne in the Rhineland, where he preached against Pope Clement VII and his supporters, that is against the Avignonese obedience of the 'great schism'. What exactly prompted his preaching and his stern stand for the Roman obedience is not known. But he seems to have found his personal mission, for wherever he went in the future he vigorously started propagating the Roman obedience. After a while the archbishop of Cologne, although of the Roman obedience himself, forbade Malkaw any further preaching activities for political reasons. The archbishop wanted to arrange a peace between the king of France (Avignonese obedience) and the duke of Geldern (Roman obedience). Apparently Malkaw's agitation was a hindrance to the archbishop's plans.[7]

Malkaw migrated some fifty miles (eighty kilometres) to Koblenz, to the south-east of Cologne, where the archbishop of Trier offered him a warm welcome. However, in less than a fortnight Malkaw managed to become acquainted with this archbishop's prison by preaching against a decree of protection for the Jews. Imprisonment was short, and Malkaw left for Mainz, some forty miles or sixty-five kilometres to the south-east of Koblenz, to advocate the Roman obedience there. Soon after he appeared at Cologne again, but nothing is known about his activities. In 1390, a year of jubilee during which a plenary indulgence could be won at Rome, Malkaw headed south to the holy city.[8] At Strasbourg in the Rhineland (see Figure 3) he stayed for more than a month, preaching. He attacked Clementists as well as those who avoided a decision for either obedience. Additionally he castigated the deplorable moral state of the clergy, especially that of the mendicant orders. His sermons split the audience. Some people, among them – not surprisingly – the mendicants, became fierce opponents of Malkaw and intended to get rid of him by any means. Others were enthusiastic supporters, so enthusiastic in fact, that after one of Malkaw's sermons a mob hurried to the Hospitaller commandery at the Grünen Wörth and drove the commander, Henry of Wolfach, out of town.[9] The Hospitallers' central convent on Rhodes was adhering to the Avignonese obedience. The Teutonic Order, by contrast, was supporting the Roman pope.[10] This may have attracted Malkaw, apart from the need to make a living.

According to his own testimony, he served the Teutonic Order as chaplain during his time at Strasbourg.[11]

Malkaw moved on to Rome. Afterwards, against the advice of the bishop of Basel, who had asked him to go back to Prussia because he had not been able to prove his priesthood in accordance with the bishop's demand, Malkaw returned to Strasbourg in the Rhineland. His opponents awaited him eagerly. Although Malkaw's episcopal permit to preach in the diocese of Strasbourg had expired, he started preaching again and was subsequently accused of heresy. The Dominican inquisitor Nicholas Böckler took charge of the case. Böckler had threatened to prosecute Malkaw before, and now he had his opportunity. Yet the trial ended fortunately for Malkaw, and in autumn 1392 Malkaw was set free.[12] The exact circumstances are not clear, but as – apparently – he had to leave Strasbourg, his opponents had achieved their principal aim. Malkaw went back to Cologne where he matriculated at the university.[13] A year later, in November 1393, he was appointed honorary papal chaplain by Boniface IX who seems to have valued Malkaw's zeal for the Roman obedience.[14] As an honorary papal chaplain Malkaw was not subject to the authority of the Inquisition.[15] The following year, on Malkaw's initiative, the University of Heidelberg declared the charges brought against him to be unjustified.[16] Thus rehabilitated, Malkaw returned to Strasbourg, where he joined the Teutonic Order as a brother-priest.

By 1396, Malkaw had become commander of the Teutonic Order's house at Strasbourg.[17] Strasbourg was one of the larger commanderies in the bailiwick of Alsace-Burgundy, but due to a loss of sources its importance has sometimes been underrated.[18] For Malkaw, the Teutonic Order and its commandery probably appeared as a firm basis in his fight for Rome. By extending the buildings and procuring new privileges he attempted to strengthen the order's spiritual and material position within the town. The number of brother-priests increased from four to seven while Malkaw was commander, whereas the number of knights never exceeded three.[19]

The rebuilding of the chapel necessitated the transfer of an altar. In February 1397 Boniface IX allowed the Teutonic Order to transfer altars in its churches without episcopal consent.[20] The privilege points to Malkaw's activities, as will be shown. In late spring 1398 a group of armed men forced their way into the order's chapel and threatened the commander. Malkaw, probably fearing for his life, left Strasbourg. He stayed at the order's commandery at Beuggen, some seventy miles or

110 kilometres to the south, during the second half of the year.[21] The
bishop-elect, William of Diest, had fuelled this incident. Michael
Tönsing has convincingly argued that the transfer of the altar without
asking for the bishop's permit may have caused this rupture.[22] Malkaw
apparently relied on the privilege of 1397 and succeeded, for in April
1400 Boniface IX issued an indulgence in favour of the new altar and
confirmed the earlier privilege concerning the transfer of altars. In
September 1400 the altar was finally consecrated.[23]

   Apart from the privilege of 1397 and the indulgence of 1400, Malkaw
is likely to have procured a range of other papal privileges, among them
several indulgences for the benefit of his commandery. On 25 February
and 22 March 1399 six charters were issued in Rome. One of these
contained an indulgence for the order's chapel in Strasbourg,[24] the
others comprised privileges of general use for the order such as an
indulgence for its *confratres* on the seven Eucharistic days that the
brothers observed,[25] several exemptions from canonical restrictions and
episcopal authority,[26] an indulgence for the sermons of the order's
clerics, who were also allowed to preach whenever and wherever they
wanted,[27] and finally the threat of excommunication against those who
impaired the order in any way.[28] Although of general use, these
privileges splendidly supported Malkaw's position in Strasbourg.[29]

   In August 1399 at least one of the charters was copied by a notary in
Basel (see Figure 3) by request of the local Teutonic commander, John
of Nollingen. John Malkaw was present. Later the transcript came into
the commandery at Ulm, some 130 miles or 210 kilometres north-east
of Basel, where someone noted on the back of the parchment: '[this]
comes from Basel' (*kimpt von Basel*).[30] Between December 1400 and
December 1402 all six papal charters were copied several times at
Strasbourg. So far, I have found twenty-four transcripts, excluding the
one made at Basel. Copies went to Marburg, Speyer, Utrecht,
Weißenburg, the bailiwick of Lorraine and even to Prussia. Today the
transcripts are kept in Vienna, Berlin, Strasbourg, Marburg, Utrecht
and possibly some other places as yet unknown.[31] These observations
suggest that Malkaw may have procured the papal charters personally
in Rome. On his way back he came through Basel where the local
commander seized the opportunity to have one or more copies of the
privileges made. Afterwards Malkaw took the original bulls with him to
Strasbourg. From there those bulls that were not specifically addressed
to the local commandery were spread within the order by means of
transcripts.

On 13 April 1400 another series of four papal charters was issued. Three of the bulls contained different indulgences for the house at Strasbourg, while the fourth confirmed several of the earlier privileges, including a Strasbourg indulgence of 1399.[32] Thus, all four bulls have a clear connection to Strasbourg. As before, the one bull that was relevant not only for the Strasbourg commandery but for the entire order was copied at Strasbourg not long after it had been issued. The pattern equals that for the first series of charters. In both cases John Malkaw seems to have been the driving force for the procurement of the bulls. He had been on friendly terms with Boniface IX since 1393 at the latest, and being an honorary papal chaplain may have helped him to obtain this set of privileges easily, although not for free: the notes on one of the surviving charters indicate that the usual taxes had to be paid to the papal chancery.[33]

Malkaw had fled to Beuggen in the summer of 1398, and he was still there in December.[34] About two months later the first series of charters was issued (February/March 1399). Malkaw may well have travelled to the Curia personally, for nothing else is heard of him until the summer of 1399. In August 1399 he was back at Basel from where he soon returned north to Strasbourg. Furnished with the new privileges he could confidently face the wrath of the bishop-elect. The successful consecration of the altar in 1400 proves that Malkaw prevailed. The three indulgences issued with the second series of charters earlier in the same year helped to increase the spiritual attraction of the refurbished chapel. No other chapel or church of the order could boast comparable papal graces at the time, if one disregards the summaries of the order's indulgence that were becoming increasingly popular.[35] Besides, the entire order was able to profit from Malkaw's initiative because he procured privileges of general use. The widespread interest in the transcripts shows that the brothers knew the potential of the bulls. The importance of Malkaw as a procurer of new privileges has not been realized, however, by historians of the Teutonic Order. Even Tönsing does not know of many of the transcripts which point to Strasbourg as the place where the original bulls were kept. Thus he still assumes that Malkaw had the transcripts made just for his own use, but this is evidently not the case.[36]

A few years later, at the end of 1404, Malkaw was no longer commander at Strasbourg. Apparently he had to step down after a rousing sermon in which he had accused citizens and clergy of moral failure. He left Strasbourg and moved to the court of the margrave of Baden.[37] At the end of 1405 the grand master (*Hochmeister*) summoned him to the general chapter in Prussia in order to discuss Malkaw's wish to leave the Teutonic Order.[38] It seems that Malkaw obtained the necessary permission to enter another form of religious life. The sources fall silent for a few years, but in 1411 Malkaw reappears as a Benedictine monk. He now campaigned against the obedience of Pisa.[39] Once more he was charged with heresy and tried at Cologne from where he fled.[40] Afterwards Pope Gregory XII employed Malkaw in his diplomatic service and furnished him with personal privileges.[41] At the Council of Constance Malkaw attempted to settle the case against him, but the exact outcome of his endeavours is unknown. After 1416 nothing else is heard of him. Neither the place nor the year nor the circumstances of his death are known.[42]

John Malkaw of Prussia was an exile of his time. After he had left Prussia for religious reasons, he was constantly on the move. For about ten years the Teutonic Order at Strasbourg offered him a field of activity allowing for fairly independent actions. Malkaw's good connections to the Roman Curia enabled him to procure a remarkable set of privileges not only for his commandery but for the whole order. From Strasbourg these privileges were distributed to other commanderies. This process points to structures of communication and mobility within the order that worked more or less independently from those directed by the order's headquarters in Prussia.

Malkaw was a remarkable figure in many respects. Born in Prussia, he was a cleric of bourgeois origin who became head of an important commandery in the empire. This combination was highly unusual. Clerics as well as men of non-noble birth could become commanders, but Prussians who left Prussia, entered the Teutonic Order elsewhere and took over a commandery were a rare occurrence indeed.[43] Possibly Malkaw is the only example of a case like this. His career – unintentional as it may have been – required his personal mobility. Had he lived in Prussia as a brother-priest of the order, he would have hardly obtained a higher office. Brothers of knightly status dominated the Prussian hierarchy.[44] Once in charge of the Strasbourg commandery he apparently enjoyed the freedom of travelling to Rome and procuring outstanding papal privileges. In this, Malkaw is an exception. His unusual career was partly due to his idiosyncratic personality, but it also indicates the degree of social and individual mobility that a military order could offer around 1400.

Notes

1 [Aloys] Schulte, [review], *Zeitschrift für die Geschichte des Oberrheins*, 46, Neue Folge, 7 (1892), 736–7, here 736.

2 Michael Tönsing, 'Johannes Malkaw aus Preußen (ca. 1360–1416): Studien und Quellen zu einem Streiter für die römische Obödienz während des Großen Abendländischen Schismas', 2 pts (Ph.D. thesis, Universität Konstanz, 1995, microfiche). Only recently printed as Michael Tönsing, *Johannes Malkaw aus Preußen (ca. 1360–1416): Ein Kleriker im Spannungsfeld von Kanzel, Ketzerprozeß und Kirchenspaltung* (Warendorf, 2004). References here are to the microfiche.

3 Tönsing, 'Johannes Malkaw', pt. 1, 9.

4 Herman Haupt, 'Johannes Malkaw aus Preußen und seine Verfolgung durch die Inquisition zu Straßburg und Köln (1390–1416)', *Zeitschrift für Kirchengeschichte*, 6 (1884), 323–89, 580–7; the text of the pamphlet can be found ibid., 365–89; for a complete edition see Tönsing, 'Johannes Malkaw', pt. 2, 6–50 no. 4.

5 Wilhelm Ribbeck, 'Beiträge zur Geschichte der römischen Inquisition in Deutschland während des 14. und 15. Jahrhunderts', *Zeitschrift für vaterländische Geschichte und Alterthumskunde*, 46, 1. Abteilung (1888), 129–56, here 133–4, 147–50; Henry Charles Lea, *Geschichte der Inquisition im Mittelalter*, 3 vols, revised and ed. by Joseph Hansen (Bonn, 1905; reprint Nördlingen, 1987), vol. 3, pp. 232–5; Josef Beckmann, 'Johannes Malkaw aus Preußen: Ein Streiter für die römische Obedienz während des großen Schismas', *Historisches Jahrbuch*, 48 (1928), 619–25.

6 Tönsing, 'Johannes Malkaw', pt. 1, 9–10; pt. 2, 13–14 (= Haupt, 'Johannes Malkaw', 370–1).

7 Tönsing, 'Johannes Malkaw', pt. 1, 10–12.

8 Ibid., pt. 1, 13–19.

9 Ibid., pt. 1, 30; for the Hospitallers at Strasbourg and their relationship with Malkaw see also ibid., pt. 1, 132, 141–3.

10 For the Hospitallers of Rhodes see Anthony Luttrell, 'The Hospitallers at Rhodes, 1306–1421', in Kenneth M. Setton (ed.), *A History of the Crusades*, vol. 4, *The Fourteenth and Fifteenth Centuries*, ed. Harry W. Hazard (Madison, 1975), p. 305; repr. in Anthony Luttrell (ed.), *The Hospitallers in Cyprus, Rhodes, Greece and the West (1291–1440)* (London, 1978), no. I. For the Teutonic Order see Jan-Erik Beuttel, *Der Generalprokurator des Deutschen Ordens an der römischen Kurie: Amt, Funktion, personelles Umfeld und Finanzierung* (Marburg, 1999), pp. 44–5.

11 Tönsing, 'Johannes Malkaw', pt. 1, 19–30; pt. 2, 16.

12 For details see ibid., pt. 1, 32–103.

13 See ibid., pt. 1, 103–6.

14 Gerd Tellenbach (ed.), *Repertorium Germanicum: Verzeichnis der in den päpstlichen Registern und Kameralakten vorkommenden Personen, Kirchen und Orte des Deutschen Reiches, seiner Diözesen und Territorien vom Beginn des*

Schismas bis zur Reformation, vol. 2, 2 pts (Berlin, 1933), here vol. 2, pt. 1, col. 710 (3 November 1393); Tönsing, 'Johannes Malkaw', pt. 2, 56–7 no. 7.

15 Tönsing, 'Johannes Malkaw', pt. 1, 106–7.

16 Ibid., pt. 1, 107–18.

17 M[oritz] Gmelin (ed.), 'Urkundenbuch der Deutschordens-Commende Beuggen', *Zeitschrift für die Geschichte des Oberrheins*, 28 (1876), 78–127, 376–438; 29 (1877), 163–260; 30 (1878), 213–322; 31 (1879), 168–233; here 30 (1878), 294–6, especially 295; Tönsing, 'Johannes Malkaw', pt. 1, 156–9.

18 See Karl Otto Müller, 'Das Finanzwesen der Deutsch-Ordensballei Elsaß-Schwaben-Burgund im Jahre 1414', *Historisches Jahrbuch*, 34 (1913), 781–823, here especially 789, 813–16; Karl Otto Müller, *Beschreibung (Status) der Kommenden der Deutschordensballei Elsaß-Schwaben-Burgund im Jahre 1393* (Stuttgart, 1958), pp. xix–xx; Tönsing, 'Johannes Malkaw', pt. 1, 153, 206; Guy Trendel, 'L'ordre teutonique en Alsace', *Recherches médiévales*, 18/19 (1987), 3–62, here 31–2; Pierre-Paul Faust, 'Der Deutsche Orden im Elsaß: Geschichte und Spuren der elsässischen Ordensniederlassungen, besonders der Kommende Rouffach-Suntheim', in Hermann Brommer (ed.), *Der Deutsche Orden und die Ballei Elsaß-Burgund: Die Freiburger Vorträge zur 800-Jahr-Feier des Deutschen Ordens* (Bühl, 1996), pp. 245–70, here pp. 248–50.

19 Müller, *Beschreibung*, p. xx (for the year 1393); Friedrich Benninghoven, 'Zur Zahl und Standortverteilung der Brüder des Deutschen Ordens in den Balleien um 1400', *Preußenland*, 26, 1 (1988), 1–20, here 7, 14 (for c. 1400); Tönsing, 'Johannes Malkaw', pt. 1, 154–5.

20 *Sincere devocionis affectus* (25 February 1397): Città del Vaticano, Archivio Segreto Vaticano (ASV), Registra Lateranensia (Reg. Lat.) 57, fol. 131r–v; Tönsing, 'Johannes Malkaw', pt. 2, 101–5 no. 37.

21 Tönsing, 'Johannes Malkaw', pt. 1, 160–2.

22 Ibid., pt. 1, 162–6.

23 *Splendor paterne glorie* (13 April 1400): ASV, Reg. Lat. 72, fol. 100r; Tellenbach, *Repertorium Germanicum*, vol. 2, pt. 1, col. 86. – Transcript (12 September 1400): Stuttgart, Hauptstaatsarchiv (HStA), B 343 U 524a; Tönsing, 'Johannes Malkaw', pt. 2, 79–81 no. 26. – Consecration (11 September 1400): Tönsing, 'Johannes Malkaw', pt. 2, 83–7 no. 29; see also ibid., pt. 1, 166.

24 *Immensa divine largitatis* (25 February 1399): ASV, Reg. Lat. 66, fol. 30r–v; Tönsing, 'Johannes Malkaw', pt. 2, 77–9 no. 25.

25 *Ad ea ex apostolice* (25 February 1399): ASV, Reg. Lat. 66, fol. 54r–v; Ernst Strehlke (ed.), *Tabulae ordinis Theutonici* (Berlin, 1869; reprint with an introduction by Hans Eberhard Mayer: Toronto, 1975), pp. 442–3 no. 697; Tönsing, 'Johannes Malkaw', pt. 2, 105–8 no. 38.

26 *Iustis et honestis* (25 February 1399): ASV, Reg. Lat. 66, fol. 53r–v; Tönsing, 'Johannes Malkaw', pt. 2, 108–12 no. 39. – *Sedis apostolice gratiosa* (25 February 1399): ASV, Reg. Lat., fol. 61r; Tönsing, 'Johannes Malkaw', pt. 2, 115–18 no. 41.

27 *Sincere devocionis affectus* (25 February 1399): ASV, Reg. Lat. 66, fols

154v–155r; Strehlke, *Tabulae*, p. 442 no. 696; ignored by Tönsing, 'Johannes Malkaw'.

[28] *Magne devocionis affectus* (22 March 1399): ASV, Reg. Lat. 66, fol. 61v; Strehlke, *Tabulae*, p. 444 no. 698; Tönsing, 'Johannes Malkaw', pt. 2, 112–15 no. 40.

[29] See Tönsing, 'Johannes Malkaw', pt. 1, 168–73.

[30] Ulm, Stadtarchiv, A Urkunden, 25 February 1399 (4 August 1399, Basel; transcript of *Sincere devocionis affectus*, 25 February 1399).

[31] Transcripts of *Iustis et honestis* (5): Vienna, Zentralarchiv des Deutschen Ordens (DOZA), Abteilung Urkunden (Urk.), 25 May 1401, 11 December 1402; Marburg, Staatsarchiv (StA), A II 24, 11 December 1402; Strasbourg, Archives départementales du Bas-Rhin (ADép), 19 J 218a, 11 December 1402; Utrecht, Archieven van de Ridderlijke Duitsche Orde, Balije van Utrecht (ARiDO), Oorkonde 90. – Transcripts of *Sedis apostolice gratiosa* (4): DOZA, Urk., 25 May 1401, 11 December 1402; Marburg, StA, A II 24, 11 December 1402; ARiDO, Oorkonde 91. – Transcripts of *Ad ea ex apostolice* (4): DOZA, Urk., 14 December 1400, 11 December 1402; Berlin, Geheimes Staatsarchiv, Preußischer Kulturbesitz (GStA-PK), XX. Hauptabteilung, Schieblade 8, Nr. 26, 16 April 1401; Marburg, StA, A II 24, 11 December 1402. – Transcripts of *Sincere devocionis affectus* (5): DOZA, Urk., 25 May 1401 (three copies); Marburg, StA, A II 24, 11 December 1402; Strasbourg, ADép, 19 J 218b, 11 December 1402. – Transcripts of *Magne devocionis affectus* (6): DOZA, Urk., 14 December 1400, 25 May 1401, 11 December 1402; Berlin, GStA-PK, XX. Hauptabteilung, Schieblade 8, Nr. 27, 11 December 1402; Marburg, StA, A II 24, 11 December 1402; Strasbourg, ADép, 19 J 218c, 11 December 1402.

[32] Indulgences for the Strasbourg commandery: *Licet is*: ASV, Reg. Lat. 72, fol. 99r; *Splendor paterne glorie*: ASV, Reg. Lat. 72, fol. 100r (transcript: Stuttgart, HStA, B 343 U 524a, 12 September 1400, Strasbourg); *Licet is*: ASV, Reg. Lat. 73, fol. 237r–v; all printed (with additional references) in Tönsing, 'Johannes Malkaw', pt. 2, 79–83 nos 26–8. – Confirmation: *Hiis que fidelibus*: Stuttgart, HStA, B 343 U 423, original; Strehlke, *Tabulae*, pp. 444–8 no. 699; Tönsing, 'Johannes Malkaw', pt. 2, 88–95 no. 31.

[33] Tönsing, 'Johannes Malkaw', pt. 2, 79 no. 26.

[34] Ibid., pt. 1, 163–4; pt. 2, 74–5 no. 23.

[35] On these summaries as well as on the indulgences of the order's churches see Axel Ehlers, 'Die Ablaßpraxis des Deutschen Ordens im Mittelalter' (Ph.D. thesis, Universität Göttingen, 2002; publication in preparation).

[36] See Tönsing, 'Johannes Malkaw', pt. 1, 168–72.

[37] Ibid., pt. 1, 176–8.

[38] Ibid., pt. 1, 178; pt. 2, 120–2 no. 44.

[39] Ibid., pt. 1, 179; pt. 2, 124–5 no. 48, here 124.

[40] Ibid., pt. 1, 181–9.

[41] Ibid., pt. 1, 189–95.

[42] Ibid., pt. 1, 196–201.

[43] See Peter Heim, *Die Deutschordenskommende Beuggen und die Anfänge der Ballei Elsaß-Burgund: Von ihrer Entstehung bis zur Reformationszeit* (Bonn-Godesberg, 1977), pp. 49–51; Erich Maschke, 'Deutschordensbrüder aus dem städtischen Patriziat' [1958], in Erich Maschke, *Domus hospitalis Theutonicorum: Europäische Verbindungslinien der Deutschordensgeschichte, Gesammelte Aufsätze aus den Jahren 1931–1963* (Bonn-Godesberg, 1970), pp. 60–8.

[44] See Klaus Militzer, *Von Akkon zur Marienburg: Verfassung, Verwaltung und Sozialstruktur des Deutschen Ordens, 1190–1309* (Marburg, 1999), pp. 65, 68.

II

Regional Studies

9

International Mobility versus the Needs of the Realm: The Templars and Hospitallers in the British Isles in the Thirteenth and Fourteenth Centuries

HELEN NICHOLSON

The brothers of the Temple and the Hospital in the British Isles were largely absent from the international stage. They seldom achieved high office in the east. From around 1330 the office of *turcopolier* in the Hospital of St John was always held by a brother from the English tongue, but none ever progressed to the grand mastership. Yet different sources of evidence give differing pictures of the international mobility of the military orders between the British Isles and the east.

The Hospitallers' records maintained at their central convent in the east give a picture of constant interchange between west and east. These records enable us to trace the careers of brothers such as John Pavely and Robert Hales from an early period on Rhodes to the priorship in England, or others such as Richard de Overton who appear holding office in England and then later as *turcopolier* on Rhodes. Some brothers (such as Robert Hales) apparently made a career in the east, not returning to the west for many years. Clearly there was a pool of brothers from the English province (the priory of England and Wales, the priory of Ireland and the commandery of Scotland) on Rhodes, albeit smaller in number than the French, the Spanish or the Italians.

In contrast, the English government records in the Public Record Office, London, provide only sporadic references to brothers coming from and going overseas. They also give evidence of considerable restrictions being placed on their movements by the English government, in the name of the needs of the realm. Finally, documents prepared by or about the brothers within the British Isles indicate that these were very insular groups, having little contact with overseas.

This chapter begins with a consideration of what international movement actually occurred in the military orders between the British Isles and the rest of Christendom during the thirteenth and fourteenth centuries. It then describes the restrictions placed on international movement by the kings of England and finally considers how far the brothers in the British Isles may have seen themselves as part of an international order.

The English government records for the thirteenth and fourteenth centuries indicate when the chief officials of the military orders within England and Ireland went overseas and returned, as they were given royal permission to travel and a royal safe-conduct. These records probably do not record every occasion that the chief officials actually crossed the sea. During times of war, written permission to leave the realm would certainly be required, but at other times perhaps nothing would be recorded in writing. In short, the lack of a record does not mean that no one went abroad in that year.

From the English government records, we see that in the thirteenth century the grand commander of the Temple left England to attend his order's chapter meeting in France in May or June, initially at five-yearly intervals from 1227 to 1236, then more intermittently – but his journeys may also have been combined with service for the king, so that the fact that he was going on his order's business was not mentioned.[1] In the 1270s there are more regular records of the grand commander going to the Holy Land.[2] In 1296 and 1304 the English grand commander went overseas to consult with the grand master.[3]

We can also see the prior of the Hospital in England going overseas in May or June (sometimes specified as 'to the Holy Land') to his order's chapter meeting, taking with him the sums due from his priory, called 'responsions'. In the thirteenth century the references are sporadic.[4] In the fourteenth century the references are a little more frequent, but this may only reflect better record-keeping.[5] The last two English priors of the fourteenth century, John Radington and Walter Grendon, had both spent their early careers on Rhodes and subsequently spent much of their period as priors in the east.[6] During the 'great schism', the English priory maintained contacts with the main convent of the order, but the Irish priory transferred its allegiance to the 'anti-grand master' in Rome, and sent a representative to his general chapter in 1384.[7]

There are fewer references to ordinary brothers going overseas, but nevertheless it is clear that there was some international movement to join the order or to trade.[8] There are also intermittent references from the thirteenth and fourteenth centuries to lesser brothers of the Hospital being sent overseas from the British Isles to the east on their order's business.[9] The records of the general chapters give some indication of the presence of 'ordinary' English brothers in the east.[10]

A major reason for international movement was to transport resources from the west to the east, especially money. The responsions had to be physically transported from the west to the east. Apart from the financial crisis of the 1320s and various limitations imposed by the English king, the English, Irish and Scottish Hospitallers apparently paid their responsions to Rhodes fairly regularly during this period.[11] The method of transporting the money to the receiver-general of the order varied. Sometimes it was taken abroad by an individual connected with the order, sometimes it was entrusted to a carrier and sometimes it was collected by a receiver who came to the British Isles.

Brother John Pavely, the lieutenant prior of the English Hospitallers, sent his responsions for 1353 to Rhodes in the care of Brother John *Paxcherius*, commander of Albi and Toulouse. On arrival, serious shortcomings were discovered in the accounts, and on 15 June 1358 the grand master instructed two leading members of the English priory to sort out the mess.[12] In February 1366 the grand master, Raymond Berenguer, instructed Brother Richard of Overton, collector of responsions in the English priory, and John of Ycle, commander of Dalby, to have the money ready to hand over to Brother Robert Hales, his *socius* or personal aide. Apparently Brother Robert Hales was coming to England to collect the money.[13] In 1382 the Scottish responsions were entrusted to a merchant of Lucca, who brought them to Avignon.[14] In 1384 the order's receiver apparently came to London to receive the money.[15] In April 1387, the receiver-general recorded that Brother Hildebrand Inge had entrusted the money for 1386 to a Genoese merchant at London, who brought it to Avignon to the receiver-general.[16] The Scottish responsions, on the other hand, were brought by a squire, Robert Gram.[17]

Not only did members of the orders travel from the British Isles to the east, but some moved in the other direction. Brothers came to take up positions in the west, such as that of Hospitaller prior of England or Ireland, but others had been given various duties, especially those of visitor. For the Temple, Brother James of Molay, the master of the order, visited England in 1294, while in the early years of the fourteenth century Brother Hugh of Pairaud, visitor of the Order of the Temple, visited England twice.[18] For the Hospital, in April 1235 King Henry III gave free leave to Peter Ferendi, a commander of the Hospital, to travel throughout his dominions in order to carry out the business of the order.[19] In 1327 Brother Leonard de Tibertis arrived in England to sort out the priory's financial problems. In 1371 the English brother Richard of Overton came as visitor.[20] In February 1382 the Hospitallers' grand master, Juan Fernández de Heredia, ordered Brother Henry de Gray to leave Rhodes for England as soon as possible. Brother Henry was sent to avoid loss to the treasury from the non-payment of responsions – presumably in the wake of the Hospitallers' losses during the English 'peasants' revolt' of 1381.[21]

Other movements are not fully explained by the records. On 24 March 1347, the grand master of the Hospital of St John, Déodat de Gozon, instructed Brother Walter *Anglicus* to leave his commandery in the Morea and proceed to England, promising that the order would supply his mount and expenses.[22] He was apparently engaged on urgent business for the order. Brothers in the east were periodically given permission to return to the west, sometimes for a limited period only.[23]

Some brothers' careers in the order of the Hospital required them to move back and forth from the British Isles to Rhodes. The most obvious examples of these are the *turcopoliers*, conventual bailiffs whose office required that they be resident in the east. For some of these men, the office of *turcopolier* was simply a stepping stone to further office: John de Pavely and John Radington advanced from the office of *turcopolier* to the priorship of England. Peter Holt combined the office with the priorship of Ireland. For other brothers, the office of *turcopolier* was the pinnacle of a long career of service in the British Isles: as for Richard of Overton, Brian de Grey and Hildebrand Inge.[24]

Robert Hales in particular was a careerist brother of the Order of the Hospital from the British Isles who moved back and forth between the west and the east during the course of his career. In February 1358 he was on Rhodes.[25] In July 1362 he must have been back in England, as he was admitted as one of the attorneys of the prior of England, John Pavely.[26] He took part in the crusade of King Peter I of Cyprus against Alexandria in October 1365, with the *turcopolier* (an Englishman) William of Middleton.[27] He was a personal aide or *socius* to the grand master on Rhodes. In spring 1366 he was given permission to return to the west (and he may have come as receiver of responsions, as already described). Hales was in England in November 1370, when he was again appointed as one of the attorneys of Prior John Pavely. By July 1372 he was prior himself.[28]

In the fourteenth century, many of the English brothers on Rhodes held office as commanders of commanderies in England, and drew the revenues from these commanderies. They would have appointed managers to run their properties in their absence: either brothers of the order or secular men.[29] In 1351 William of Middleton was anxious to have two brothers assigned to his commanderies in England (Ribston and Wetherby, Mount St John and Cowton or Couton, all in Yorkshire), which had been depopulated by the Black Death.[30] He needed to have brothers on the spot to manage his properties for him.

The greatest limitation on the brothers' movements was the king of England. The brothers of the orders were expected to go overseas in the king's service to meet the needs of the realm, or to play a role within the king's government that necessitated their remaining within his domains.[31] In addition, the king of England often prevented the brothers from carrying out their order's commands, forbidding them to cross the sea or to take money overseas.

In the thirteenth century, the leading officials of the Temple and the Hospital in the British Isles were often used as ambassadors overseas.[32] In particular, the military orders played an important role as messengers to King Louis IX between 1261 and 1265, during Henry III's dispute with his barons. They acted as messengers on both sides, both for the king and for his enemies led by Simon de Montfort.[33] Many leading churchmen supported Montfort's regime and were willing to act as envoys for him. Following the destruction of Montfort's cause at the battle of Evesham on 4 August 1265, the military orders did not reappear as royal ambassadors until the late fourteenth century, except as envoys to the east, although they were occasionally called upon to go overseas with the king.[34]

King Henry III also relied on the brothers of the Temple and the Hospital to carry money overseas for him: for himself when he was overseas,[35] to his allies in France,[36] and in 1241 to his younger brother Richard, earl of Cornwall, who was then in the Holy Land.[37] Again, although Edward I and Richard II employed the Hospitaller prior of England as royal treasurer, the orders were not used to carry the king's money abroad after the troubles of the 1260s.

In addition, the king forbade the brothers to travel overseas when he was at war with the king of France. As the military orders were supranational, predominantly French and based overseas, in times of war they could be regarded as possible traitors to the king.[38] In April 1243, while Henry III was in Bordeaux, campaigning in France to defend his territorial claims to Aquitaine, he issued instructions to the bailiffs of the Cinque Ports in England to prevent the grand commander of the Temple in England from going overseas. The grand commander had been summoned to the Holy Land, but Henry had written to the master in the east and told him to revoke the summons.[39] In February 1342 Philip de Thame, prior of the Hospital in England, was forbidden to go overseas on any pretext; he was later allowed to go, on condition he return quickly.[40] In March 1345 King Edward III again forbade him to go abroad because he needed Philip's counsel for his difficult business and that of the realm during his wars.[41] In February 1346 Philip was allowed to go to a council at Arles on condition he return immediately.[42]

During internal crises or external wars, the king of England would not allow the orders to export their responsions to the east.[43] In particular, at the beginning of the Anglo-French war in January 1337, Edward III issued a general ban on any religious order which was based overseas but had houses in England from exporting money.[44] Philip de Thame, prior of England, was ordered to appear before the king's court because he had sent great sums of money overseas – the responsions – thereby reducing the Hospital's resources, which (Edward said) he should be using to defend the realm against foreign invaders.[45] The brothers who had carried the responsions were accused of being 'adherents of the king's enemies overseas'.[46]

The long war with France left the realm impoverished and added to political upheaval within England, so that the export of money overseas became still less desirable in royal eyes. At the Parliament of 1385 a 'petition from the commons' asked that the money in the hands of the prior of St John of Jerusalem in England 'called responsions' be used to the profit and honour of the lord king, to relieve and support his poor people, rather than being sent to the east. King Richard II's reply was that he wished the money to be taken to the convent on Rhodes to maintain the war against the infidel; but, if the prior preferred, he would take advice from his nobles and his council as to how the money could be best used.[47] The actual views of Richard II in this situation are not clear; perhaps he was hoping to persuade the prior to halt the payment of responsions of his own free will. Prior John Radington, however, continued to pay his responsions. One way around the problem was to send cloth in place of cash.[48]

It is difficult to tell how far the brothers of the British Isles regarded these royal restrictions as unreasonable. On the one hand, they continued to send responsions to the east in defiance of royal orders and heavy hints. On the other, many leading brothers were heavily involved in the royal service, and while some brothers in the crises of the early 1260s had apparently supported Simon de Montfort, in the 1370s and early 1380s the leading Hospitallers supported the king of England. If many of the brothers within the British Isles had never been overseas, they might have regarded the king of England as their natural lord.

It is not easy to ascertain what proportion of the brothers had been overseas and how many came from outside the British Isles. The report of the English prior Philip de Thame to the convent on Rhodes, 1338, does include the names of the brothers in England. Although at this period surnames were not a safe guide to a brother's place of origin, it is interesting that most of the surnames of the Hospitaller brothers in England in 1338 appear to be from Britain or from Ireland. There are brothers 'de Norfolk', 'de Wincester', 'Waleis' (Welsh), 'Fitz Neil', 'de Draycote', 'de Huntingdon', a Philip Ewyas from the Herefordshire/Monmouthshire border, a Reginald of Coventry, a Walter of Coventry and so on.[49] Other surnames, such as Macey, were not place-specific.

The interrogations of the brothers of the Temple in the British Isles, which took place between October 1309 and the end of June 1311, give some indication of international movement. A total of 108 brothers were interrogated. Most of the brothers in England and Ireland had English or Anglo-Norman surnames. One was 'of Kilros' in Ireland. A few were surnamed 'Scot'.[50] The Irish interrogations very helpfully inform us which diocese the brothers came from as well as where they were received. All came from dioceses in either England or Ireland: eleven from England, three from Ireland.[51] Overall, it appears that most of the Templars in the British Isles came from the British Isles.

There was more variation in where they were received. In Ireland, eight of the fourteen interrogated brothers had been received in England and five in Ireland, including two born in England. So some of the brothers in Ireland had been transferred there from Britain by their order, some were 'home-grown', and some were drawn from the Cymro-Norman/Anglo-Norman families who were moving into Ireland. Some, such as Brother Thomas of Toulouse, moved back and forth across the Irish Sea. Brother Thomas had been received at Temple Dinsley in Hertfordshire, England, in around 1266; in 1285 and the early 1290s he was commander of Ireland, but by the beginning of the fourteenth century he was a commander in the diocese of York, and in 1307 he was commander of the commandery at Upleadon (Bosbury) in Herefordshire in England.[52]

How many had been in the east? Brothers apparently had to pay a *passagium* in order to be admitted, implying that they would be sent overseas, but one brother complained that he had got nothing in return for his payment.[53] Setting the great officials aside, many of the testimonies of the ordinary brothers indicate that they had never left the British Isles. Brother William de Sautre, an important brother who had been present at many receptions, when asked whether the reception of brothers was the same everywhere, replied that he believed it was, as far as he had seen in England, but he had never been out of England.[54] Neither of the brothers assigned to the two Scottish commanderies, who were both of English origin, had ever been out of the British Isles.[55] Some testimonies projected a particularly English 'national' pride. Brother John of Euleye, asked about the charge that there was public scandal about the Templars' errors and that many had confessed to them, replied that he did not know what the brothers had confessed to or done outside England but God was content about the things that were done in the order in England (although apparently doubtful about the things that were done outside England).[56] Yet, despite these apparently narrow, localized viewpoints, many brothers noted that one of the vows that they made on joining the order was to help the Holy Land as far as they could.[57] One brother stated that there was some relaxation in regard to penance for brothers travelling to the east.[58] There are also some references in the proceedings to four brothers from England who were overseas: two of these had actually been received in France and Apulia respectively, not in England.[59] However, two other brothers who had been received in England but who were in Cyprus during the trial were not mentioned by the English brothers.[60] Six brothers in the British Isles during the trial had been received outside the British Isles;[61] one of these remarked that he had attended chapter in France.[62] Brother Henry Tanet or Danet, commander of Ireland, had spent two years overseas, *in ultramarinis partibus*, where, according to a hostile witness, he had been the master's *socius* (companion) and had been given the command of Ireland as a personal favour.[63]

The Templar trial proceedings, therefore, indicate that there was some movement of brothers in and out of the British Isles. Some men were admitted overseas and returned to the British Isles; some came and went. Clearly some overseas kept in touch with their colleagues at home in so far as brothers in the British Isles were aware that they were overseas and alive; others were apparently forgotten. For those brothers who had never been overseas, there was little knowledge of the order overseas, and some, apparently, did not greatly care. However, most did remember that the purpose for their joining the order was to help the Holy Land.

Although it may appear with hindsight that the kings of England placed the greatest restrictions on the international movement of personnel and resources between the Hospital's properties in the British Isles and in the east, the members of the order actually blamed individual brothers for problems rather than the king of England or other factors. When responsions failed to arrive in the east, or the accounts did not add up, visitors were sent to check up on the brothers rather than to argue with the king. In June 1360 the Hospitallers of Ireland complained to Edward III that they had been unable to support the Hospital on Rhodes effectively. Similar complaints were made in 1381.[64] They blamed not the king of England, but their own prior of Ireland. The solution applied by the grand master and convent was to make appointments of men previously based on Rhodes (in the English priory)[65] or to allow the local Hospitallers to choose local men (in Ireland)[66] rather than attempting to insist on the order's independence from royal interference. After all, the convent might have argued, the order relied on the good will and protection of kings to continue its operations, and a good prior should be able to resist unreasonable royal demands.

Notes

Part of this article was researched and written with the assistance of a British Academy/Leverhulme Trust Senior Research Fellowship which I held in the academic session 2003–4 for a project entitled: 'The Trial of the Templars in the British Isles'.

[1] *Patent Rolls of the Reign of Henry III Preserved in the Public Record Office, Printed under the Superintendence of the Deputy Keeper of the Records* (London, 1901–3), *1225–1232*, p. 433; *Calendar of the Patent Rolls Preserved in the Public Record Office, Prepared under the Superintendence of the Deputy Keeper of the Records* (London, 1891–1939) (*CPR*), *Henry III, 1232–1247*, pp. 120, 147; ibid., *1258–1266*, p. 78; *Close Rolls of the Reign of Henry III*

Preserved in the Public Record Office, Printed under the Superintendence of the Deputy Keeper of the Records (London, 1902–38), *1254–1256*, p. 423; ibid., *1264–1268*, p. 256; ibid., *1268–1272*, p. 127. During the trial of the Templars, the Templar brother William of Middleton stated that the English grand commander attended chapter in France every five years: Oxford, Bodleian Library, MS Bodley (MS Bod.) 454, fol. 157r; David Wilkins, *Concilia magnae Britanniae et Hiberniae*, vol. 2 (London, 1737), p. 381. The commanders of the Temple in Ireland and in Scotland were supposed to attend the English Templars' chapter meeting each year. In fact the Irish attended only every two or three years: MS Bod. 454, fols 66v, 67r (omitted in Wilkins, *Concilia*).

2   *CPR, Henry III, 1266–1272*, pp. 541, 542; *Calendar of the Close Rolls Preserved in the Public Record Office, Prepared under the Superintendence of the Deputy Keeper of the Records* (London, 1892–1963) (*CCR*), *Edward I, 1272–1279*, pp. 115, 331, 336; *CPR, Edward I, 1272–1281*, pp. 208, 308.

3   *CCR, Edward I, 1288–1296*, p. 511; ibid., *1302–1307*, p. 208. On this last occasion, according to the Templar brother William of Middleton, the visitor Hugh of Pairaud acted as lieutenant grand commander in his absence: MS Bod. 454, fol. 156v; Wilkins, *Concilia*, p. 381.

4   1214: *Rotuli litterarum patentium in Turri Londinensi asservati*, ed. Thomas D. Hardy (London, 1835) (*Rot. lit. pat.*), p. 138; 1238; *CPR, Henry III, 1232–1247*, p. 209; 1257: *CPR, Henry III, 1247–1258*, p. 561; 1269: ibid., *1266–1272*, p. 348; 1273: *CCR, Edward I, 1272–1279*, p. 50; February 1274: *CPR, Edward I, 1272–1281*, p. 44; November 1287: ibid., *1281–1292*, p. 278.

5   1317: *CCR, Edward II, 1313–1318*, p. 453; 1319: *CPR, Edward II, 1317–1321*, p. 403; 1330: *CCR, Edward III, 1330–1333*, p. 142; *CPR, Edward III, 1327–1330*, p. 531; 1331: *CPR, Edward III, 1330–1333*, pp. 323, 325; 1341: *CCR, Edward III, 1341–1343*, p. 133; 1346, 1348: ibid., *1346–1349*, pp. 45–6, 554, 558. See also: Charles Tipton, 'The 1330 general chapter of the Knights Hospitaller at Montpellier', *Traditio*, 24 (1968), 293–308, here 302; Charles Tipton, 'The English Hospitallers during the Great Schism', *Studies in Medieval and Renaissance History*, 4 (1967), 91–124.

6   Tipton, 'English Hospitallers', 109–21.

7   Malta, Valletta, National Library, Archives of Malta (AOM) 281, fol. 9r; Charles Tipton, 'The Irish Hospitallers during the Great Schism', *Proceedings of the Royal Irish Academy*, 69 C (1970), 33–43, here 36.

8   *Rotuli litterarum clausarum in Turri Londinensi asservati*, ed. Thomas D. Hardy, 2 vols (London, 1833–44) (*Rot. lit. claus.*), vol. 1 (1204–1224), p. 599; *Patent Rolls, 1216–1225*, pp. 469, 517, 531; *CPR, Henry III, 1225–1232*, pp. 24, 105, 196–7, 368; *Close Rolls, 1227–1231*, pp. 291, 368, 477, 518–19; Geoffrey of Bauzan: *CPR, Henry III, 1232–1247*, p. 161; ibid., *1247–1258*, p. 44.

9   1250: *CPR, Henry III, 1247–1258*, p. 68; 1265: *Close Rolls, 1264–1268*, p. 31; 1267: *CPR, Henry III, 1266–1272*, pp. 76, 78; 1270: ibid., p. 438; 1348: *CCR, Edward III, 1346–1349*, pp. 554, 558; 1358: AOM 316, fols 201v–202r (now 200v–201r), 202v (now 201v); *CPR, Edward III, 1358–1361*, p. 187.

[10] 1332: AOM 280, fol. 29v (three brothers from the English tongue 'retained' for the grand master's service); 1335: AOM 280, fol. 33r (Brother John Pavely, *turcopolier*, present); 1337: AOM 280, fols 39r, 42r–v (Brother John Pavely, *turcopolier*, present and eight brothers from the English tongue retained); 1340: AOM 280, fols 45v, 46r (Brother John Pavely, *turcopolier*, present, and two brothers from the English tongue retained); 1344: AOM 280, fols 50v, 51v (three brothers from the English priory retained *citramare*, on this side of the sea, i.e. on Rhodes; and seven *ultramare*, as well as one brother from Ireland).

[11] References given in Helen Nicholson, 'The Hospitallers of England, the kings of England, and relations with Rhodes in the fourteenth century', *Sacra Militia*, 2 (2001), 25–45, here 27 note 7.

[12] Letter to Nicholas of Hales and John de Eyton, AOM 316, fol. 199v (now 198v).

[13] AOM 319, fol. 173r (now 179r).

[14] AOM 48, fol. 59r.

[15] Tipton, 'English Hospitallers', 107–8 and note 71: 'receu a londre', quoting AOM 48, fol. 88v.

[16] AOM 48, fol. 146r.

[17] Ibid., fol. 146v.

[18] Alain Demurger, *Jacques de Molay: le crépuscule des templiers* (Paris, 2002), p. 381; MS Bod. 454, fol. 157r; Wilkins, *Concilia*, p. 381.

[19] *CPR, Henry III, 1232–1244*, p. 100.

[20] Leonard de Tibertis (1327): *Calendar of Entries in the Papal Registers Relating to Great Britain and Ireland (CEPR): Papal Letters*, ed. William H. Bliss et al., 14 vols (London, 1893–1960), vol. 2, p. 484; *CPR, Edward III, 1327–1330*, p. 138; *CCR, Edward III, 1327–1330*, pp. 220–1. Richard of Overton (1371): *CPR, Edward III, 1370–1374*, p. 92.

[21] AOM 321, fol. 137r (now 146r).

[22] AOM 317, fol. 130 (now 142r).

[23] On 30 October 1351, Brother Richard de Den of Ireland was given permission by the grand master, Déodat de Gozon, to return to Ireland: AOM 318, fol. 133v (now 141v). On 15 March 1352, Brother William of Middleton, commander of Ribston, was given permission by the grand master to go overseas (i.e. from Rhodes) and return to Rhodes within two years: AOM 318, fol. 123v (131v).

[24] On this see Tipton, 'English Hospitallers', *passim*.

[25] *CEPR: Petitions to the Pope, A.D. 1342–1419*, ed. William H. Bliss (London, 1896), p. 347. For the date of the general chapter see Joseph Delaville le Roulx, *Les Hospitaliers à Rhodes, 1310–1421* (Paris, 1913; reprinted London, 1974), p. 136.

[26] *CPR, Edward III, AD 1361–1364*, p. 233.

[27] Anthony Luttrell, 'English contributions to the Hospitaller tower at Bodrum in Turkey, 1407–1437', in Helen Nicholson (ed.), *The Military Orders*, vol. 2, *Welfare and Warfare* (Aldershot, 1998), pp. 163–72, here p. 164; AOM 319, fol. 171r (now 177r).

[28] Tipton, 'English Hospitallers', 96, 99–100; *CPR, Edward III, 1370–1374*, pp. 4, 8 (acting as attorney for Prior John Pavely, November 1370), p. 188 (as prior, July 1372).

[29] Michael Gervers (ed.), *The Cartulary of the Knights of St. John of Jerusalem in England: Secunda camera, Essex* (Oxford, 1982), pp. lx–lxiii; Michael Gervers (ed.), *The Cartulary of the Knights of St. John of Jerusalem in England, Part 2: Prima camera, Essex* (Oxford, 1996), pp. lxxxi–lxxxii; Gregory O'Malley, 'The English Knights Hospitaller, c.1468–1540' (unpublished Ph.D. thesis, University of Cambridge, 1999), pp. 63, 71, 261. I am grateful to Dr O'Malley for permission to cite his thesis.

[30] AOM 318, fol. 123v (now 131v): Grand Master Déodat de Gozon to Philip de Thame. In 1338 there had been four brothers resident at these commanderies: *The Knights Hospitallers in England, Being the Report of Prior Philip de Thame to the Grand Master Elyan de Villanova for A.D. 1338*, ed. Lambert B. Larking, introduction by John Mitchell Kemble, Camden Society, First Series 65 (1855), pp. 47–8, 135–8.

[31] See, for example, Helen Nicholson, 'Serving king and crusade: the military orders in royal service in Ireland, 1220–1400', in Norman Housley, Marcus Bull, Peter Edbury and Jonathan Phillips (eds), *The Experience of Crusading* (Cambridge, 2003), pp. 233–52, here pp. 249–51.

[32] *Rot. lit. pat.*, p. 155 (1215); *Rot. lit. claus.*, vol. 2 (1224–1227), pp. 4, 11, 71, 197; *Calendar of the Liberate Rolls Preserved in the Public Record Office, Prepared under the Superintendence of the Deputy Keeper of the Records: Henry III* (London, 1914–64) (*CLR*), *1226–1240*, pp. 47, 160, 334; ibid., *1240–1245*, p. 94; ibid., *1251–1260*, pp. 15, 133; *Patent Rolls, 1216–1225*, p. 558; *CPR, Henry III, 1232–1247*, p. 120; ibid., *1247–1258*, pp. 68, 118; *Close Rolls, 1251–1253*, pp. 108, 186–7, 191–2, 208, 225, 241–2.

[33] *CPR, Henry III, 1258–1266*, pp. 189, 275, 366, 476–7; John R. Maddicott, *Simon de Montfort* (Cambridge, 1994), p. 242; see ibid., pp. 272–306 on Montfort and his supporters.

[34] For example, *CPR, Edward I, 1281–1292*, pp. 245, 279, 367. See also Simon D. Phillips, 'The Role of the Prior of St John in Late Medieval England, c.1300–1540' (unpublished Ph.D. thesis, University College Winchester, 2005), pp. 86–93.

[35] *CPR, Henry III, 1247–1258*, p. 326; *Close Rolls, 1253–1254*, p. 320.

[36] *CPR, Henry III, 1232–1247*, p. 75; ibid., *1247–1258*, pp. 364, 367, 386, 405, 412; *CLR, 1251–1260*, pp. 159, 168, 177, 180.

[37] *CPR, Henry III, 1232–1247*, p. 250.

[38] *Close Rolls, 1242–1247*, pp. 73, 283; ibid., *1247–1251*, p. 263.

[39] *Close Rolls, 1242–1247*, p. 19. The Cinque Ports (or 'five ports') are the ancient port towns on the south coast of England which in the Middle Ages were given special rights in exchange for providing ships in times of war. The original five were Hastings, Sandwich, Dover, Romney and Hythe, but Rye and Winchelsea were soon added, while other smaller towns such as Folkestone and Margate were included as dependants of the larger ports.

40 *CCR, Edward III, 1341–1343*, pp. 474, 668, 670; *CPR, Edward III, 1340–1343*, p. 560.

41 *CCR, Edward III, 1343–1346*, p. 555. See also ibid., *1360–1364*, p. 99; ibid., *1369–1374*, p. 568.

42 *CPR, Edward III, 1345–1348*, p. 50.

43 *Close Rolls, 1247–1251*, p. 251; *Foedera, conventiones, litteræ, et cujuscunque generis acta publica*, ed. Thomas Rymer et al., revised by Adam Clark et al., 4 vols in 7 (London, 1816–69), vol. 2, pp. 618–19; *CCR, Edward II, 1323–1327*, pp. 544–5; ibid., *1337–1339*, pp. 140, 290; ibid., *1346–1349*, pp. 45–6, 554; ibid., *1349–1354*, p. 379.

44 *CCR, Edward III, 1333–1337*, p. 643. On this see also Nicholson, 'Hospitallers of England', 35–6.

45 *CCR, Edward III, 1339–1341*, pp. 256–7; ibid., *1341–1343*, pp. 137–8.

46 *CPR, Edward III, 1340–1343*, p. 203.

47 *Rotuli Parliamentorum ut et petitiones, et placita in Parliamento*, ed. R. Blyke et al., 6 vols (London 1767–77), vol. 3, pp. 179 (1383), 213 (1385); *CPR, Richard II, 1385–1389*, p. 95.

48 See, for example, AOM 48, fol. 39v; see also *CCR, Edward I, 1288–1296*, p. 511 and *CCR, Henry IV, 1399–1402*, p. 374. For the fifteenth and early sixteenth century see Jürgen Sarnowsky, *Macht und Herrschaft im Johanniterorden des 15. Jahrhunderts: Verfassung und Verwaltung der Johanniter auf Rhodos (1421–1522)* (Münster, 2001), pp. 483, 507, 540, 545.

49 *Knights Hospitallers in England*, ed. Larking and Kemble, pp. lxi–lxiii.

50 William de Scotho: MS Bod. 454, fol. 18r; Wilkins, *Concilia*, p. 339. Robert the Scot: MS Bod. 454, fol. 46v; Wilkins, *Concilia*, p. 345.

51 MS Bod. 454, fols 134–149r; Wilkins, *Concilia*, pp. 373–7.

52 *Calendar of Documents Relating to Ireland, Preserved in Her Majesty's Public Record Office, London*, ed. H. S. Sweetman et al., 5 vols (London, 1875–86), vol. 3, p. 30 no. 57; MS Bod. 454, fols 24r, 29v, 58v, 148v, 149r; Wilkins, *Concilia*, pp. 340, 341, 347 (other references omitted in Wilkins, *Concilia*). Receptions in England and Ireland were normally carried out by the provincial commander. As Brother Thomas of Toulouse was receiving brothers in Ireland in the early 1290s he was probably commander of Ireland at that time.

53 Brother Geoffrey de Gonneville, commander of Aquitaine, received at London, referred to the many commanders and others who had helped to pay his *passagium*: MS Bod. 454, fol. 93v 'plures preceptores + alij de ordi[n]e multa dederant sibi pro passagio suo'; exactly the same words appear in Jules Michelet (ed.), *Le procès des Templiers* (Paris, 1841–51; reprinted Paris, 1987), vol. 2, p. 400. Wilkins, *Concilia*, p. 361, has amended to 'pro itinere suo', a translation rather than a transcription. Brother Roger of Dalton had paid sixty marks but seen nothing for it: 'dicit t[ame]n q[uo]d receptio sua costitit sibi sexaginta marcas et nu[n]q[uam] aliquid recepit a domo Templi': MS Bod. 454, fol. 77v (omitted in Wilkins, *Concilia*). While he does not call this a *passagium*, given that it is a round-figure sum that he had paid when

100   HELEN NICHOLSON

he was admitted, he expected some return for it that he had not received,
and since he had not been sent overseas, it seems reasonable to assume that
it was a *passagium*. If it were simply a simoniacal admission payment, he
had already received his return for it when he was admitted.

54   MS Bod. 454, fol. 26r. For the receptions at which he was present, see fols
     26r, 28v, 30v, 34v, 37r, 38v, 40r, 45v, 49v, 104v, 105r, 106v, 110r, 128r, 130v,
     131v. See also fol. 53v; Wilkins, *Concilia*, pp. 341–5, 365–6, 372, 373.

55   MS Bod. 454, fols 156r–157r; Wilkins, *Concilia*, pp. 380–1.

56   MS Bod. 454, fol. 46r: 'Respondit q[uo]d nescit quid confessi sunt vel
     fecerunt extra Angliam sed deus est contentus de hiis que fiunt in ordine
     predicto in Anglia.' See also ibid., 34r: 'contenta in dictis articulis negavit et
     maxime in Anglia.' These passages were omitted in Wilkins, *Concilia*.

57   For example, MS Bod. 454, fols 24r, 25r, 26r, 27r, 28r, 28v, 30v, 31v, 32v,
     36r–v, 37v, 38v, 39v, 40v, 41r, 42r, 43v, 44v–45r, 46v, 47v, 48r, 49r, 49v, 50v,
     51v, 52r, 53v, 54r, 55v, 56r, 57r; see Wilkins, *Concilia*, pp. 340–2, 344, 346.

58   MS Bod. 454, fol. 74v: 'ip[s]e dicit q[uo]d f[rat]rib[u]s transfretantib[u]s ult[ra]
     mare Grecie suspend[u]nt[ur] p[er] f[rat]rem confessore[m] cap[e]ll[anu]m
     donec venirent ad quiete[m]'; omitted in Wilkins, *Concilia*.

59   Roger de la More 'the Englishman': MS Bod. 454, fols 31v, 55r; Wilkins,
     Concilia, pp. 342, 346; *The Trial of the Templars in Cyprus: A Complete
     English Edition*, trans. Anne Gilmour-Bryson (Leiden, 1998), p. 99. Richard
     of Grafton, priest-brother: MS Bod. 454, fols 39v, 55r; Wilkins, *Concilia*,
     pp. 343, 346. Richard 'the Englishman' (the same?): *Trial in Cyprus*, trans.
     Gilmour-Bryson, pp. 81–2 and note 34, p. 87 note 69, p. 99 note 140, p. 175.
     John *Anglicus*: *Trial in Cyprus*, trans. Gilmour-Bryson, p. 107 and MS Bod.
     454, fol. 56r; Wilkins, *Concilia*, p. 346. Brother Nicholas *Peccia* or de Peche:
     Trial in Cyprus, trans. Gilmour-Bryson, pp. 80–1 and MS Bod. 454, fol. 42r;
     Wilkins, *Concilia*, p. 344. Alan Forey notes that Richard of Grafton was
     receiving a pension from an English diocese in 1313. It is possible that the
     brothers in Cyprus were sent back to England after the dissolution of the
     order to perform their penance: Alan Forey, 'Ex-Templars in England',
     Journal of Ecclesiastical History, 53 (2002), 18–37, here 36 note 101.

60   Hugh and Stephen de Mally: *Trial in Cyprus*, trans. Gilmour-Bryson, pp. 87,
     96.

61   Brothers John of Stoke, called 'of Sutton', Robert the Scot, William of
     Winchester, Thomas of Staunford, Ralph of Ruston, Richard of Burthesham
     (or Bustleham or Bristelesham?): MS Bod. 454, fols 42v–43r and 79r, 46v
     and 70v, 110v (and see 122v), 126r, 126v, 134r; Wilkins, *Concilia*, pp. 344,
     345, 366, 372, 373. See also *Trial in Cyprus*, trans. Gilmour-Bryson, p. 137
     and note 333.

62   MS Bod. 454, fol. 79r (omitted in Wilkins, *Concilia*). See also Brother
     Robert of Arnoldon or Hameldon, who had seen receptions outside England:
     MS Bod. 454, fol. 121r (omitted in Wilkins, *Concilia*).

63   MS Bod. 454, fols 139v, 151v: 'fuit socius collat[er]al[is] + concubilaris
     magni mag[ist]ri ord[in]is in p[ar]tib[us] t[r]ansmarinis a quo magnu[m]

honore[m] equitata vestib[us] + in alio app[ar]atu necno[n] + tocius ord[in]is in Hib[er]n[ia] ad vita[m] suam s[i] placu[er]it recepit et optinuit', and fol. 153v: 'maxi[m]e de fr[atr]e Henr[ico] Danet q[uod] cons[er]vabat[ur] cu[m] magno mag[ist]ro p[er] annu[m] + ampli[us] valde sp[eci]ali[ter] + familiarit[er] q[uod] recognov[i]ᵗ p[ro]ut bulla testat[ur] se co[n]misisse illa nephanda c[ri]mina in bulla contenta + id[e]m fr[ater] Henr[icus] creat[us] fuit p[er] d[ic]t[u]m magnu[m] mag[ist]r[u]m + magnu[m] p[re]ceptore[m] in Hib[er]n[ia]'; Wilkins, *Concilia*, pp. 376, 378 (abridged; the final witness is omitted in Wilkins, *Concilia*).

64 *CCR, Edward III, 1360–1364*, pp. 39–40; Tipton, 'Irish Hospitallers', 38–9; AOM 321, fol. 138r–v (now 147r–v).

65 John Pavely, Robert Hales, John Radington and Walter Grendon.

66 Richard White, Robert White, Thomas Butler: see Tipton, 'Irish Hospitallers', 38–42.

10

Mobility of Templar Brothers and Dignitaries: The Case of North-Western Italy

ELENA BELLOMO

D ue to the lack of detailed study on the presence of the Order of the Temple in Italy, the mobility of Templar brothers and dignitaries within the peninsula is difficult to assess. However, research into the Templar settlements of north-western Italy (in an area covering the modern Valle d'Aosta, Piedmont, Liguria and Lombardy) is particularly rewarding. The many published and unpublished sources dealing with the military orders in this region have been examined in recent studies. These studies have not only revealed the existence of a flourishing network of (around fifty) Templar houses; they have also highlighted that the local nobility responded to the Templars' recruitment efforts in a positive way and that there were many complex relationships between the Templars and other local lay and ecclesiastical institutions.[1]

Considering the Templars' positive involvement with local society, it is interesting to investigate the mobility of the brothers and officials of the order in north-western Italy. An initial census of the brothers of the Temple from this area, based exclusively on local documents, shows that the knights and sergeants of the order rarely moved away from the region. The movements that are visible from local documents show mobility on a very limited scale, namely transferrals within the confines of medieval Lombardy. One of the few exceptions was John of Milan, who, in 1196, found himself in Barletta (Apulia).[2]

This is the extent of the limited information contained in local archives. More important sources for the study of the movements of Lombard Templars are the records of the trial of the order. The fragmentary documentation from the inquiry that took place in north-western Italy does not contain any mention of Templar brothers from distant parts of Italy or other European countries.[3]

An examination of the trial records from other countries is more revealing. For example, several Lombard Templars were arrested and prosecuted in Cyprus. The mere presence of these brothers in Cyprus is a significant detail. Their testimonies are important for a study of the Templars' mobility because they not only record the provenance of the brother in question, but also the place where he was admitted into the order and the names and origins of the brothers who attended the reception ceremony. Thus the records allow us to ascertain some of the movements of the interrogated brothers and to pinpoint particular regions where Templars from north-western Italy can be located. Francis of Genoa,[4] for example, was received in Dalmatia, and one of those present at this ceremony was Francis *de Valegi*, who may have originated from the diocese of Troyes, but could also have been from Valeggio sul Mincio.[5] Nicholas of Montecucco,[6] the natural brother of James of Montecucco, the Templar master of Lombardy, was admitted in Asti in the presence of this same James and in the presence of Otto of St George, who was probably a member of an important noble family from north-western Italy, namely the counts of Biandrate.[7] Peter *Cadelli* of *Castro Gyra* (Provence) may have come from Monferrat and was admitted into the order by William *de Noves*, Templar master of Lombardy. His reception took place in Venice in the presence of Templars from Piedmont and Emilia.[8] John *Panis* of Vienne confirmed that Bartholomew of Cremona and *Genisus* of *Cremena* (a possible corruption of Cremona) were both present at his reception in France.[9] Finally, the reception of William *de Garent* took place in Piedmont before William of Canelli, master of Lombardy, and other Templars from Monferrat and Emilia.[10]

The records of the trial in France contain hardly any references to Templar brothers from north-western Italy.[11] The only case of interest is that of Anthony, nephew of *Ugucciono* of Vercelli, master of Lombardy, who, according to one deposition, was admitted into the order in the east.[12] The presence in 'outremer' of two close relatives of provincial masters, Anthony and the aforementioned Nicholas of Montecucco, is fairly important, since a personal acquaintance between a candidate and members of the order's leadership could have been a crucial factor in later nominations for the position of provincial master.[13]

It is apparent that, in contrast to the local documentation, there is a lot more information to be gained from the trial records. They show, for brothers of north-western Italian origin, a certain level of mobility: some of them obviously did leave the confines of medieval Lombardy and created communication links between this region and the east and, also, with territories across the Alps.

With regard to the mobility of Templar dignitaries from north-western Italy, there is relatively little information available. It is not even possible to make any general assumptions about the movements of these dignitaries. However, a study of the limited amount of sources does reveal some uniquely 'Italian' factors – logistic, diplomatic and political – that probably influenced the mobility of these Templar officials. First of all, it must be noted that the Templar masters of Lombardy mentioned in the sources are all Italians and mainly Lombards – William *de Noves*, also referred to as William *Provincialis* (a *Lombardie preceptor* in 1285–6), being the only exception.[14] The leadership of the Templar province of Lombardy was, more or less, entirely monopolized by the nobility from Monferrat and from Emilia.[15]

There is only one instance that shows one of these masters in the Latin east. In 1167, Boniface, the first master of Lombardy to be found in the documents, was in Jerusalem. In the spring of that year, according to the wishes of the order's master, Boniface had carried out the sale of some Templar properties in Bavaria to Otto of Wittelsbach. The document confirming the sale was then signed by some forty German nobles, who had travelled to the Holy Land on an Easter pilgrimage. Among these pilgrims were Welf VI of Bavaria and Frederick of Wittelsbach, Otto's brother.[16] It is conceivable that Boniface had journeyed to the east in the company of these important members of the imperial faction.[17] Actually, in the fifties and sixties of the twelfth century, Lombard Templars had important and positive links with the imperial party and Frederick I Barbarossa. In 1158, the emperor, while laying siege to Milan, stayed in the local Templar house.[18] Some scholars have speculated that Boniface, the master of Lombardy in 1167, may have been identical with a certain Boniface who was master of the Templar house of Milan in 1149.[19] Unfortunately, there is no evidence to back up such a claim. There is, however, the possibility that Boniface may have come into contact with the imperial court sometime before his voyage to Jerusalem. In 1160, the master of the Templar house of Rome was present at the council of Pavia which approved the election of the antipope, Victor IV.[20] Four years later, the counts of Biandrate, supporters of the emperor, made a large donation to the Temple.[21] In 1167, after he had returned from the Holy Land, Boniface is referred to as *de rebus Templi in Italia magister et procurator*.[22] It is therefore possible to speculate that his official powers had been increased during his stay in Jerusalem. Boniface's voyage to 'outremer' is clearly of great significance, not just for its potential political implications but also for the institutional development of the Order of the Temple in Italy.

A second important example of mobility is that of *Barotius magister Lombardie*, probably from 1200. He participated in the Fourth Crusade, and on this occasion he played an important role with regard to the relationship between the new Latin Emperor Baldwin of Flanders and Pope Innocent III. An early letter from Innocent, written in October 1204, recounts how, after the conquest of Constantinople, *Barotius*, on behalf of Emperor Baldwin, was carrying some precious gifts intended for the pope when his ship was attacked by Genoese pirates. A second letter, also written in 1204 by Pope Innocent, clarifies what exactly *Barotius*'s mission had been on this occasion: *Barotius* had carried a letter from Emperor Baldwin to the pope; in this letter Baldwin had reported the conquest of Constantinople and justified the founding of the new empire.[23] Hence, the delicate task of informing the pope about the definitive conquest of Constantinople had fallen to the Templar *Barotius*. *Barotius* was certainly a person who was well received by the papal court. In 1204, Innocent III referred to him as *dilectus filius*; four years earlier, in 1200, the pope had dealt with a difficult conflict between this Templar master of Lombardy and the bishop of Tortona, and the Templars had emerged victorious.[24]

The good relations between the papacy and the Lombard Templars that can be inferred from the incident involving *Barotius*, intensified in the course of the thirteenth century when several Templar officials were promoted to papal *cubicularii, hostiarii* and *marescalci*. The first master of Lombardy to become papal chamberlain was *Ugucciono* of Vercelli. Both Martin IV and Nicholas IV assigned him important tasks, and he seems to have held the title of *cubicularius* as early as 1278.[25] In 1283, *Ugucciono* became castellan of the fortress of Ponte della Badia near Tuscania.[26] He was also sent to Sicily. Nicholas IV entrusted to him the delivery of letters concerning the controversial possession of a castle in Abruzzo[27] and, in 1290, rewarded him for his dedication by giving him the fief of Miranda, near Narni.[28] Between 1296 and 1302, *Ugucciono* was in the service of Boniface VIII.[29]

The case of *Ugucciono* of Vercelli shows, for the first time, how the responsibility for the Templar houses of northern and central Italy was combined with various tasks on behalf of the Holy See (above all inside the papal state), and that a single master oversaw the province of Lombardy and that of Tuscany, the march of Ancona, Rome, the duchy of Spoleto, Campania, Marittima and Sardinia. The geographic expanse of this area would have compelled *Uguccione* to travel a great deal. However, most of his mobility had to do with following the pope or carrying out papal assignments. The documentation shows that *Uguccione* was usually far away from Lombardy. From 1299 on, James of Montecucco seems to have been active in Lombardy as his lieutenant.[30] By 1304, James was the new master of Lombardy, and in the same year he became *cubicularius* to the papal court in Perugia.[31]

The relocation of the Holy See to the other side of the Alps made the mobility of some Italian dignitaries of the Temple even more pronounced. In 1307, James of Montecucco was in Poitiers in his capacity as *cubicularius* to the new pope, Clement V.[32] It was in France that James was arrested: a *comanador de Lombardia* is mentioned in the sources reporting the early stages of the proceedings against the Templars.[33] However, James managed to escape in February 1309, thus provoking the anger of the pope, who dubbed him *falsus religiosus vir* and put a price on his head. In the same year, James probably returned to Lombardy, where he waited for the trial to come to an end.[34]

Finally, a very particular reason for mobility has to be considered, namely political upheavals. A well-documented case is that of the Canelli family, relatives of Bianca Lancia d'Agliano who was the wife of Frederick II and the mother of their son Manfred.[35] A letter of recommendation written by Manfred in 1262 is the first reference to Albert of Canelli, Templar master of Sicily.[36] After Manfred's death, Albert had to leave southern Italy. He was forced to begin his career anew in his homeland. In 1268, he was responsible for several Templar houses in Piedmont, and three years later he served as commander of Asti.[37] Later on, the court of Aragon, ruled by Constance, daughter of Manfred and wife of Peter III, required his services.[38]

A second member of the Canelli family, William, was master in Sicily in 1287.[39] When he was removed from this office, Queen Constance asked William of Beaujeu, the master of the Temple, to reinstate him, but to no avail.[40] Only after William of Beaujeu's death did William of Canelli succeed in becoming master of Lombardy, an office that he held at least until 1296.[41] Meanwhile, the kings of Aragon continued to promote his career and wrote him a letter of recommendation in 1294.[42] Eventually, William was sent to Hungary,[43] and he died soon after his return to Italy.[44]

The developments in the Italian imperial faction had a strong influence on the Canellis' careers in the Order of the Temple.[45] The interests of rulers such as Manfred, Constance and Peter III were often decisive in granting them promotions or in causing their removal from offices that were then assigned to other dignitaries supporting the Angevin faction.[46] This did not change until the political conditions in southern Italy had become more stable, as the career of *Albertinus* of Canelli reveals. *Albertinus* was received into the Temple in Asti by his relative William.[47] In 1305, he served as *hostarius pontificius* at the court of Pope Benedict XI,[48] and he then became the lieutenant of the Templar commander of Lombardy.[49] The administration of the Templar province of Sicily was also entrusted to *Albertinus*.[50] Unlike other members of the Canelli family, *Albertinus*'s career does not appear to have been influenced by political developments. It is exemplary of the Canellis' ability to build new connections with the papacy. *Albertinus*'s mobility was a result of the administrative needs of the order: he had to 'take the place' of the Lombard regional master whenever that official was absent, and he had to oversee the Templar province of Sicily. He also had to accompany Benedict XI and Clement V to France, where he, too, was arrested and put on trial, along with the other Templars.[51]

A short study of the function of the Templar bases in north-western Italy with regard to the movements of the brothers and dignitaries of the order will conclude this regional study. One would expect that the ports on the Ligurian coast played an important role for these movements, but in reality, there are very few references to Templars in this region. Only four Templar houses can be confirmed with certainty: Albenga, Genoa, Osiglia and Ventimiglia.[52] The activities of the Order of the Temple in 'outremer', particularly the order's links with Venice during the war of St Sabas, probably hindered the development of the Templars' Ligurian houses.[53] It is significant that the Italian documentation does not mention any Ligurian Templars in connection with the crusade ventures in which Genoa took part. The Ligurian documents do not contain any evidence to suggest that the local Templars used the Genoese docks.[54] However, the *Falcon*, the ship commanded by Brother Roger de Flor, was a Genoese vessel.[55]

It was not until the end of the thirteenth and the beginning of the fourteenth century that the links between Genoa and the Templars improved. The cartulary of a Ligurian notary named Lamberto di Sambuceto, who was active in Cyprus at this time, contains several documents that testify to both the development of good relations between the Genoese and the Templars, and the chartering of Ligurian vessels by members of the order.[56] One such document, dating back to 1301, actually contains the only record of a Templar ship bound for Genoa: the *St Anna*, captained by the Templar commander Peter *Visianus*.[57]

To sum up: the lack of information in the local archives makes a precise description of the movements of those Templars who originated in north-western Italy or who were active in this area impossible.[58] Nevertheless, other sources show that certain degrees of mobility were undoubtedly a part of the lives of Templars of all ranks. With regard to the higher-ranking officials of the order, this analysis has shown that mobility within Italy had its unique characteristics – partly because of the role that the Italian port cities played in the crusades and in the Latin east, but mostly because of the links that connected the Italian Templars with the two great medieval powers, namely the papacy and the Holy Roman Empire. It was to be in Italy that these two giants would clash, forcing the military orders to take a clear stance as well.

Notes

[1] For the Templars in this area see Luigi Avonto, *I Templari in Piemonte* (Vercelli, 1982); Giampietro Casiraghi, 'Fondazioni templari lungo la via Francigena: Da Torino a Chieri e da Testona-Moncalieri a S. Martino di Gorra', in Giuseppe Sergi (ed.), *Luoghi di strada nel Medioevo: Fra il Po, il mare e le Alpi occidentali* (Turin, 1996), pp. 125–45; Elena Bellomo, 'La milizia del Tempio in Italia nord-occidentale (XII–metà XIV secolo)' (unpublished Ph.D. thesis, Università Cattolica del Sacro Cuore, Milan, 2000). For the Hospitallers see Josepha Costa Restagno (ed.), *Cavalieri di San Giovanni e territorio: La Liguria tra Provenza e Lombardia nei secoli XIII–XVII* (Genoa, 1999); Tomaso Ricardi di Netro and Luisa Clotilde Gentile (eds), '*Gentilhuomini Christiani e Religiosi Cavalieri': Nove secoli dell'ordine di Malta in Piemonte* (Milan, 2000); Renato Bordone, Alberto Crosetto and Carlo Tosco (eds), *L'antico S. Pietro in Asti: Storia, architettura, archeologia* (Turin, 2000); Josepha Costa Restagno (ed.), *Riviera di Levante tra Emilia e Toscana: Un crocevia per l'ordine di San Giovanni* (Genoa, 2001).

[2] Giovanni Guerrieri, *I cavalieri templari nel Regno di Sicilia* (Trani, 1909), p. 89–91. Professor Hubert Houben has drawn my attention to this Lombard Templar.

[3] For the trial in this region see Renzo Caravita, *Rinaldo da Concorezzo, arcivescovo di Ravenna (1303–1321) al tempo di Dante* (Firenze, 1964), pp. 97–160.

[4] Konrad Schottmüller (ed.), *Der Untergang des Templer-Ordens* (Berlin, 1887), vol. 2, pp. 191, 320–23; *The Trial of the Templars in Cyprus: A Complete English Edition*, trans. Anne Gilmour-Bryson (Leiden, 1998), pp. 115–16, 286–8.

[5] Schottmüller, *Untergang des Templer-Ordens*, vol. 2, p. 191 note 3; Jules Michelet (ed.), *Le procès des Templiers* (Paris, 1841–51), vol. 2, pp. 411, 417; Lorenzo Tacchella, *Gli insediamenti dei Templari a Nice e Grasse, in Lombardia e Veneto* (Milan, 1999), p. 148.

[6] Schottmüller, *Untergang des Templer-Ordens*, vol. 2, pp. 198–9, 341–3; Gilmour-Bryson, *Trial of the Templars in Cyprus*, pp. 125–7, 321–7. Nicholas of Montecucco can be identified with the *Nicola Lombardus* quoted in Schottmüller, *Untergang des Templer-Ordens*, vol. 2, p. 131; Gilmour-Bryson, *Trial of the Templars in Cyprus*, pp. 60–1 note 107.

[7] A Templar who attended this reception, Raymond *de Canetis*, may have been Spanish, but he can also be identified with a member of the Canelli family: Gilmour-Bryson, *Trial of the Templars in Cyprus*, p. 126 note 283. For these families see Antonio Raggi, *I conti di Biandrate* (Novara, 1933); Giancarlo Andenna, 'I conti di Biandrate e le città della Lombardia occidentale (secoli XI e XII)', in *Formazione e strutture dei ceti dominanti nel Medioevo: Marchesi, conti e visconti nel regno italico (secc. IX–XII)* (Rome, 1996), pp. 57–84; Alessandro Barbero, 'I signori di Canelli fra la corte di re Manfredi e gli ordini monastico-cavallereschi', in Renato Bordone (ed.), *Bianca Lancia d'Agliano: Fra il Piemonte e il regno di Sicilia* (Alessandria, 1992), pp. 219–33.

[8] Schottmüller, *Untergang des Templer-Ordens*, vol. 2, pp. 209–10; Gilmour-Bryson, *Trial of the Templars in Cyprus*, pp. 140–1, 367–70.

[9] Schottmüller, *Untergang des Templer-Ordens*, vol. 2, pp. 186, 304–8; Gilmour-Bryson, *Trial of the Templars in Cyprus*, p. 109. In the records of the trial in Cyprus we find an *Ymberta de Cremena*. This person has been identified with the Templar Humbert of Cremona, *Cremi* or *Crimen*, mentioned during the trial in France, or with a *soror* of the order: Gilmour-Bryson, *Trial of the Templars in Cyprus*, p. 110, note 203; Michelet, *Procès*, vol. 2, pp. 352, 366; Heinrich Finke, *Papsttum und Untergang des Templer-ordens* (Münster, 1907), vol. 2, pp. 359–60; Francesco Tommasi, 'Uomini e donne negli ordini militari di Terrasanta: Per il problema delle case doppie e miste negli ordini giovannita, templare e teutonico (secc. XII–XIV)', in Kaspar Elm and Michel Parisse (eds), *Doppelklöster und andere Formen der Symbiose männlicher und weiblicher Religiosen in Mittelalter* (Berlin, 1992), pp. 177–202, here p. 196 note 79.

[10] Schottmüller, *Untergang des Templer-Ordens*, vol. 2, pp. 74–5, 256–60; Gilmour-Bryson, *Trial of the Templars in Cyprus*, pp. 90–1, 203–8.

[11] According to the testimony of the Lombard master *Albertinus* of Canelli, arrested in France, a *Garinus, miles Provincialis*, was present at his reception in Asti: Michelet, *Procès*, vol. 1, pp. 425–6.

[12] Ibid., p. 562.

[13] See Alan Forey, *The Templars in the Corona de Aragón* (London, 1973), pp. 309–10.

[14] He may have been the member of a family from Avignon with connections to the Templars: Léon-Honoré Labande, *Avignon au XIIIe siècle: L'évêque Zoen Tencarari et les Avignonnais* (Paris, 1908), pp. 9, 84, 323, 342, 365; Émile-G. Léonard, *Introduction au cartulaire manuscrit du Temple (1150–1317), constitué par le marquis d'Albon et conservé à la Bibliothèque nationale, suivie d'un tableau des maisons françaises du Temple et de leurs précepteurs* (Paris, 1930), p. 53. Damien Carraz kindly provided these references. See henceforth also his Ph.D. thesis, 'Ordres militaires, croisades et sociétés méridionales: L'exemple de l'ordre du Temple dans la basse vallée du Rhône (1124–1314)' which is now in progress at the Université d'Avignon.

[15] Bellomo, 'La milizia del Tempio in Italia nord-occidentale', 139–62.

[16] Hermann Grauert, 'Eine Tempelherrenurkunde von 1167', *Archivalische Zeitschrift*, 3 (1878), 294–309, here 294–5; Otto of Freising and Rahewin, *Gesta Friderici I imperatoris, appendix annorum 1160–1170*, ed. Roger Wilmans, in *Monumenta Germaniae historica, Scriptores*, vol. 20 (Hannover, 1868), p. 492.

[17] Michael Schüpferling, *Der Tempelherren-Orden in Deutschland* (Bamberg, 1915), p. 70.

[18] 'Narratio de Lombardie obpressione et subiectione', ed. Franz Josef Schmale, in Franz Josef Schmale (ed.), *Italische Quellen über die Taten Kaiser Friedrichs I. in Italien und der Brief über den Kreuzzug Kaiser Friedrichs I.* (Darmstadt, 1986), p. 258; Otto Morena and his continuators, 'Libellus de rebus a Frederico imperatore gestis', ed. Franz Josef Schmale, in Schmale (ed.), *Italische Quellen*, p. 84.

[19] See, for instance, Fulvio Bramato, *Storia dell'ordine dei Templari in Italia*, 2 vols (Rome, 1991–4), vol. 1, p. 57 note 109; Alessandro Colombo, 'I Gerosolimitani e i Templari a Milano e la via della Commenda', *Archivio Storico Lombardo*, third series, 53 (1926), 185–240, here 214–15 no. 2.

[20] *Ottonis Epicopi Frisingensis et Rahewini, seu, rectius Cronica*, ed. Franz Josef Schmale (Darmstadt, 1974), p. 674.

[21] Amedeo Ponziglione, 'Saggio storico intorno ai Templari del Piemonte e degli altri Stati del Re', *Ozi Letterari*, 3 (1791), 109–173, here 151 no. 1 (here the date of the document is incorrect; see Bellomo, 'La milizia del Tempio in Italia nord-occidentale', 188).

[22] Paolo Accame, *Notizie e documenti inediti sui Templari e Gerosolimitani in Liguria* (Finalborgo, 1902), p. 46 no. 6.

[23] *Die Register Innocenz' III, 7. Pontifikatsjahr, 1204/1205*, ed. Othmar Hageneder, Andrea Sommerlechner et al. (Vienna, 1997), pp. 235–6 no. 147, pp. 262–3 no. 152.

[24] 'Decretales Gregorii IX', ed. Emil Albert Friedberg and Emil Ludwig Richter, in *Corpus iuris canonici*, vol. 2, second edition (Leipzig, 1879), 1. II, tit. XIII, *c.*12, cols 285–6 (X 2.13.12); Augustin Theiner (ed.), *Vetera*

monumenta Slavorum meridionalium historiam illustrantia, 2 vols (Osnabrück, 1968), vol. 1, p. 61 no. 190.

25 Friedrich Baethgen, 'Quellen und Untersuchungen zur Geschichte der päpstlichen Hof-und Finanzverwaltung unter Bonifaz VIII.', *Quellen und Forschungen aus italienischen Archiven und Bibliotheken*, 20 (1928–9), 114–237, here 196–9, 201, 204.

26 Anthony Luttrell, 'Two Templar-Hospitaller preceptories north of Tuscania', *Papers of the British School at Rome*, 39 (1971), 90–124, here 105.

27 *Les Registres de Nicolas IV*, ed. Ernest Langlois, 3 vols (Paris, 1886–93), vol. 2, pp. 966–7 nos 7144–6, p. 1047 nos 7653–4.

28 Ibid., p. 993 no. 7276, p. 998 no. 7313; Agostino Paravicini Bagliani, *La vita quotidiana alla corte dei papi nel Duecento* (Bari, 1996), p. 62. This work was first published as Agostino Paravicini Bagliani, *La cour des papes au XIIIe siècle* (Paris, 1995).

29 Giulio Silvestrelli, 'Le chiese e i feudi dell'Ordine dei Templari e dell'Ordine di San Giovanni di Gerusalemme nella regione romana', *Rendiconti della Reale Accademia dei Lincei: Classe di scienze morali, storiche e filologiche*, fifth series, 26 (1917), pp. 491–539, here 494 note 1; *Les Registres de Boniface VIII*, ed. Georges Alfred Laurent Digard et al., 4 vols (Paris, 1884–1939), vol. 3, col. 664 no. 5032.

30 Telesforo Bini, 'Dei Tempieri e del loro processo in Toscana', *Atti della Reale Accademia Lucchese di Scienze, Lettere ed Arti*, 15, no. 9 (1845), pp. 465, 478, 479, 486; Francesco Tommasi, 'Interrogatorio dei Templari a Cesena (1310)', in Francesco Tommasi (ed.), *Acri 1291: La fine della presenza degli ordini militari in Terra Santa e i nuovi orientamenti del XIV secolo* (Perugia, 1996), pp. 265–300, here pp. 288, 293.

31 Anne Gilmour-Bryson (ed.), *The Trial of the Templars in the Papal State and the Abruzzi* (Città del Vaticano, 1982), pp. 132, 252; Francesco Tommasi, 'L'ordine dei Templari a Perugia', *Bollettino della Deputazione di Storia Patria per l'Umbria*, 78 (1981), 5–80, here 19 and 60 no. 17; Pietro Maria Campi, *Dell'historia ecclesiastica di Piacenza*, 3 vols (Piacenza, 1651; reprinted 1995), vol. 3, pp. 34–5; Emilio Nasalli Rocca di Corneliano, 'Della introduzione dei Templari a Piacenza', *Bollettino Storico Piacentino*, 36 (1941), 97–102, 37 (1942), 16–20: here 19; Bellomo, 'La milizia del Tempio in Italia nord-occidentale', 159.

32 *Regestum Clementis papae V*, ed. *Monachi ordinis Sancti Benedicti*, 9 vols and appendix (Rome, 1885–92), vol. 7, reg. 513 no. 7138.

33 Finke, *Papsttum und Untergang*, vol. 2, p. 59 no. 39.

34 Archivio di Stato di Milano, Fondo Religione, Miscellanea Materiale Restaurato, cart. 5 (6 April 1308); Colombo, 'I Gerosolimitani e i Templari a Milano', 220 no. 8. A Brother James of Moncucco was in Ivrea in 1314 and 1316. Archivio Storico della Diocesi di Ivrea, XII.5.AM.313/317/1, fol. 31r–v, VIII.3.310/320/1, fol. 23v.

35 Barbero, 'I signori di Canelli', pp. 228–33.

36 Marie Luise Bulst-Thiele, *Sacrae domus militiae Templi Hierosolymitani*

magistri: Untersuchungen zur Geschichte des Templerordens 1118/19–1314 (Göttingen, 1974), p. 246.

[37] Ezio Trota, 'L'ordine dei cavalieri templari a Modena e l'ospitale del ponte di S. Ambrogio', *Atti e Memorie della Deputazione di Storia Patria per le Province Modenesi*, 16 (1984), 29–56, here 48, 52.

[38] According to Bulst-Thiele, he finished his career in Spain. Bulst-Thiele, *Magistri*, p. 278.

[39] David Wilkins, *Concilia magnae Britanniae et Hiberniae*, vol. 2 (London, 1737), p. 372; Bulst-Thiele, *Magistri*, pp. 279–80.

[40] Heinrich Finke, *Acta Aragonensia: Quellen zur deutschen, italienischen, französischen, spanischen, zur Kirchen- und Kulturgeschichte, aus der diplomatischen Korrespondenz Jaymes II. (1291–1327)*, 3 vols (Berlin, 1908–22) (AA), vol. 3, p. 10 no. 5.

[41] Schottmüller, *Untergang des Templer-Ordens*, vol. 2, pp. 174–5; Gilmour-Bryson, *Trial of the Templars in Cyprus*, p. 90; Bini, 'Dei Tempieri e del loro processo in Toscana', pp. 465, 474; Gilmour-Bryson, *Trial of the Templars in the Papal State*, pp. 189, 201.

[42] Finke, AA, vol. 3, p. 36 no. 18; Barbero, 'I signori di Canelli', pp. 230–1.

[43] At the end of the thirteenth century, other dignitaries were sent from Lombardy to Hungary. In 1290, James *de Monte Regali* (Mondovi?) and, in 1292, William *de Noves* served as Templar masters of the Hungarian province. Zsolt Hunyadi kindly provided this information.

[44] Gilmour-Bryson, *Trial of the Templars in the Papal State*, pp. 189, 201.

[45] The same is valid for Boniface of Calamandrana, Hospitaller dignitary, a relative of the Canelli family: Barbero, 'I signori di Canelli', pp. 232–3.

[46] Bulst-Thiele, *Magistri*, pp. 246–8, 278–9.

[47] Michelet, *Procès*, vol. 1, pp. 424–5.

[48] Tommasi, 'L'ordine dei Templari a Perugia', 18, 60 no. 17.

[49] Gilmour-Bryson, *Trial of the Templars in the Papal State*, p. 216.

[50] Michelet, *Procès*, vol. 1, p. 424. He could be identified with *Ubertinus de Cavelle*, mentioned in the records of the trial of the Templars in Tuscany. Bini, 'Dei Tempieri e del loro processo in Toscana', p. 478.

[51] Michelet, *Procès*, vol. 1, pp. 424–8.

[52] Bellomo, 'La milizia del Tempio in Italia nord-occidentale', 87–9, 298–309, 323–9, 454–7, 459–61.

[53] Georg Caro, *Genova e la supremazia sul Mediterraneo, 1257–1311*, 2 vols (Genoa, 1974–5), vol. 1, pp. 46–79. This work was first published as Georg Caro, *Genua und die Mächte am Mittelmeer, 1257–1311*, 2 vols (Halle, 1895–9).

[54] They are not even mentioned in Luigi T. Belgrano (ed.), *Documenti inediti riguardanti le due crociate di S. Ludovico IX, re di Francia* (Genoa, 1859), pp. 28–9 nos 3–4, p. 89 no. 67, pp. 135–7 nos 129–32.

[55] Ramón Muntaner, *Crónica Catalana*, ed. Antonio de Bofarull y de Brocá (Barcelona, 1860), pp. 368–9.

[56] Bellomo, 'La milizia del Tempio in Italia nord-occidentale', 93–6.

[57] Romeo Pavoni (ed.), *Notai genovesi in Oltremare: Atti rogati a Cipro da Lamberto di Sambuceto, gennaio–agosto 1302* (Genoa, 1987), pp. 132–3 no. 104, pp. 179–80 no. 150, pp. 184–5 no. 155, p. 192 no. 162.

[58] A Templar commander of Antioch named William of Monferrat is mentioned in the 'Annales de Terre Sainte', but he actually was from Montferrand. It is also certain that Frederick, *preceptor de Alamannia*, mentioned in the records of the trial in Cyprus, was not a member of a Savoy family. 'Annales de Terre Sainte', ed. Reinhold Röhricht and Gaston Raynaud, *Archives de l'Orient Latin*, 2 (1884), documents, 427–61, here 439; Schottmüller, *Untergang des Templer-Ordens*, vol. 2, p. 197; Gilmour-Bryson, *Trial of the Templars in Cyprus*, p. 125.

11

The Mobility of Templars from Provence

CHRISTIAN VOGEL

The Templar province of Provence (*Provincia*) was – with France (*Francia*), the Auvergne (*Avernia*) and Aquitaine (*Aquitania*) – one of the order's four provinces in the territory of modern-day France. It was certainly in existence by 1143 and originally consisted of Provence, Languedoc, Gascony and northern Italy.[1] Until 1240, this province and the order's possessions in Aragon, Catalonia and the Roussillon were under joint management and referred to as *Provincia et partes Hispaniae*.[2] After the council of Troyes (1129),[3] the Templars' possessions increased dramatically, especially in the Languedoc, although the Hospitallers, who were already widely established in southern France, continued to be significant competitors.[4] The mobility of the Templars' provincial masters, local commanders and simple brothers – particularly those from Provence – will be examined in this chapter.

The Templars' dedication to the protection of pilgrims in the Holy Land required extensive manpower. Brothers from the west had to travel to the east where they served for a limited period of time before returning to the west.[5] However, the Templars not only moved from their western commanderies to the Holy Land and back. Apparently, the brothers were not attached to particular houses in the west either. The order's trial records reveal the busy movement of some Templars within France.[6] Gerard *de Passagio*, a brother-sergeant, – for example – can be found in a number of different houses over a period of fifteen years: originally from the diocese of Metz, he spent three years in Cyprus, then returned to France where he spent time in the diocese of Langres as well as in Lorraine, Picardy and the diocese of Vienne, before he accompanied the commander of Trier to the general chapter in Paris.[7]

The cartularies of the Templars in the west further confirm this notion of mobility. St Gilles is a case in point. In one of the earliest documents, dated March 1150, three Templar brothers appear as representatives of *St Egidius*, the Templar house in St Gilles – among them the commander Bernard *Catalanus* and one William *de Riallaco*, who would be in charge of the order's house in Jalez the following year.[8] It seems that in 1156 a considerable number of Templars assembled in St Gilles to hold a provincial chapter: more brothers than usual, as well as the provincial master and at least two commanders were in attendance.[9] It is safe to assume that a provincial chapter was also held in St Gilles in September 1217: in addition to the provincial master William *de Monterotunda* (titled *magister in Provincia et in Hispania*), thirteen Templars were present – among them William *de Alliaco* (titled *magister Templi Provinciae*), the commander and the sub-commander of St Gilles, the commander of Arles and three brothers with no title who, however, can be traced in earlier or later documents as commanders in Marseille, Montpellier, Pézenas, Bailles and Toulouse.[10] A similar assembly of prominent figures, including the provincial master, also came to St Gilles in November 1234.[11]

The charters of the Templar house of *St Egidius* reveal that non-local commanders visited the house at St Gilles even when no provincial chapter was in session.[12] In April 1175, Peter *de Tolosa*, at the time commander of Toulouse (*magister Tolosanus*), appears at St Gilles as the first of seven witnesses.[13] In July 1187, William *de Solario*, the order's commander of Arles, is mentioned as a witness at St Gilles.[14] In November 1213, Peter *de Castronovo* from Arles visited St Gilles.[15] The commanders of houses that were subordinated to St Gilles, particularly those of Montfrin and Saliers, frequently functioned as witnesses at St Gilles. However, St Gilles was not an exceptional case. The mobility of commanders from Provence can be seen at Arles as well. Bernard *Catalanus*, the aforementioned commander of *St Egidius*, served as a witness at Arles in May 1189.[16] In November 1234, a provincial chapter seems to have been held in Arles: four commanders and the provincial master were in attendance.[17] Many of the other Templar witnesses found at Arles later served as commanders of other houses.

However, not only the commanders were travelling. Simple brothers were not submitted to any *stabilitas loci* either. The witness lists in the cartularies indicate that the 'crew' of a Templar house was anything but permanent. At St Gilles, there are only a few names that appear repeatedly over extended periods of time. Raymond *Imbertus* can be found several times between January 1173 and May 1184.[18] John *de Aiguno*, who served as sub-commander in the 1180s, can be found in St Gilles during a period of approximately ten years (April 1175–November 1185).[19] Gontard *Rebollus* and Stephen *Rebollus* appear in the witness lists of St Gilles over a thirteen-year period.[20] In later decades, there were longer intervals between the appearances of certain Templars at St Gilles, while the number of those who governed houses subordinate to St Gilles increased (as did the number of such houses and the possessions attached to them). At all times, however, names can be found which are mentioned only once. Whether the respective brothers left the house in order to join the order's troops in the Holy Land is unknown. It does, however, seem certain that they did not stay long at St Gilles.

An analysis of the cartularies of Arles,[21] Jalez,[22] Toulouse,[23] La Chapelle-Livron[24] and Montsaunès[25] leads to similar results. One Templar (Pons *Rufus*), who was in St Gilles in 1177 and 1184, appeared in the neighbouring house in Arles in 1178.[26] Bernard *Bedocius*, sub-commander in St Gilles in 1191–2, was a brother and representative of the house in Arles in August 1192.[27] Except for a few recurring names, there were no permanent 'crews' in the other above-mentioned houses (Jalez, Toulouse, La Chapelle-Livron and Montsaunès) either. Furthermore, the time period over which a name continues to surface in the lists seldom exceeds a decade. For the years between 1184 and 1193, there are five references to the Templar Peter *Aicardi*'s presence in Arles.[28] There are four references to Peter *de Mosterio*'s presence in Arles for the time period between 1184 and 1189.[29] A certain Peter Astruc seems to have been in Arles for as long as seventeen years, however, he is mentioned only three times, namely in 1188, 1198 and 1205.[30] Unfortunately, the documentation for Arles is not as good as for St Gilles. The Templar house of Mas-Deu may have been an exception: in 1310, eighteen of twenty-five brothers – twenty-five being an exceptionally high number of Templar brothers for a western commandery – had stayed in Mas-Deu since their reception into the order.[31]

Amédée Trudon des Ormes has suggested that the mobility of brothers (even of those without special functions) served to maintain the exchange of information within the order.[32] However, it is conceivable that this flow of information was only one aspect of a broader strategy. It will, therefore, be useful to take a closer look at institutionalized mobility within the Order of the Temple, namely travels, special commissions and transfers of officials. For the commanders, the requirement to attend the meetings of the provincial chapters was an important and recurrent reason to travel. At these annual assemblies, the commanders rendered their accounts, the order's statutes were enforced, administrative affairs were discussed and new commanders were assigned to the order's houses.[33] On a higher level, the general chapter was a reason for the provincial masters to travel. At the general chapter, the provincial masters and other high officials for the order's eastern and western territories were nominated.[34] This system of chapters connected the provinces with the order's central administration.[35] However, not only *ex-officio* participants joined the sessions of the chapters. Brothers who had violated the order's statutes were not always tried in their respective houses. Despite the costs and dangers of the long journey, some 'offenders' were sent to the east in order to be judged by the order's master and general chapter.[36]

Brothers and provincial officials were summoned from the west to come to the central convent where visitors were appointed to oversee the management of the western provinces.[37] An impressive example is the mobility of the French visitor Hugh of Pairaud.[38] In 1291 or 1292, he was near Lyon, in 1293 near Châlons and during the years 1294, 1297, 1303 and 1307 he was in Paris. He visited Sommereux at least three times (1297, 1298 and 1300), he travelled to Templar houses in the dioceses of Troyes and Langres and he visited various other houses of the order (including Mormant, Montélimar, Messelan and Beaune). In most cases, he presided over chapter meetings.[39] Concurrently with serving as visitor, Hugh of Pairaud was master of France and, temporarily, replaced the provincial master of England.[40] This illustrates very strong ties to the order's central government which seem to have existed since the Templars' earliest days; extensive travelling between east and west – to assume administrative functions or to carry out specific missions – can be documented as early as the first half of the twelfth century.[41]

The ties between the order's headquarters in the east and its houses in the west were also strengthened by those officials who, in the course of their careers, held offices in the east and the west. Before being appointed as provincial masters in the west, several Templars had served their order meritoriously in the east.[42] Thus, Gilbert Eral, who originated from the Templar province of *Provincia*, had served as grand commander in Jerusalem in 1183, as provincial master of Provence (*magister Provinciae et in partibus Hispaniae*) between 1185 and 1189 and as master of the west (*magister cismare*) in 1194 before he was elected master of the order.[43] One of his successors, William of Sonnac, was commander of Auzon in 1224 and provincial master of Aquitaine between 1236 and 1246 before assuming the office of master of the order.[44] William's immediate successor, Rainald of Vichiers, probably hailed from Champagne, served as commander of the Templar palace in Acre in 1240, returned to France as provincial master (1242–8), assumed the office of marshal in 1249 and became master in 1250.[45]

A Templar by the name of William Cadel (or William *Catelli*), probably a native of southern France, held offices in Provence, north and south of the Pyrenees, as well as in the Holy Land. He served as commander of St Gilles (1201–3), as *magister Provinciae* (1205–9), as commander of Monzón (1210–12) and as *magister Provinciae et Hispaniae* (1212); he assumed this latter office for a second time in 1231–2. In the interval, he functioned as master of the west (*magister cismare*; 1216) and – probably in his capacity as the order's grand commander – travelled with a delegation from the Holy Land to Rome (1222–3) and then on to France and England.[46]

Geoffrey *Fulcherii*, who originated from Burgundy, was a busy traveller as well.[47] After stays in the Holy Land (1144), Spain (1146) and the Holy Land once again (1151), he travelled to Rome and Cîteaux and then returned to the Holy Land where he stayed from 1156 until 1160. He subsequently visited France and England (1163–4) and returned to the east to serve in a high office in the order's central convent.[48] He eventually left the Holy Land again and became master of the west (*magister cismare*). In this latter capacity, he travelled to Paris, Catalonia and Flanders.[49]

The transfer of high officials was not limited to an east–west exchange. Some of the Templars' provincial masters successively managed different provinces of the order. Thus, the English master Aimery of St Maur (1200–20) had been master of Aquitaine earlier in his career.[50] A certain Amblard first served as master of England (1261–6) and later as master of Aquitaine (1278–95); he probably originated from southern France and may have served as marshal in the Holy Land in 1271.[51] Considering the political ties between England and Aquitaine, the exchange of Templar officials between these two regions makes much sense. However, there was not only an exchange between England and Aquitaine. Guy of Bazainville became Templar master of Aquitaine in 1262 after having served as provincial master of France from 1243 until 1255.[52] His successor, Imbert of Pairaud, followed in his footsteps, first as provincial master of France (1261–4), then as provincial master of Aquitaine and visitor general (1266–9), and as provincial master of England (1268–71).[53] John *le Franceys*, on the other hand, was provincial master of Aquitaine (1269–76) before he became provincial master of France (*c.*1279). However, he had been commander of Paris (in the province of France) in 1269 before he was promoted to provincial master of Aquitaine. Thus, the England–Aquitaine career-sequence was followed by a France–Aquitaine career-sequence. Around the same time, there was also an England–Provence career-sequence. Roncelin of Fos originally came from a noble family residing near the Rhône delta. He served as *magister Provinciae* from 1248 until 1250 and from 1260 until 1278; in between, from 1252 until 1255, he was provincial master of England.[54]

During the reign of Charles I of Anjou, Sicily was considered a potential career-station for French Templars as well. In 1266, Pope Clement IV tried to persuade the order's master to transfer Amaury *de Rupe* (or La Roche),[55] the provincial master of France, to Sicily.[56] While Amaury, a Templar of presumably southern French origin, never took the office of provincial master in Sicily, it is conceivable that he visited the court of Charles of Anjou.[57] In each case, there were probably specific reasons why an official was moved from one province to another; however, all these transfers have one thing in common: those who relocated were of French origin or career-background and, thus, fluent in the language (or variations thereof) that was spoken in France, in England, in their order's central convent and at the court of Charles of Anjou in Sicily.

The appointment procedures of these officials certainly played an important role as well. The Templars' provincial masters were not elected by their subordinates or by the local commanders in their respective provinces; they were appointed by the general chapter or by the master and his convent.[58] After approximately four years of service and before their appointments could be renewed, the order's provincial masters had to render an account of their administration.[59] As the provincial masters were appointed at the order's headquarters, it is not surprising that they were often Templars who were directly known to the master and the central convent: Geoffrey of Goneville, for example, had served as the master's legate to the Curia prior to his appointment as provincial master of Aquitaine.[60]

The Templars' local officials, namely the commanders of the houses, were transferred far more frequently than the order's provincial masters. According to Trudon des Ormes's analysis of the Templars' trial records,

Baldwin of St Just and Robert of Beauvais (a brother-priest) served
successively as commanders of Sommereux, Beauvais and Ponthieu.[61]
The lists of commanders compiled by Émile Léonard for the Templars
in France and by Alan Forey for the Templars in Aragon reveal that
these northern French cases of Baldwin and Robert are absolutely no
exception: most commanders were transferred – after a short term – to
another house.[62]

However, there seem to have been a few exceptions: Bernard *Catalanus*,
one of the commanders of *St Egidius*, the Templar house in St Gilles,
proved remarkably immobile. According to Léonard, Bernard served
as commander of *St Egidius* for almost half a century (1151–96)
without interruption.[63] The cartulary of this house confirms Léonard's
observation. Bernard was apparently absent between November 1185
and April/June 1186;[64] a sub-commander appears in the documents
during those few months, which suggests that Bernard was absent but
still in charge.[65] Again, in May 1189, he was absent briefly as he was
functioning as a witness in the nearby Templar house of Arles.[66] Bernard
Catalanus must have been one of the first Templar brothers of *St
Egidius* in St Gilles. He and several other brothers received donations
on behalf of this house, but they probably did not travel around for this
purpose: Bernard consistently appears in St Gilles. From approximately
1159 on, he occupied a position of leadership, which indicates that the
position of commander emerged at St Gilles at that time.[67]

The successors of Bernard *Catalanus* held the office of commander of
St Gilles only for very short terms and were often successively in charge
of a number of houses. Bernard's immediate successor, Bertrand *de
Bellicadro*, served for only two years (1196–8 and again 1234–5) and
appeared afterwards as commander of Palau. Bernard *de Casa* was
commander of *St Egidius* for two brief terms (1199–1200 and 1204), but
in the years between 1200 and 1227 he served as commander of the
Templar houses in Arles, Marseille, Montpellier, Pézenas and Montfrin
(the latter being a house that was subordinated to *St Egidius*).

The commanders of the houses in Provence moved within the geographical boundaries of the province to houses located both north
and south of the Pyrenees. Peter *de Deo*, a simple Templar witness in St
Gilles in 1185,[68] later reappeared as commander of St Gilles (1208);[69]
he also served as commander in Horta (1202), Miravet (1205) and
Zaragoza (1218 and 1229), then again in St Gilles (1221) and in Toulouse
(1228).[70] Among the twenty-eight commanders of *St Egidius* listed by
Léonard there are only five who do not seem to have held an office

outside St Gilles. The commanders moved on to important as well as less important houses: Arles, Carcassonne, Jalez, Le Puy, Marseille, Mas-Deu, Miravet, Montfrin, Montpellier, Monzón, Palau, Peyrens, Pézenas, Richerenches, Rué, St Eulalie, St Pierre-de-Camp-public, Tortosa, Toulouse, Villedieu, Villel and Zaragoza. In Arles, the situation was apparently similar. Bertrand Hugh was the first commander of Arles who, after his time in Arles (1184–5), subsequently served as commander in other houses: he first became sub-commander of St Gilles (1187–9) and then commander of Rué (1195).

Early on, the Templar houses of Arles and St Gilles established a considerable number of new houses which were subordinated to their respective jurisdiction.[71] In St Gilles, Bernard *Catalanus* promoted this development,[72] and his long tenure as commander may have contributed favourably to this commandery's expansion. The house of Douzens began as early as the mid-twelfth century to establish subordinate houses.[73] The transfer of officials did not follow jurisdictional hierarchies.[74] The commanders and sub-commanders of St Gilles often moved on to become commanders of the subordinated house of Montfrin and for the commanders of Arles the subordinated house of Avignon sometimes was a subsequent career-station. In addition to that, there were certain houses – such as Montpellier, Rué and Toulouse – which served as career-stations for Templars from St Gilles as well as for their colleagues from Arles.

It is very difficult to identify any clear or typical pattern of transfer. In the twelfth century, some commanders were transferred between Jalez and St Eulalie; later on, such transfers took place between Jalez and Pézenas. In the mid-thirteenth century, two of the commanders of St Eulalie had previously held an office south of the Pyrenees, that is prior to the establishment of a separate Spanish province. Apparently there was also some kind of connection between the houses in La Chapelle-Livron and La Selve: in the second half of the thirteenth century, three Templar commanders successively presided over these two houses.[75]

Much like the transfer of officials between houses, the careers of the brothers did not follow any clear pattern, as the following examples from Provence show. The Templar commander Bernard *de Casa* moved from St Gilles to Arles (in 1201), from there to Marseille and eventually back to St Gilles. His transfer from St Gilles to Arles can hardly be seen as a 'step up' in his career: fifteen years earlier, a former commander of Arles (Bertrand Hugh) had taken the office of sub-commander in St Gilles. However, Bernard *de Casa*'s career continued. After holding the office of commander in Montpellier and Pézenas, he finally reached Montfrin, a *dépendance* of his first commandery, St Gilles. Montpellier, too, was not a 'step up' in his career: one of its commanders, Gilbert *de Costabella* (1184 and again 1191–2), became sub-commander in St Gilles after serving in Montpellier and returned to Montpellier after serving in St Gilles. Likewise, Pézenas was not a 'step up' from Montpellier: in the mid-thirteenth century, Raymond *de Amenlerio* served in Pézenas before becoming commander of Montpellier; incidentally, his career had begun in Montfrin where the career of Bernard *de Casa* had ended. Apparently, Joseph Delaville le Roulx's statement concerning the careers of the Hospitallers' high officials can be applied to the Templars' careers as well: these careers were chaotic.[76] The word 'career' may even be quite inappropriate. After all, the Templars regarded the holding of an office as a trust and responsibility rather than a reward. By frequently transferring their officials, they ensured that no single person would enjoy permanent control over a small community and the possessions of a commandery.[77] Thus local ties and loyalties were less likely to have a significant impact on the administration of a province or a house.[78] Any conflict between the order's master and a provincial master over the appointment of a local commander may be seen as an indicator that the master was attempting to increase his control in the west by appointing a confidant.[79]

Transfers of commanders seem to have occurred only within the boundaries of a province.[80] This can be established clearly for the Templar province of Provence by comparing the situation before and after the separation of the *partes Hispaniae*. However, Provence was not an exception: apparently the commanders of the other French provinces also changed commanderies only within their respective provinces, though not as frequently as their colleagues in southern France and not until the later part of the thirteenth century. It seems that the custom of transferring commanders to other houses, as it had been established in *Provincia* since the twelfth century, was not introduced in the north until a century later.

In the province of *Provincia et partes Hispaniae*, the Templars' mobility involved locations both north and south of the Pyrenees. Administrative personnel could be moved around the entire province. The Templar commander William of *Saignone* moved from Arles to Alfambra (1207); he then returned to Arles and became provincial master in 1214. The Templar commander William of Solesas moved from Pézenas to Alfambra (1221) and then on to Jalez. Peter of Camphaet held the commanderies of Alfambra, Villel and Gardeny in the *partes Hispaniae* and afterwards those of St Eulalie, Pézenas and Espalion. Peter *de Deo* transferred from Horta in Spain to St Gilles, then to Toulouse and eventually back to Spain, to the commandery of Zaragoza (1218, 1229).[81]

After 1240, that is after the separation of *Provincia* from the *partes Hispaniae*, this connection across the Pyrenees came to an end.[82] The case of the Templar commandery of Mas-Deu in the county of Roussillon, which joined the new province of Aragon and Catalonia after the division in 1240, illustrates this particularly well. Raymond *de Caneto* was commander of Mas-Deu in 1165 and 1191; in the interval, he served as commander in St Eulalie (1181) and as *magister Provinciae et Hispaniae* (1184–9). William *de Solario* changed from Mas-Deu to Arles in 1186. Fulk *de Montepesato* oversaw his order's houses in Jalez, Mas-Deu, Le Puy and Pézenas before becoming provincial master. Peter of Malon began his 'career' in 1230 as commander in Peyrens, was transferred to St Gilles, served as commander in Mas-Deu from 1233 until 1239 and subsequently governed the commandery of St Gilles again. His successor in Mas-Deu (1240–1), Martin of Nissa, was a former commander of Argenteins and Toulouse. Things changed after the division of the province in 1240. After 1240, no commander of Mas-Deu was a former or future Provençal office-holder, but the ties to the increasing number of houses in Aragon and Catalonia became more intense.[83]

The appointment procedures for commanders of houses can serve as an explanation of why provincial boundaries were strictly upheld. The commanders of houses were usually appointed for a certain term by the provincial master, sometimes by the order's master,[84] usually during the holding of the annual provincial chapter.[85] Marion Melville has suggested that these officials were frequently taken from the lower nobility of the region in order to connect the order's houses to the local elite.[86] For the Templars' houses in Rouergue, Alain Demurger has shown family connections between the Templar commanders and the local nobility. At Montsaunès all of the known commanders came from the aristocracy of Comminges.[87] However, as has been indicated previously, the commanders were regularly transferred from one commandery to the other. Thus, Peter of Sombrun was commander in Montsaunès in 1270–1 and would later govern the houses in Bordères and Argenteins. His successor Peter *de Gavaretto* had been entrusted with Gimbrède before becoming commander in Montsaunès; he later moved on to

Bordères and finally to Toulouse. However, all these transfers took place within the province: the provincial chapters, where commanders of houses were usually appointed, were assemblies of one province. The provincial master, who appointed the commanders with the advice of the provincial chapter, only oversaw the commanderies and brothers of his province; therefore, he could never appoint a brother to a house outside his province or summon a brother from another province.[88] Any exchange with personnel outside the provincial boundaries was only possible when so ordered by the order's master and central convent or general chapter.

In the Order of the Temple, the monastic *stabilitas loci* gave way to *mobilitas loci*. The brothers served in the Holy Land and spent the rest of their life not just in one commandery, but were frequently transferred from one house to another. This also applies to the order's officials. Because of the order's strict centralization it was possible to transfer officials frequently. The order was conceived as an integrated whole – a centrally governed federation of commanderies. To a Templar, any house of the order could become a temporal 'home'. However, on the level of the commanders of houses, there was no exchange of personnel across provincial boundaries. The main reason for this was not that provincial boundaries followed language boundaries. Rather, the structure of the order's provincial government precluded the inter-provincial exchange of commanders.

Notes

1 Joseph-Antoine Durbec, *Templiers et Hospitaliers en Provence et dans les Alpes-maritimes* (Grenoble, 2001), p. 57; first published as 'Les Templiers en Provence', *Provence historique*, 9, nos 35 and 37 (1959).

2 For the Templars' western provinces see Alain Demurger, *Vie et mort de l'ordre du Temple* (Paris, 1985), p. 85. It has been speculated that the north of France and the British Isles might have originally belonged to one and the same province; see Henri de Curzon (ed.), *La règle du Temple* (Paris, 1886), p. 80 note 4; Judi Upton-Ward, *The Rule of the Templars* (Woodbridge, 1992), p. 41 note 87.4. This idea has been contested by Jochen Burgtorf, 'Führungsstrukturen und Funktionsträger in der Zentrale der Templer und Johanniter von den Anfängen bis zum frühen 14. Jahrhundert' (Ph.D. thesis, Heinrich-Heine-Universität Düsseldorf, 2001), 63 note 11.

3 Marion Melville, *La vie des Templiers*, second edition (Paris, 1974), p. 32.

4 Demurger, *Vie et mort*, p. 50.

[5] Alan Forey, 'Towards a profile of the Templars in the early fourteenth century', in Malcolm Barber (ed.), *The Military Orders*, vol. 1, *Fighting for the Faith and Caring for the Sick* (Aldershot, 1994), pp. 196–204, here p. 201.

[6] Amédée Trudon des Ormes, *Étude sur les possessions de l'ordre du Temple en Picardie* (Amiens, 1892), pp. 29–31; his study is based on Jules Michelet (ed.), *Le procès des Templiers* (Paris, 1841–51). Forey, 'Towards a profile of the Templars', p. 203, provides an example illustrating the mobility of an English Templar within Britain.

[7] Michelet, *Procès*, vol. 1, pp. 215–18.

[8] Paris, Bibliothèque Nationale (BN), nouvelles acquisitions latines (n.a.l.), vols 1–71 (Marquis d'Albon, manuscript 'Cartulaire du Temple'), here vol. 5, fol. 11 (witness-list).

[9] BN, n.a.l., vol. 5, fol. 13; witness-list: ibid., fol. 15.

[10] BN, n.a.l., vol. 6, fol. 122; a witness-list, ibid., fol. 125, features Bernard *de Casa* (who served consecutively as commander in St Gilles, Arles, Marseille, St Gilles, Montpellier, Pézenas and Montfrin), Raymond Chausoart (who served consecutively as commander in Arles, Bailles and Toulouse) and William *Pelliparius* (commander of Pézenas). Details about these commanders are based on Émile-G. Léonard, *Introduction au cartulaire manuscrit du Temple (1150–1317), constitué par le marquis d'Albon et conservé à la Bibliothèque nationale, suivie d'un tableau des maisons françaises du Temple et de leurs précepteurs* (Paris, 1930).

[11] BN, n.a.l., vol. 5, fol. 238.

[12] Ibid., vols 5 and 6.

[13] Ibid., vol. 5, fol. 88.

[14] Ibid., vol. 5, fol. 196.

[15] Ibid., vol. 7, fol. 18.

[16] Ibid.

[17] Ibid., vol. 7, fol. 193.

[18] Ibid., vol. 5, fols 74, 87–8, 90, 97, 100, 107, 129, 130, 138, 152.

[19] Ibid., vol. 5, fols 86, 118, 121, 143, 146, 151, 152, 154, 156, 158, 163–5, 170, 172, 178.

[20] Gontard is mentioned between April 1175 (ibid., vol. 5, fol. 86) and December 1188 (ibid., vol. 5, fol. 228). Stephen appears, though fairly infrequently, between July 1202 (ibid., vol. 6, fol. 18) and June 1215 (ibid., vol. 6, fol. 108).

[21] Ibid., vol. 7.

[22] Ibid., vol. 13.

[23] Ibid., vol. 32.

[24] Ibid., vol. 23.

[25] Ibid., vol. 34.

[26] Pons *Rufus* appears towards the end of witness-lists in St Gilles in 1177 (ibid., vol. 5, fol. 107) and 1184 (ibid., vol. 5, fol. 158) and in Arles in 1178 (ibid., vol. 7, fol. 14).

[27] Ibid., vol. 7, fol. 24.

[28] Ibid., vol. 7, fols 15, 17–19, 28.

29   Ibid., vol. 7, fols 15, 17–19.

30   Ibid., vol. 7, fols 17, 45, 64.

31   Forey, 'Towards a profile of the Templars', p. 202.

32   Trudon des Ormes, *Étude sur les possessions*, p. 31.

33   For the provincial chapters see Alan Forey, *The Military Orders from the Twelfth to the Early Fourteenth Centuries* (London, 1992), pp. 160–1.

34   Melville, *La vie des Templiers*, p. 98; Burgtorf, 'Führungsstrukturen und Funktionsträger', 62–3 with reference to Curzon, *Règle*, no. 88.

35   Laurent Dailliez, *Les Templiers en Provence* (Nice, 1979), p. 8. For the order's chapters see Laurent Dailliez, *Les Templiers: Gouvernement et institutions* (Nice, 1980), pp. 261–79.

36   Marie Luise Bulst-Thiele, *Sacrae domus militiae Templi Hierosolymitani magistri: Untersuchungen zur Geschichte des Templerordens 1118/19–1314* (Göttingen, 1974), p. 194 note 27 with reference to Curzon, *Règle*, nos 585 and 607.

37   Demurger, *Vie et mort*, p. 86.

38   Amédée Trudon des Ormes, *Liste des maisons et de quelques dignitaires de l'Ordre du Temple en Syrie, en Chypre et en France d'après les pièces du procès* (Paris, 1900), p. 23; first published in *Revue de l'Orient Latin*, 5 (1897), 389–459; 6 (1898), 156–213; 7 (1900), 223–74, 504–89.

39   Ibid.

40   Bulst-Thiele, *Magistri*, pp. 297–8.

41   See Burgtorf, 'Führungsstrukturen und Funktionsträger', 63.

42   Bulst-Thiele, *Magistri*, p. 41.

43   Ibid., p. 135; Burgtorf, 'Führungsstrukturen und Funktionsträger', 489–95.

44   Bulst-Thile, *Magistri*, p. 217.

45   Ibid., p. 226.

46   For William *Catelli* see Marie Luise Bulst-Thiele, 'Templer in königlichen und päpstlichen Diensten', in Peter Classen and Peter Scheibert (eds), *Festschrift Percy Ernst Schramm* (Wiesbaden, 1964), vol. 1, pp. 289–308, here pp. 297–8; Burgtorf, 'Führungsstrukturen und Funktionsträger', 727–33.

47   For Geoffrey *Fulcherii* see Bulst-Thiele, 'Templer in königlichen und päpstlichen Diensten', p. 290; Burgtorf, 'Führungsstrukturen und Funktionsträger', 503–8; Melville, *La vie des Templiers*, p. 81.

48   Melville, *La vie des Templiers*, p. 81.

49   Ibid., p. 86.

50   Bulst-Thiele, 'Templer in königlichen und päpstlichen Diensten', p. 297.

51   Ibid., p. 300; Burgtorf, 'Führungsstrukturen und Funktionsträger', 379–85.

52   Burgtorf, 'Führungsstrukturen und Funktionsträger', 512–16. For lists of the Templars' provincial masters see Léonard, *Introduction au cartulaire manuscrit du Temple*. Subsequent details (given in the text of this chapter) of the order's officials are based on Léonard's work unless indicated otherwise.

53   Bulst-Thiele, *Magistri*, p. 300 note 29. Léonard, *Introduction au cartulaire manuscrit du Temple*, p. 96.

[54] Bulst-Thiele, *Magistri*, p. 249 note 68.

[55] For Amaury of La Roche see Burgtorf, 'Führungsstrukturen und Funktionsträger', 371–9.

[56] Édouard Jordan (ed.), *Les Registres de Clément IV (1265–1268)* (Paris, 1893–1945), no. 418.

[57] Bulst-Thiele, 'Templer in königlichen und päpstlichen Diensten', p. 303; Burgtorf, 'Führungsstrukturen und Funktionsträger', 374–5.

[58] Forey, *Military Orders*, p. 154.

[59] Bulst-Thiele, *Magistri*, p. 279 with reference to a letter by the order's master William of Beaujeu, published in Heinrich Finke, *Acta Aragonensia: Quellen zur deutschen, italienischen, französischen, spanischen, zur Kirchen- und Kultur-geschichte, aus der diplomatischen Korrespondenz Jaymes II. (1291–1327)*, 3 vols (Berlin, 1908–22), vol. 3, p. 10.

[60] Bulst-Thiele, *Magistri*, p. 309.

[61] Trudon des Ormes, *Étude sur les possessions*, pp. 28–9. For these examples see Michelet, *Procès*, vol. 1, pp. 241, 371, 374, 471; for Robert see ibid., p. 291.

[62] Léonard, *Introduction au cartulaire manuscrit du Temple*; Alan Forey, *The Templars in the Corona de Aragón* (London, 1973), pp. 266, 420–50.

[63] Léonard, *Introduction au cartulaire manuscrit du Temple*, p. 30.

[64] Bernard *Catalanus* appears one last time in October 1185 (BN, n.a.l., vol. 5, fol. 176). In late November 1185, John *de Aiguno* received a donation as sub-commander (ibid., vol. 5, fol. 178). In late April 1186, Peter of St Tiberias appears as sub-commander (ibid., vol. 5, fol. 179). In these two latter cases, Bernard is not mentioned in the witness-lists. However, in June 1186, Bernard appears again as commander (ibid., vol. 5, fol. 181).

[65] It seems that, during Bernard's absence, there was never another commander in his place. The documents either mention a Templar without any title (ibid., vol. 5, fols 99, 161) or a sub-commander (ibid., vol. 5, fols 185, 207, 225, 228). Thus, it may be safe to assume that Bernard continued as commander until 1196. See also Dominic Selwood, *Knights of the Cloister: Templars and Hospitallers in Central-Southern Occitania, 1100–1300* (Woodbridge, 1999), p. 153.

[66] BN, n.a.l., vol. 7, fol. 18.

[67] Until 1158, all donations seem to have been received by several brothers. It is possible that all these brothers belonged to this particular Templar house at St Gilles, however, usually not all brothers were listed by name (instead, the phrase *ceterisque fratribus* appears). Perhaps (and in contrast to the witness-lists) only those brothers were named as recipients who held leading offices or belonged to a higher social rank. In 1159, Bernard *Catalanus* and Rigaud *Severicus* were called *fratres fratrum* (ibid., vol. 5, fol. 27); one year later, Bernard appears alone as *frater fratrum*, whereas the other brothers mentioned by name seem to have formed an advisory group (*cum consilio*: ibid., vol. 5, fol. 32).

[68] Ibid., vol. 5, fol. 162. Peter *de Deo* appears as the third of eight witnesses.

[69] Ibid., vol. 6, fol. 36.

[70] The details concerning the Templar possessions in Aragon and Catalonia are based on the lists of commanders given by Forey, *The Templars in the Corona de Aragón*, pp. 420–50. Unless indicated otherwise the data for the commanders of the Templars' French commanderies are based on Léonard, *Introduction au cartulaire manuscrit du Temple*.

[71] Dailliez, *Les Templiers en Provence*, p. 10.

[72] Durbec, *Templiers et Hospitaliers en Provence*, pp. 84–5.

[73] Jonathan Riley-Smith, 'The origins of the commandery in the Temple and the Hospital', in Anthony Luttrell and León Pressouyre (eds), *La Commanderie: institution des ordres militaires dans l'occident médiéval* (Paris 2002), pp. 9–18, here p. 14.

[74] Dailliez, *Les Templiers en Provence*, p. 8, stresses the limitations caused by these jurisdictional ties.

[75] See above, note 70.

[76] Joseph Delaville le Roulx, *Les Hospitaliers en Terre Sainte et à Chypre (1100–1310)* (Paris, 1904), pp. 326–7.

[77] Forey, *The Templars in the Corona de Aragón*, p. 266. Forey, *The Military Orders*, p. 152, compares the military orders' practice of appointments with the 'rapid changes of personnel' in the office of 'podestà' in Italian cities. The military orders' officials must have possessed a certain degree of administrative experience. Assigning commanderies for short terms prevented individuals from establishing a power base.

[78] Forey, 'Towards a profile of the Templars', p. 203.

[79] Forey, *The Templars in the Corona de Aragón*, p. 264, suggests that the Templar master was petitioned by members of the order in the east who sought an office as a means of returning to western Europe.

[80] See Dailliez, *Les Templiers en Provence*, p. 8; Forey, 'Towards a profile of the Templars', p. 203.

[81] See above, note 70.

[82] Forey, *The Templars in the Corona de Aragón*, p. 89.

[83] See above, note 70.

[84] Forey, *The Templars in the Corona de Aragón*, p. 264. The notion that the provincial master appointed the commanders is confirmed by a certificate of appointment addressed to the commander of the commandery in La Chapelle-Livron. It is unclear why this certificate was issued: perhaps the appointment had not taken place during a chapter, or perhaps there were some quarrels within the commandery about an interim commander. BN, n.a.l., vol. 23, fol. 211: '[12 October 1263] Noverint universi presentes [. . .] et futuri quod nos, frater R. de Fos, domorum milicie Templi magister in Provincia, dilectum nostrum fratrem Petrum Boneti, de consilio et voluntate fratrum nostrorum, facimus et constituimus, creamus et ordinamus procuratorem sindicum et auctorem bajulie domus Capelle in omnibus causis . . .'.

[85] Forey, *The Templars in the Corona de Aragón*, p. 265; Forey, *Military Orders*, p. 161.

[86]   Melville, *La vie des Templiers*, p. 42.

[87]   Demurger, *Vie et mort*, p. 77.

[88]   Joseph Delaville le Roulx (ed.), 'Un nouveau manuscrit de la règle du Temple', *Annuaire-Bulletin de la Société de l'histoire de France*, 26 (1889), 185–214, here no. 18 which shows the limits of command of a provincial master. The new edition is Judi Upton-Ward (ed.), *The Catalan Rule of the Templars* (Woodbridge, 2003), p. 22 no. 43.

12

Templar Mobility in the Diocese of Limoges According to the Order's Trial Records

JEAN-MARIE ALLARD

Before the French Revolution, the former diocese of Limoges in the centre of France consisted of a territory almost identical with the three modern-day *départements* of Creuse, Haute-Vienne and Corrèze. In 1317, Pope John XXII divided it into fifty parishes to create the small additional diocese of Tulle. Located on the western plateau of the Massif Central and nowhere exceeding an altitude of 1,000 metres, the area corresponds to the historical provinces of La Marche and the Limousin. The military orders surfaced here considerably later and more modestly than they had in the south of France. At the end of the twelfth century, there were two Hospitaller houses and six Templar houses in the northeast of the diocese. The thirteenth century brought around fifty dependencies, each referred to as *domus* (house) in the sources. Twenty-four Hospitaller houses and thirty-six Templar houses have been identified.[1] Even though many of these are fairly modest, the question arises why so many houses were established. We may speculate that this interest in the military orders, and thus in the crusades, was connected to a long history of involvement in the crusades, which originally began with Pope Urban II's visit to the region at Christmas 1095, just one month after the Council of Clermont. It is also possible that donations to the military orders were considered more beneficial for the salvation of the soul than those directed at other religious institutions. We may also speculate that the influence of the many local lords who had departed for the Holy Land played a part in encouraging local donations to the military orders. One of the best known of these was Gouffier of Lastours whose actions at Antioch and Maᶜarrat-an-Nuᶜman are reported in Gregory Béchade's

Canso d'Antiochia, written around 1130. He belonged to the crusading contingent of Raymond of St Gilles and was regarded as one of the incarnations of the *chevalier au lion*: according to a later legend, he rescued a lion from the mortal grip of a snake, like Yvain in the work of Chrétien de Troyes.[2] The present study, however, is concerned not with the establishment of the military orders in the Limousin but with the mobility of their members after their establishment.

While the medieval archives of the military orders in the Limousin are sparse, the records of the trial of the Templars reveal certain aspects concerning the mobility of the Templars from this region. However, the information that can be obtained largely depends on what the inquisitors wanted to know, for the interrogation of the accused Templars focused rather less on their careers than on the alleged deviant practices condemned by the Church. Nevertheless, the depositions do provide some insights. The diocese of Limoges belonged to the Templar province of Auvergne-Limousin which stood under the command of an official who is referred to as *preceptor Alvernie, preceptor domorum militie Templi in Lemovicinio*, or as *preceptor Alvernie et Lemovicensis*, occasionally even as *preceptor seu magister domorum militie Templi in Lemovicinio et in Arvernia*. The title varied according to the degree the official's business pertained to the order's houses in the Auvergne or the Limousin.[3] A Templar commander is first mentioned in the Limousin in 1188.[4] It seems that the province was among the order's smallest, since it basically consisted of only the former dioceses of Limoges and Clermont.[5] This Templar province was, however, considerably older than the corresponding Hospitaller priory of Auvergne, which was created around 1243.[6] The trial records enable us to identify ninety-eight Templar knights, priests or sergeants who originated from the diocese of Limoges.[7] In addition, ten Templars can be linked to the area because they served as commanders or priests of houses in the Limousin, and for six others local origin can be established,[8] thus bringing the number up to 114.[9] They are not always easy to identify as their names were frequently misrepresented or in various ways 'corrected' by the notaries, despite the fact that two of the notaries who served alongside the papal commission in Paris were locals (i.e. canons from the diocese of Limoges), namely *Chatardus de Penna Varia, canonicu[s] Sancti Juniani, diocesis Lemovicensis*, and *Bernardus Filholi, ecclesie Rausoliensis, canonicus Lemovicensis*. Even though Reynald of La Porte, the bishop of Limoges, was a member of the commission, the scribes were not familiar with Occitan names. While the number of brothers has thus to be regarded with some caution, it does provide a sense of the extent of the material available for this study. While seventeen Templars from the Limousin were interrogated at Clermont,[10] the number of Templars who were arrested in the diocese of Limoges is unknown. Similarly, it is impossible to ascertain the number of brothers from the diocese of Limoges who were captured in the order's houses outside the province. Some of them were questioned at Cahors and Poitiers in 1307 and 1308.[11] Eight coming from Poitiers were present in Paris on 17 February 1310 and nine were brought from Bourges on 27 March 1310.[12] Four brothers were brought from Tours, Moissac, Rouen and Le Mans.[13] Can this be seen as an illustration of the mobility of the Templars from the Limousin? Were they stationed outside their original province or were they travelling on a mission from their province?

Of the 114 brothers mentioned earlier, only very few, namely ten, had been to 'outremer'. One brother explicitly declared before the commission in Paris that he had not been there.[14] When he was interrogated at Clermont, he remembered that he had heard many brothers say that there was a 'head' in a Templar house in 'outremer'.[15] If the men travelled little outside France, such mere rumour became fact for them. The case of Peter of Noblat (*Petrus de Nobiliaco*) is unique: before he entered the order, he had spent six years in the east in the service of Gerard of Sauzet at a time when William of Beaujeu was master of the order. When he was questioned in Paris on 10 May 1311, Peter stated that he had not heard any talk about the idol which Antonio Sicci di Vercelli, a lay notary formerly employed by the Templars, had mentioned in his deposition several days earlier. His stay in the east brought back memories of William of Beaujeu's actions: Peter of Noblat claimed that the master's friendship with the sultan and the Muslims allowed the order to maintain its presence in the Holy Land.[16] Hugh *de Fauro* had also served in 'outremer': he had spent fourteen years there and had assisted with numerous receptions into the order at Tortosa. On 12 May 1311, he also stated that Thomas *Berardi*, the order's master between 1256 and 1273, had purchased the city of Sidon. Hugh was in his fifties and his deposition was rather long-winded. He related that at some point two brothers *de crimine sodomitico diffamati* (accused of sodomy) were arrested at Château Pèlerin ('Atlīt); one was killed when he tried to escape, the other was sentenced to life in prison.[17] Then, however, he continued his recollections with a story about necrophilia which he had heard from the royal bailli of Limassol when he had taken refuge in Cyprus after the fall of Acre:

a certain noble had deeply loved a certain damsel of the castle of Maraclea in the County of Tripoli, and since he could not have her in her lifetime, when he heard that she was dead, he caused her to be exhumed, and had intercourse with her. Afterwards he cut off the head for himself, and a certain voice rang out that he should take good care of the said head, since whoever saw the head would be totally destroyed and routed.[18]

The nobleman kept the head in a chest, but one day, when he was travelling by ship to attack Constantinople, his old nurse opened the chest, thus causing a sea storm which sank the ship. According to Brother Hugh, the story was known by the sailors who survived the shipwreck. He added, however, that this head had never belonged to the Order of the Temple, neither had that other head mentioned by Antonio Sicci di Vercelli on 4 March. The two versions of the head are only slightly different. They reflect old legends based on the story of Perseus and Medusa.[19] However, another witness declared on 19 May that he had never heard of these heads, but that long before the foundation of the Orders of the Temple and the Hospital, a head used to appear in the Gulf of Satalia, threatening the boats that would venture into those parts.[20] Hugh concluded his deposition with an account of the Templars' internal rivalries which became evident after the death of Master Theobald *Gaudini*. Supposedly, two parties had emerged: the brothers from the province of Auvergne-Limousin, who were in the majority in the convent and who wanted to see Hugh of Pairaud elected as master, and a minority leaning towards the election of James of Molay. One certainly cannot accept this as a fact. The province of Auvergne-Limousin was hardly that influential. Also this would mean that many of their representatives would have had to be present at the chapter of 1292. However, the fact that only few brothers from the Limousin are reported to have spent time in the east does not make such a presence very likely. It is, of course, nevertheless conceivable that the chapter was divided between two candidates.[21] On occasion, the election of abbots in other orders even turned violent. The definitive answer as to what happened in 1292 is not at stake here. Rather, one can see that his stay in the east gave Hugh *de Fauro* the opportunity to express himself in detail about a variety of subjects. The subject of the head was, of course, connected to one of the accusations levelled against the Templars, and its discussion kept the focus on the order's alleged reproachable activities, even if, as in this case, the order was not involved at all. One has to wonder what may have caused Hugh to bring up this story. Was he afraid?[22]

Other brothers were less talkative. From three of them, we learn a few details. On 1 July 1308, the Templar knight Gerald of St Martial stated that he had spent twenty-four years in 'outremer' shortly after entering the order.[23] Another knight, William of Limoges, had been received into the order at Nicosia by the commander of Cyprus in the presence of five or six brothers, more than twenty years before the trial deposition he made on 1 July 1308 at Poitiers.[24] On All Saints' Day 1281, the Templar sergeant Durand of Limoges (deceased at the time of the trial), had assisted with a reception at Tripoli in the presence of numerous brothers.[25] In his testimony given in Paris, the Templar knight Reynald *de Bort* mentioned an interesting detail: around 1279, he had participated in the reception of Bertrand of Sartiges at Tortosa, an event which was interrupted by a (providential?) Muslim attack (which prevented any dubious practices). The fighting lasted for one day and one night.[26] At Clermont, where he abjured his errors, he did not mention this reception.[27] Had his resolve been shaken, as the editors of the trial of Clermont seem to believe?[28] Two brothers had personally experienced the enemy's prisons.[29] On 12 May 1311, Hugh *de Fauro* referred to Amblard of Aix (from the diocese of Limoges) as *captum in Paganismo* (captured by the 'infidel').[30] Andrew of Ventadour (*Andreas de Venthodoro*), probably a member of the family of the viscounts of Ventadour, was captured by the Muslims at Tortosa.[31] Undoubtedly, he was one of the forty Templars captured in 1300–2 and referred to in a testimony given at Cyprus.[32] The Templars' unfortunate military venture at Tortosa, intended to establish an operational base on the Syrian coast in conjunction with the crusaders' alliance with the Mongols of Persia, must have been one of the last real efforts to regain the Holy Land.[33]

The last two brothers from the Limousin who are known to have made the trip to 'outremer' are better known. According to the deposition of a brother whom he received into the order in 1291, Gerard of Sauzet – who is said to have been commander of Auvergne between 1284 and 1294, but may not have been nominated for the post until 1289 – originated from the diocese of Limoges.[34] His previous conduct in office caused his transfer into this province. At the time of the trial, he was deceased. A dramatic episode that took place in the Holy Land is linked to his name: the fall of the Templar castle of Baghras (Gaston) which was taken by Baybars in 1268 without a fight. At the time, Gerard was *comandaor de la terra d'Antiochia* (commander of the land of Antioch). Because of an apparent lack of arms, provisions and experienced troops, and because he was surprised by an act of treason, he decided to flee together with his garrison to another Templar fortress, namely La Roche Guillaume. He was then accused of insufficiently dismantling the castle and of not destroying all provisions and ammunitions, which earned him a penance of one year and one day.[35] He is the only Templar from the Limousin (mentioned in the trial records) with a story from his military life.

One aspect of how military service was rendered in the order can be gathered from the testimony of a former Templar, the knight William *de Rezes*, who probably originated from the Limousin and had been received into the order in 1288 at Paulhac: immediately after his reception, he was sent to the east, where he stayed for three years.[36] Was it a common practice to send new recruits to fight for a limited time on the battlefield?[37] The second and last brother from Limousin who is known to have served in the east is William of *Chamborand* or *Chamborent*, commander of Blaudeix from 1304/5 until 1307. Because of reading errors, this knight, who was one of the four procurators linked to the defence of the order, is often wrongly referred to as William of *Chambonnet*. He appeared several times in April and May of 1310 during the trial at Paris,[38] and he is mentioned in all works dealing with these proceedings.[39] However, on 17 December 1310, he relinquished his charge while two of the procurators were absent. According to one deposition, he assisted James of Molay on Cyprus with a reception ceremony conducted at Limassol between Easter and Pentecost of 1304 and attended by over 120 brothers.[40] Undoubtedly, he was participating in a general chapter there.[41] With the exception of his presence on Cyprus in 1304, we know nothing about his career between his reception in 1276 and his first known transaction in 1305.

With regard to some forty Templars from the diocese of Limoges (apart from those questioned elsewhere, such as at Poitiers and Clermont), the trial records allow us to follow a portion of their careers and transfers. We have no information concerning the reasons for their distance from their region of origin. Were they on a mission? Were they residing in some distant house? Was their presence elsewhere a coincidence? Twenty-five brothers were transferred only within the borders of the diocese. That is more than half of those under consideration, and it shows just how limited mobility was in many cases. Ten brothers can be traced in neighbouring regions. The sergeant Peter *de Claustro*, for example, had been received in 1300 in the diocese of Saintes.[42] John *Durandi* spent his entire career, from his reception in

1289 until his arrest, in the neighbouring diocese of Poitiers. The other eight had very similar careers. Two of them had been received in houses that were further away. The Templar knight Peter *de Conders*, commander of a house in the Limousin in 1307, came from Picardy, in the north of modern-day France, where he had made his profession in 1293 before Geoffrey of Vichiers, the Templar visitor of France.[43] The aforementioned Peter of Noblat, who recalled the tenure of the Templar master William of Beaujeu in the Holy Land, had been received into the order in Bordeaux in 1291 and was present in Angers in 1299 when Geoffrey of Gonneville, the master of Poitou, received two brothers from the *lingua gallicana* into the order. This incident alludes to the linguistic differences between the north and the south of France.[44] The Templar sergeant Gerald *de Augnihaco* was the last commander of Nantes.[45] He had been received into the order in the diocese of Angoulême in 1291 and can be found in two different houses in Poitou in 1299 and 1303.[46] During his interrogation in Paris on 20 March 1311, he stated that the Holy Cross was venerated in 'outremer'.[47]

Three Templars with ties to the Limousin stand out. These are, first of all, two of the provincial masters of Auvergne-Limousin, namely Gerard of Sauzet and *Franco de Bort*. Between 1289 and 1291, Gerard's office took him very frequently from one house to the other.[48] We know of one of his receptions in the diocese of Autun in 1291, as well as ten others in less distant locations. *Franco de Bort*, who is less well known, nevertheless had a more impressive career.[49] His presence at a reception ceremony in the neighbouring diocese of Poitiers is recorded for 1249.[50] According to a sergeant from the diocese of Clermont, he himself received around 120 brothers into the order.[51] These receptions took place between 1267 and 1291, all of them (with one exception) in the dioceses of Limoges and Clermont. He served as commander of Aquitaine in 1261, of Provence in 1267 and then of Auvergne-Limousin between 1274 (or 1279) and 1289, but was also the commander of various houses in 1269, 1286 and 1291. He functioned as visitor *citra mare* in 1271–3 and 1279.[52] In June 1261, he was the lieutenant of Guy of Bazainville, the master of the Templar houses in France.[53] Thus, he was a fairly well-travelled man who had held a number of different offices in the order as was customary for the Templars' leadership personnel.[54] His career is somewhat difficult to follow as most of the information pertaining to him comes from the Templars' trial testimonies. Did their memory never betray them? When using the trial records as sources, we find ourselves confronted with the problem of their reliability. Since *Franco de Bort* passed away before the trial, we do not have his own deposition to confirm or to correct the depositions of others. The last person of interest here is the Templar Humbert of Comborn, a member of one of the four great local vicecomital families. He served as the commander of the house of Paulhac between 1298 and 1306, and in this function he moved around a great deal considering the fairly low level of this appointment. Having been received in a house in the diocese of Poitiers in 1295 or 1296, this knight conducted around ten reception ceremonies in the diocese of Limoges. We also find that three of the last provincial masters of Auvergne-Limousin, namely Peter of Madic, Gerard of Sauzet and Raymond of Mareuil, came to the house of Paulhac to hold chapter meetings there, which reveals this house as one of the most important of the entire region.[55]

On the basis of so few examples, it is difficult to present definitive conclusions. However, it seems that the material surveyed here suggests that most of the Templars of the Limousin were moved around within their province. Several years ago, Alan Forey came to very similar findings with regard to Mas-Deu, Lérida and the British Isles. He also noted that most of the Templars interrogated at Clermont had in fact been received into the order in the province of Auvergne. For him, receptions that had taken place in houses located further away were the exception.[56] Could this have to do with the fact that the Templars' 'glory days' were more or less over? Since 1291, the Templars participated in very few military expeditions. Their needs were different. Forey has compared the Templars' mobility with that of the mendicant orders where the new recruit joined an order and not a particular house, but has also pointed out that the mobility of personnel between provinces was more important in the mendicant orders than in the Order of the Temple.[57] Jürgen Sarnowsky has interpreted the mobility in the military and mendicant orders by describing them as the 'military and spiritual arms of the papacy'.[58] Of the sixty-nine Templars interrogated at Clermont, forty-nine originated from the diocese of Clermont and seventeen from the diocese of Limoges.[59] Would an investigation conducted fifty or one hundred years earlier have yielded the same results? Perhaps one would find a greater mobility between east and west, between front line and rearguard, in the days when those who had been lost needed to be replaced.

(Translated from the French by Jochen Burgtorf)

Notes

[1] Jean-Marie Allard, 'Templiers et hospitaliers en Limousin au Moyen Âge: État de la recherche et nouvelles considérations', *Revue Mabillon*, 14 (2003), 53–7.

[2] Rita Lejeune, 'L'esprit de croisade dans l'épopée occitane', *Cahiers de Fanjeaux*, 4 (1969), 143–73; Antoine Thomas, 'Le roman de Gouffier de Lastours', *Romania*, 34 (1905), 55–65; Gaston Paris, 'La Chanson d'Antioche provençale et la *Gran conquista de Ultramar*', *Romania*, 17 (1888), 513–41, 19 (1890), 562–91, 22 (1893), 345–63; Paul Meyer, 'Fragment d'une chanson d'Antioche en provençal', *Archives de l'Orient Latin*, 2 (1884), 467–509; *The Canso d'Antioca: An Occitan Epic Chronicle of the First Crusade*, ed. Carol Sweetenham and Linda M. Paterson (Aldershot, 2003). The grateful lion faithfully followed Gouffier on his travels and even wanted to accompany him to France. When the commander of the ship prohibited the animal from coming on board, the lion, according to the legend, jumped into the water, but later drowned from exhaustion.

[3] Amédée Trudon des Ormes, *Liste des maisons et de quelques dignitaires de l'ordre du Temple en Syrie, en Chypre et en France d'après les pièces du procès* (Paris, 1900), p. 204.

[4] Émile-G. Léonard, *Introduction au cartulaire manuscrit du Temple (1150–1317), constitué par le marquis d'Albon et conservé à la Bibliothèque nationale, suivie d'un tableau des maisons françaises du Temple et de leurs précepteurs* (Paris, 1930), p. 165.

[5] Alain Demurger, *Jacques de Molay: Le crépuscule des templiers* (Paris, 2002), p. 103.

[6] Jean-Marie Allard, 'Complément sur les origines du prieuré d'Auvergne de l'ordre des Hospitaliers de Saint-Jean de Jérusalem', *Bulletin de la Société archéologique et historique du Limousin*, 130 (2002), 91–7.

[7] This paper mainly relies on the following editions: Jules Michelet (ed.), *Le procès des Templiers*, 2 vols (Paris, 1841–51); Konrad Schottmüller (ed.), *Der Untergang des Templer-Ordens*, 2 vols (Berlin, 1887); Heinrich Finke, *Papsttum und Untergang des Templerordens*, 2 vols (Münster, 1907); Roger Sève et Anne-Marie Chagny-Sève, *Le procès des templiers d'Auvergne (1309–11): Édition de l'interrogatoire de juin 1309* (Paris, 1986).

[8] Eight commanders, two priests, two brothers who had been received in a house in the diocese of Limoges, one residing in one of the local houses and three brothers identified by their patronymics (Durand of Limoges, William of Limoges and Peter of Limoges).

[9] Nine brothers were at some point in a Templar house in the Limousin; however, it is unclear whether they originated from the area. Therefore, they have not been included in this survey. One of them, a knight, was imprisoned in Avignon in 1311 (Michelet, *Procès*, vol. 2, p. 222). The editors of the trial of the Templars at Clermont estimate the number of Templars originating from the diocese of Limoges at ninety-seven (Sève, *Le procès des templiers d'Auvergne*, pp. 31–2).

[10] Sève, *Le procès des templiers d'Auvergne*, p. 31.

[11] For Cahors, see Finke, *Papsttum und Untergang des Templerordens*, vol. 2, pp. 316–17 and Louis Esquieu, 'Les templiers de Cahors', *Bulletin de la Société des études littéraires, scientifiques et artistiques du Lot*, 23 (1898), 176–7, 24 (1899), 5–7. For Poitiers, see Schottmüller, *Untergang des Templer-Ordens*, vol. 2, pp. 9–71 and Finke, *Papsttum und Untergang des Templerordens*, vol. 2, pp. 332–4.

[12] Michelet, *Procès*, vol. 1, pp. 75–7, 98–9.

[13] Ibid., vol. 1, pp. 62, 82, 86, 230.

[14] Stephen *de Glotonis*, a forty-year-old sergeant, on 22 May 1311 (Michelet, *Procès*, vol. 2, p. 254).

[15] Sève, *Le procès des templiers d'Auvergne*, p. 164 (interrogation), 61 and 76. He did not mention this at Paris. He seemed *valde simplex* (very ignorant) to the members of the papal commission, but it was noted that he understood Latin (Michelet, *Procès*, vol. 2, p. 256).

[16] Michelet, *Procès*, vol. 2, p. 215: *Dixit tamen quod dictus frater Guillelmus habebat magnam amiciciam cum soldano et Saracenis, quia aliter non potuisset ipse vel ordo tunc ultra mare remansisse*; see also Demurger, *Jacques de Molay*, p. 79. Alan Forey mentions Peter of Noblat in 'Recruitment to the military orders (twelfth to mid-fourteenth centuries)', *Viator*, 17 (1986), 139–71, here 170. The accusation is contained in a speech made by William of Plaisians at the first consistory at Poitiers on 29 May 1308; see Georges Lizerand, *Le dossier de l'affaire des templiers* (Paris, 1923), pp. 122–3.

[17] This is so like the case related in the order's own records that it presumably refers to the same case: Henri de Curzon (ed.), *La règle du Temple* (Paris, 1886), pp. 297–8 no. 573.

[18] Malcolm Barber, *The Trial of the Templars*, second edition (Cambridge, 1993), p. 186.

[19] Michelet, *Procès*, vol. 2, pp. 222–4; Salomon Reinach, 'La tête magique des templiers', *Revue de l'histoire des religions*, 63 (1911), 32–4; Barber, *Trial of the Templars*, pp. 186–8.

[20] Michelet, *Procès*, vol. 2, p. 238.

[21] Ibid., vol. 2, pp. 224–5; Demurger, *Jacques de Molay*, pp. 101–8; Barbara Frale, *L'ultima battaglia dei Templari* (Roma, 2001), pp. 17–19, does not question this testimony.

[22] He had been absolved by the bishop of Limoges (Michelet, *Procès*, vol. 2, p. 220).

[23] Schottmüller, *Untergang des Templer-Ordens*, vol. 2, p. 65.

[24] Ibid., vol. 2, p. 52. Finke, *Papsttum und Untergang des Templerordens*, vol. 2, p. 317, believes that his reception took place at Acre.

[25] Michelet, *Procès*, vol. 2, p. 16 (interrogation of Thomas de *Panpalona* on 9 March 1311).

[26] Ibid., vol. 2, p. 153. At Clermont, Bertrand of Sartiges did not mention the Muslim attack during his reception into the order, but rather indicated that

Reynald *de Bort* was present at the event (Sève, *Le procès des templiers d'Auvergne*, p. 220).

[27] Sève, *Le procès des templiers d'Auvergne*, p. 221.

[28] Ibid., p. 81.

[29] They probably died in captivity. Alan Forey, 'The military orders and the ransoming of captives from Islam (twelfth to early fourteenth centuries)', *Studia monastica*, 33 (1991), 259–79, here 279: 'for those in the East the chances of liberation were probably smaller than in the Iberian peninsula'.

[30] Michelet, *Procès*, vol. 2, p. 221.

[31] Ibid., vol. 2, p. 222. Hugh *Fauro* stated: *Citra mare autem vidit recipi fratrem Andream de Venthodoro militem quondam de Lemovicinio, captum apud Tortosis per Saracenos, in dicta capella de Bella Chassanha.*

[32] Schottmüller, *Untergang des Templer-Ordens*, vol. 2, p. 160. Trudon des Ormes, *Liste des maisons*, p. 39.

[33] Alain Demurger, *Chevaliers du Christ: Les Ordres religieux-militaires au Moyen Âge, XIe–XVIe siècle* (Paris, 2002), p. 217.

[34] Michelet, *Procès*, vol. 2, p. 99 (23 March 1311). This is the only time when his geographical origin is clearly indicated; note on Gerard of Sauzet in Sève, *Le procès des templiers d'Auvergne*, pp. 294–5.

[35] Joseph Delaville le Roulx (ed.), 'Un nouveau manuscrit de la règle du Temple', *Annuaire-Bulletin de la Société de l'histoire de France*, 26 (1889), 185–214, here 208–11. The new edition is Judi Upton-Ward (ed.), *The Catalan Rule of the Templars* (Woodbridge, 2003), pp. 80–7 no. 180. See Marion Melville, *La vie des templiers*, second edition (Paris, 1974), pp. 256–8 and Judi Upton-Ward, 'The surrender of Gaston and the rule of the Templars', in Malcolm Barber (ed.), *The Military Orders*, vol. 1, *Fighting for the Faith and Caring for the Sick* (Aldershot, 1994), pp. 179–88, here 186–7.

[36] Schottmüller, *Untergang des Templer-Ordens*, vol. 2, pp. 18–19. Upon his return to France, he received permission from Peter of Madic, the Templar master of Auvergne-Limousin, to leave the order (in 1291/2, during a general chapter held in the Auvergne). During his interrogation at Poitiers, William *de Rezes* was referred to as *miles, olim templarius* (a knight, a former Templar).

[37] Alan Forey, 'Towards a profile of the Templars in the early fourteenth century', in Barber (ed.), *Military Orders*, vol. 1, pp. 196–204, here 201.

[38] Note on William of *Chamborand* in Sève, *Le procès des templiers d'Auvergne*, pp. 278–9.

[39] He is already mentioned with the cognomen *Chambonnet* in Pierre Dupuy, *Traittez concernant l'histoire de France, sçavoir la condamnation des templiers* (Paris, 1654), pp. 146–7, 155, 160.

[40] Michelet, *Procès*, vol. 1, p. 562.

[41] Trudon des Ormes, *Liste des maisons*, p. 48.

[42] Schottmüller, *Untergang des Templer-Ordens*, vol. 2, p. 16.

[43] Ibid., vol. 2, p. 49; Trudon des Ormes, *Liste des maisons*, pp. 29, 164, 216.

[44] Michelet, *Procès*, vol. 2, p. 214; Trudon des Ormes, *Liste des maisons*, pp. 5, 187.

45 Michelet, *Procès*, vol. 2, p. 82; Trudon des Ormes, *Liste des maisons*, p. 188; Amédée Guillotin de Corson, *Les templiers et les hospitaliers de Saint-Jean de Jérusalem dits chevaliers de Malte en Bretagne* (Nantes, 1902), p. 173, calls him 'Gérald Le Juge d'Augniac'.

46 Michelet, *Procès*, vol. 2, pp. 84, 90, 102; Trudon des Ormes, *Liste des maisons*, pp. 196, 186. He is referred to as *Gerardus de Anguihaco alias Judicis* in 1299 and as *Gerardus Judicis de Auginhaco* in 1303.

47 Michelet, *Procès*, vol. 2, p. 83.

48 The editors of the trial of the Templars at Clermont believe that this level of appointment was preceeded by a career in 'outremer' (Sève, *Le procès des templiers d'Auvergne*, p. 25).

49 Note in Sève, *Le procès des templiers d'Auvergne*, p. 275.

50 Michelet, *Procès*, vol. 2, p. 7.

51 Ibid., vol. 1, p. 513.

52 Léonard, *Introduction au cartulaire manuscrit du Temple*, p. 17; Sève, *Le procès des templiers d'Auvergne*, p. 221.

53 Melville, *La vie des templiers*, p. 254.

54 Alain Demurger, *Vie et mort de l'ordre du Temple* (Paris, 1989), p. 193; Dominic Selwood, *Knights of the Cloister: Templars and Hospitallers in Central-Southern Occitania, 1100–1300* (Woodbridge, 1999), p. 155.

55 Michelet, *Procès*, vol. 2, p. 124, where Brother *Bertrandus de Villaribus, de diocesi Lemovicensi oriundus*, states that *fratres Petrus de Mandito, Gerardus de Sanzeta et Raymundus de Marolio, preceptores Alvernie successive, dicebant et faciebant predicta quando tenebant eorum capitulia in dicto loco de Paulhaco.* Trudon des Ormes, *Liste des maisons*, p. 211. This house at Paulhac is mentioned more than twenty times in the trial records, which is further proof of its importance.

56 Forey, 'Towards a profile of the Templars', p. 203.

57 Ibid., p. 202: 'Templars joined an Order rather than a house, and there was more mobility within the Temple than among Cluniacs or Cistercians; in this respect the Templars and members of other military orders were more comparable with friars.'

58 Jürgen Sarnowsky, 'Regional problems in the history of the mendicants and military orders', in Jürgen Sarnowsky (ed.), *Mendicants, Military Orders and Regionalism in Medieval Europe* (Ashgate, 1999), pp. 1–18, here pp. 2–5.

59 Sève, *Le procès des templiers d'Auvergne*, p. 31.

13

Hospitaller Officials of Foreign Origin in the Hungarian-Slavonian Priory (Thirteenth and Fourteenth Centuries)

ZSOLT HUNYADI

For quite some time now, scholars have been emphasizing the international character of the Hospital and its French dominance from the late twelfth to the fourteenth century. However, apart from research on the order's central administration, only very few studies have addressed the horizontal mobility of the Hospitallers' provincial officials. With regard to the order's Hungarian-Slavonian priory, most historians have acknowledged the presumably foreign origin of the priory's officials, but few historians have made any efforts to identify these Hospitaller individuals and their origins. The recent research of Anthony Luttrell and Karl Borchardt has shed much light on the Hospital's thirteenth- and fourteenth-century central European dignitaries. Thus, the – still incomplete – list of the Hungarian-Slavonian priory's high officials can now be reconstructed; augmented with the results of my own research, a more thorough picture of the officials' mobility and the order's activities emerges.

Nameless Hungarian Hospitaller priors appear in the charters in the early thirteenth century, for example in 1208,[1] 1217 (specified as *P*)[2] and 1222,[3] and a certain *R* (or *B*), Hospitaller proctor *in Hungaria*, is mentioned in 1216.[4] As was customary in Europe at the time, the title *procurator* was used in a variety of different contexts: in the early decades it may have referred to an officer in charge of a commandery, but later it was also given to lieutenants, deputies, visitors and – occasionally – officials entrusted with particular cases (*procurator in hac causa*).

Two identifiable officials surface in the second quarter of the thirteenth century. A charter dating from 1226 mentions a *magnus magister* named John, even though the circumscription of his seal attached to the same charter refers to him as prior (*S. Prioris Vngarie Hospitalis*).[5] For 1225, that is one year earlier, a *procurator*, whose name is abbreviated as *R* and who may have been Rembald of Voczon, can be identified.[6]

Rembald appears in the sources between 1232 and 1254 as the provincial master of Hungary and Slavonia, grand commander, prior and *preceptor in partibus cismarinis*. Conrad IV, king of the Romans, referred to him as grand commander of Italy, Hungary and Austria in 1253 and 1254;[7] this title is, however, not recorded in any Hungarian sources. Neither John's nor Rembald's origin can yet be ascertained with certainty. However, with regard to Rembald, Jean Raybaud's suggestion is worth considering. According to him, Rembald may have originated from Beauson (Provence) and may have been identical with the commander of Dua Lamec.[8] He served as *visitator* in the priory of St Gilles in 1246. It is likely that he stayed abroad for a longer period of time since he is not recorded in any Hungarian source between 1244 and 1247. Rembald's extensive horizontal mobility supports the assumption of his foreign origin. He was a very active figure during the second quarter of the thirteenth century, functioning as a deputy of King Andrew II (1205–35) in Rome in 1232 and playing an important role as a judge-delegate of the Holy See.

In 1243, a certain Ambrose, canon of the Buda collegiate chapter, served as the Hospital's general proctor and lieutenant master during the Mongol invasion.[9] He was the first and, for a long time, only high official of presumably Hungarian origin, which can perhaps be explained by the extraordinary situation caused by the Mongols.

According to historical tradition,[10] a certain Jordan heads the list of the Hospital's Hungarian-Slavonian officials for the second half of the thirteenth century. It is, however, doubtful whether he was even a Hospitaller. There is no contemporary source confirming that he belonged to the order. What is more, a charter issued by King Béla IV in 1259 reports that one Arnold was Rembald's immediate successor as grand commander.[11] It seems that Ede Reiszig and subsequent historians mistook Jordan, the Templar master of the Hungarian province between 1256 and 1258, for a Hospitaller.[12] However, there can be no doubt that Arnold led the Hungarian-Slavonian priory in 1259, and it is quite probable that he was in office as early as 1255.

By 1262, Arnold had been succeeded by a certain Ferrustan of unknown origin.[13] Two Frenchmen followed, namely Pons of Fay (1267–76) from Auvergne[14] and Hugh Boraldy who served as Pons's lieutenant in 1275.[15] There is a hiatus between the tenure of Ferrustan and that of Pons of Fay: all that is known for this period is that the German Henry of Fürstenberg served as grand commander of the German, Hungarian, Bohemian, Polish and Scandinavian priories (1266). This suggests that one of the above-mentioned officials was – still or already – in charge of the Hungarian-Slavonian priory.[16] A somewhat similar situation occurred about a decade later: in 1279, Hermann Brunshorn served as grand (*summus*) commander of the Austrian, Bohemian, Moravian, Polish and Hungarian priories while a year later he was named as lieutenant master (*gerensque vices summi magistri*).[17]

In the last decades of the thirteenth century, the Hungarian-Slavonian priors continued to be of foreign, admittedly non-identifiable, origin. Most of them seem to have arrived from Italy or governed the priory from Italy. This situation became an obvious parallel to the consolidation of the rulership of the Neapolitan Angevin king, Charles Robert, in the first half of the fourteenth century. At least two dozen Hospitallers of Italian origin can be identified in Hungary on the basis of charters issued between 1315 and the 1340s. Among them, the Italian Gragnanas are probably the most remarkable: Rolando (1315)[18] and Filippo de Gragnana (1317–29) acted as priors, while Francesco (1319–20)[19] and Girardo de Gragnana (1321–2, 1326–8)[20] were lieutenants and proctors in the priory. The last representative of the Gragnana 'clan' was Pietro[21] who, in 1329, served as commander of several Hungarian commanderies. Until recently, I shared Anthony Luttrell's opinion concerning the origin of the Gragnanas, namely the idea that they came from northern Tuscany, from the Garfagnana region.[22] However, so far no unequivocal source has come to light proving that the members of the Gragnana 'clan' (provided that they were related at all and not merely fellow townsmen) did, in fact, come from Tuscany. Utilizing a charter from 1294,[23] one may now be able to trace them in a different direction, namely to the priory of Venice. This charter is the first known written evidence establishing a half-way link between the Gragnanas and Hungary. It features Engherrand de Gragnana, prior of Venice,[24] one of the very first Gragnanas who had a 'career' as a Hospitaller. In the charter he is named as *Angeran de Grignano*. The town of Grignano lies in the Italian region of Friuli, which formed a part of the Hospitaller priory of Venice.[25] The Gragnanas' origin is probably to be sought here.

This hypothesis may be strengthened by the activity of Rolando de Gragnana in Hungary in 1315: just prior to coming to Hungary he had served in Friuli as a Hospitaller brother in the commandery of Sacile.[26] Moreover, Francesco de Gragnana, the Hungarian-Slavonian proctor in 1319–20, also later returned to Sacile where he was commander between 1322 and 1349.[27] It seems that the Italians replaced the French leadership at the turn of the thirteenth and fourteenth centuries, but at the present stage of my research it is not clear whether this was due to the Italian connections of the new dynasty ruling Hungary (Anjou) or to the geographical position of the territory of Friuli – between Venice and the Istrian peninsula, which also belonged to the Hospitaller priory of Venice, and was next door to Hungary. The fact that John of Pula from the Istrian peninsula served as commander of Újudvar (1326) and Bela (1329) seems to confirm the latter notion.[28]

After the 'rule' of the Gragnanas over the Hungarian Hospitallers, the order's grand master in 1330 retained the priory and its incomes.[29] In 1335, the same grand master, Helion de Villeneuve appointed the Provençal Pierre [*Peyre*] Cornuti for five years to the priory,[30] and this appointment was renewed in 1340.[31] It seems that the grand master and the order's convent were satisfied with Pierre's activities, for he was still in office in 1348. One of the reports of the investigation of 1338 conducted in the priory of St Gilles may help to identify Pierre Cornuti. The report on the commandery of Lardiers lists Pierre and Raybaud Cornuti among the *donati* of the commandery.[32] At the same time, a third Cornuti, Hugh, had a *stagia* (residence) in the adjacent commandery of Manosque; earlier, that same Hugh had also been associated with Lardiers.[33] The Cornutis' appearance in Provence as well as in Hungary is not a coincidence. In 1338, one can find a certain Fulk Rocafolii among the brothers of Lardiers. Two years later he served as Pierre Cornuti's lieutenant in Hungary.[34] Moreover, James *de Roderterio*, one of the former *donati* of Lardiers, became commander of a Hungarian commandery by 1350.[35] The Provençal origin of the high officials of the Hungarian-Slavonian priory may explain a unique incident which occurred in 1348: Grand Master Déodat de Gozon exiled François Furoni, the former commander of Santo Stefano di Monopoli (Apulia),[36] who had fallen into the sin of sodomy, to Hungary by asking the prior there to provide François with a *stagia*. François had served the order in southern Italy, but he was originally from Provence.[37]

Pierre was succeeded by another Cornuti in 1348. However, there was a strange interlude preceding the priorship of Baudon Cornuti (1348–74). The Hungarian ruler, King Louis I, had given the priory to the infamous condottiere, the Provençal Montreal du Bar also known as Frà Moriale,[38] who would later be executed for his misdeeds in Rome in 1354.[39] His peculiar role is mirrored in the clause of a charter issued in 1347, reporting that the seal of the priory had been taken away by the rebellious Montreal who alienated many goods of the priory with the help of its seal.[40] Thus, Montreal's priorship was rather memorable, though it was very short and he was quickly stripped of his title. Baudon Cornuti became lieutenant prior in the spring of 1348,[41] and from the autumn of the same year until 1374 he bore the title of prior without interruption.[42]

The postlude to Baudon's priorship proved problematic, as King Louis I used the vacancy to interfere in the affairs of the order again. He wanted a certain Provençal Hospitaller to take over the Hungarian-Slavonian priory, namely Raymond de Beaumont (*Bellomonte*) who had served as commander of Csurgó and Újudvar since 1366 and as lieutenant prior in 1373.[43] However, Pope Gregory XI wanted to give the priory to another Provençal, namely the influential Bertrand Flotte. When the Hospitaller grand master installed a third candidate – Giovanni Rivara, the order's prior of Venice[44] – the king objected to Giovanni and Bertrand by referring to an agreement of the *langues* (or tongues) of Italy and Provence, enacted in November 1373 when Baudon had still been alive.[45] According to this agreement, the first vacancy in the office gave the grand master the right to appoint the Hungarian prior, but subsequent priors were supposed to be elected alternately from the *langues* of Italy and Provence.[46] Considering the bitter memory of his previous wars with Venice, the Hungarian king resented the appointment of Giovanni Rivara despite Pope Gregory XI's assurances that Rivara was not of Venetian origin, but from Piedmont. The papal intervention was disregarded and the prior's seat was given to Raymond de Beaumont, who then held it until 1381.[47] Raymond resumed the office again in 1384 while also serving as commander of Csurgó.[48]

Similarly to the various Italian Gragnanas and the various Provençal Cornutis, Raymond was not the only Provençal Beaumont in the Hungarian-Slavonian priory.[49] While Raymond held the office of prior, Arnold de Beaumont served as lieutenant prior, and the same Arnold can also be documented as commander of Csurgó and Újudvar.[50]

The Great Schism of 1378 divided the Hungarian-Slavonian priory as well. Prior Raymond de Beaumont decided to follow Pope Urban VI, but an ambitious Hungarian Hospitaller, John of Palisna (1379–83, 1386/7–1391/2), attempting to ingratiate himself with the order's grand master, Juan Fernández de Heredia, took the side of Pope Clement VII.

John started to bear the title of the Hungarian-Slavonian prior as early as 1379[51] but was not officially appointed until 1382.[52] The following year, despite the fact that he was now the 'legitimate' prior and despite an explicit request from the grand master, John did not attend the general chapter in Valence-sur-Rhône,[53] perhaps because he was already hindered by the active role he had played in the struggles for the Hungarian throne. From then on, Heredia[54] and the Anti-Master Ricardo Caracciolo alternately assigned commanders to Hungarian commanderies, although there is no sign of *responsiones* or other dues paid during this time.

The peculiarity of the whole situation is well demonstrated by the case of the commandery of Dubica. In March 1383, after Dubica's commander (Alfred) had died, Juan Fernández de Heredia assigned Jacopo de Leone, the Hospitaller captain of Smyrna, as commander of Dubica for ten years.[55] Jacopo did not finish his tenure there – not because he was reported dead in July 1386,[56] but because, in May 1384, the Anti-Master Riccardo Caracciolo had appointed Arnold de Beaumont as commander of Dubica.[57] Two months later, Heredia moved Jacopo to a vacant commandery in the priory of Venice, perhaps as a move to compensate him for the loss of Dubica.[58] By April 1385, however, a certain Lucas[59] governed the commandery of Dubica, and since he was an adherent of John of Palisna, he may have been appointed by Heredia. The later career of Lucas is unknown, but in July 1386 Gérard Cornuti was installed as commander of Dubica for ten years.[60] Thus Dubica had four different commanders within three years.

After the rebellion of John of Palisna against the queens (Maria, the daughter of Louis I, and her mother Elizabeth), the development picked up speed.[61] In 1384, Raymond de Beaumont was back as prior, indicating that the 'Roman' obedience had countervailed, and the Anti-Master Ricardo Caracciolo assigned Arnold de Beaumont and Baudon *de Monte Iustino* to several Hungarian commanderies for ten years.[62] The following spring, a new prior was in office, namely the Hungarian John of Hédervár. By the summer of 1386, John was bishop-elect of Györ,[63] but he must have resigned the Hospitaller priorship earlier, because a new prior was in office as early as September 1385, namely *Ranforsatus de Castellana. Ranforsatus*'s activities imply that he had been appointed by Grand Master Heredia, but he did not enjoy the incomes of the priory for long, because the Anti-Master Ricardo Caracciolo appointed Gérard Cornuti, an adherent of the 'Roman' obedience, as *procurator* of the priory of Vrana on 15 June 1386.[64] Only three weeks earlier, on 23 May 1386, in a charter issued in Genoa, Caracciolo had referred to John of Palisna as *gubernator* of the priory.[65] Gérard Cornuti's appointment did not hinder Palisna from usurping the title of prior until his death in 1391/2.[66] Formally, neither Heredia nor the pope deprived Palisna of the priorship. Palisna's priorship still awaits a thorough analysis; he was an important figure in the long process of bringing native Hungarians to prominence in the governance of the Hungarian-Slavonian priory.

A development very similar to the one just outlined for the provincial priors of Hungary and Slavonia can be seen, for the same time period, with regard to the higher officials of individual Hungarian-Slavonian commanderies. In many cases the personnel of commanderies can be reconstructed from the lists of dignitaries (*series dignitatum*) inserted into the closing passages of charters or from the activities registered in charters issued by Hospitaller commanderies which served as places of authentication (*loca credibilia*).[67] A recent survey[68] shows that with some exceptions the high officials of the commanderies – commanders, priors and *custodes* – were of foreign, presumably French and Italian origin until the end of the 1370s.[69] The first commander of evident Hungarian origin was a certain Peter (1308–21), the descendant of a well-to-do family from Sopron on the westernmost edge of the kingdom.[70] In the course of the fourteenth century more and more officials of probable local origin appear: Simon (Csurgó), Andrew (Dubica), John (Gora, Našice-Martin, Újudvar), Robert, Benedict and Michael (Székesfehérvár). The process that took place in the leadership of the Hungarian-Slavonian priory found its counterpart in one of the most significant commanderies of the kingdom. In the commandery of Székesfehérvár, the brothers of minor rank, namely the choir priests, were natives as early as the middle of the fourteenth century, while their superiors were not primarily of Hungarian origin until the end of the same century.[71]

The question of origin raised in connection with Hospitallers who appear in the Hungarian sources can often be answered indirectly. In this respect, one needs to consider the activities of nine Hungarian Hospitaller commanderies, namely the ones that served as places of authentication: the mere fact that they fulfilled this function implies that some of their brothers must have spoken the vernacular as well as studied customary law, that they must have been familiar with local customs (*consuetudo terrae*) or with the customs of the realm (*consuetudo regni*).[72] Partly as a consequence of this activity, the proportion of the native members of the order gradually increased, but foreigners continued to play a prominent role in the leadership of the Hungarian-Slavonian priory until the beginning of the sixteenth century. However, it is unknown to what extent foreign officials actually participated in the administrative interaction between the commanderies and the outside world. At times at least, these foreign priors were represented by their native chaplains, thus obviating the need for direct contact: thus in 1315 Rolando de Gragnana was represented by his chaplain Nicholas, while in 1325 Filippo de Gragnana was represented by chaplain George (who was *presbyter, capellanus et scriptor* of the order).[73] The question of how these foreign officials interacted with the local Hungarians is a matter for future research.

Notes

[1] Georgius Fejér (ed.), *Codex diplomaticus Hungariae ecclesiasticus ac civilis*, 11 vols (Buda, 1829–44), vol. 3, pt. 1, pp. 56–7; Vilmos Fraknói (ed.), *Veszprémi püspökség római oklevéltára: Monumenta romana episcopatus Wesprimiensis, 1103–1526*, 3 vols (Budapest, 1896–1907), vol. 1, p. 17; Joseph Delaville le Roulx (ed.), *Cartulaire général de l'ordre des Hospitaliers de Saint-Jean de Jérusalem (1100–1310)* (Paris, 1894–1905), vol. 2, no. 1302.

[2] Gusztáv Wenzel (ed.), *Codex diplomaticus Arpadianus continuatus*, 12 vols (Pest, 1860–74), vol. 6, pp. 380–3; Delaville, *Cartulaire*, vol. 2, no. 1605.

[3] Fejér, *Codex diplomaticus*, vol. 3, pt. 1, pp. 383–4; vol. 3, pt. 5, p. 383; Delaville, *Cartulaire*, vol. 2, no. 1747.

[4] László Erdélyi and Pongrác Sörös (eds), *A pannonhalmi Szent-Benedek-rend története* (History of the Benedictine Order of Pannonhalma), 12 vols (Budapest 1902–16), vol. 1, pp. 164, 638; Wenzel, *Codex diplomaticus*, vol. 6, pp. 377–9; Fraknói, *Veszprémi püspökség*, vol. 1, pp. 36–7; Delaville, *Cartulaire*, vol. 2, no. 1472.

[5] Erdélyi and Sörös, *A pannonhalmi*, vol. 1, pp. 672–3; Fraknói, *Veszprémi püspökség*, vol. 1, p. 70; Ferdinandus Knauz et al. (eds), *Monumenta Ecclesiae Strigoniensis*, 4 vols (Esztergom/Budapest, 1874–1999), vol. 1, pp. 260, 278; Wenzel, *Codex diplomaticus*, vol. 1, pp. 222–3.

[6] Augustinus Theiner (ed.), *Vetera monumenta historica Hungariam sacram illustrantia, 1216–1352*, 2 vols (Rome, 1859–60), vol. 1, pp. 61–2; Fraknói, *Veszprémi püspökség*, vol. 1, p. 66; Knauz, *Monumenta Ecclesiae Strigoniensis*, vol. 1, p. 254; Wenzel, *Codex diplomaticus*, vol. 1, pp. 211–12.

[7] Delaville, *Cartulaire*, vol. 2, nos 2615, 2638, 2663; see Karl Borchardt, 'The Hospitallers, Bohemia, and the empire, 1250–1330', in Jürgen Sarnowsky (ed.), *Mendicants, Military Orders and Regionalism in Medieval Europe* (Ashgate, 1999), pp. 201–32, here pp. 205–6.

8   Jean Raybaud, *Histoire des grands prieurs et du prieuré de Saint-Gilles*, 3 vols (Nîmes, 1904–6), vol. 1, pp. 156, 163.

9   Ede Reiszig, *A jeruzsálemi Szent János lovagrend Magyarországon* (The Order of the Knights of St John of Jerusalem in Hungary), 2 vols (Budapest, 1925–8), vol. 2, p. 58; see also Zsolt Hunyadi, 'Cruciferi domus hospitalis per Hungariam et Sclavoniam: A johanniták Magyarországon a 14. század végéig' (The Hospitallers in Hungary up to the end of the fourteenth century), *Aetas*, 17, 4 (2002), 52–76, here 66.

10 Reiszig, *A jeruzsálemi*, vol. 1, p. 68; vol. 2, p. 164.

11 Fejér, *Codex diplomaticus*, vol. 4, pt. 2, pp. 492–5; Wenzel, *Codex diplomaticus*, vol. 9, pp. 456–7; Delaville, *Cartulaire*, vol. 2, no. 2932; Marko Kostrenčić Tadija Smičiklas (eds), *Codex diplomaticus regni Croatiae, Dalmatiae ac Slavoniae*, 18 vols (Zagreb, 1904–90), vol. 5, pp. 135–6.

12 Smičiklas, *Codex diplomaticus*, supplement 1, pp. 206–8.

13 Fejér, *Codex diplomaticus*, vol. 4, pt. 3, pp. 98–9; vol. 6, pt. 2, p. 110; Kálmán Géresi (ed.), *A nagy-károlyi gróf Károlyi család oklevéltára* (Charters of the Károlyi family), 5 vols (Budapest, 1882–97), vol. 1, pp. 2–3; Delaville, *Cartulaire*, vol. 3, no. 3030.

14 See Anthony Luttrell, 'The Hospitaller province of Alamania to 1428', in Zenon Hubert Nowak (ed.), *Ritterorden und Region: Politische, soziale und wirtschaftliche Verbindungen im Mittelalter*, Ordines militares, Colloquia Torunensia historica, vol. 8 (Toruń, 1995), pp. 21–41, here p. 29; Alan Forey, 'The military orders and holy war against Christians in the thirteenth century', *English Historical Review*, 104 (1989), 1–24, here 3.

15 Wenzel, *Codex diplomaticus*, vol. 9, pp. 128–30; Delaville, *Cartulaire*, vol. 3, no. 3572; Smičiklas, *Codex diplomaticus*, vol. 6, p. 137.

16 Delaville, *Cartulaire*, vol. 3, no. 3219; see also Borchardt, 'The Hospitallers, Bohemia, and the empire', pp. 207, 209.

17 Delaville, *Cartulaire*, vol. 3, nos 3692, 3729. According to recent research, Hermann Brunshorn originated from the region around the Rhine and the Moselle; see Borchardt, 'The Hospitallers, Bohemia, and the empire', p. 211.

18 Imre Nagy and Gyula Tasnádi Nagy (eds), *Anjoukori Okmánytár: Codex diplomaticus Hungaricus Andegavensis*, 7 vols (Budapest, 1878–1920), vol. 1, pp. 376, 389–90.

19 Nagy, *Codex diplomaticus*, vol. 1, pp. 514–15; Fejér, *Codex diplomaticus*, vol. 8, pt. 3, p. 341; Smičiklas, *Codex diplomaticus*, vol. 8, pp. 556–9; National Archives of Hungary, *Collectio Antemohacsiana* (henceforth Dl. and Df.), Dl. 34297.

20 Nagy, *Codex diplomaticus*, vol. 2, pp. 55–6; Smičiklas, *Codex diplomaticus*, vol. 9, pp. 97–8; Fejér, *Codex diplomaticus*, vol. 8, pt. 2, pp. 362–3, 543–5, 562; ibid., vol. 8, pt. 3, p. 341.

21 Df. 257974; Df. 258481.

22 Anthony Luttrell, 'The Hospitallers of Rhodes between Tuscany and Jerusalem: 1306–1431', *Revue Mabillon*, 64 (1992), 117–38, here 121, 134; Anthony Luttrell, 'The Hospitaller priory of Venice in 1331', in Enzo Coli,

Maria De Marco and Francesco Tommasi (eds), *Militia Sacra: Gli ordini militari tra Europa e Terrasanta* (Perugia, 1994), pp. 101–43, here pp. 106, 112–13; Anthony Luttrell, 'The Hospitallers in Hungary before 1418: problems and sources', in Zsolt Hunyadi and József Laszlovsky (eds), *The Crusades and the Military Orders: Expanding the Frontiers of Medieval Latin Christianity* (Budapest, 2001), pp. 269–81, here p. 273.

23   Smičiklas, *Codex diplomaticus*, vol. 7, pp. 171–2.

24   The duration of Engherrand de Gragnana's tenure of office as prior of Venice has been subject to debate. According to Luttrell, 'The Hospitaller priory of Venice', p. 106, he served from 1263 until 1293. See also Jonathan Riley-Smith, *The Knights of St. John in Jerusalem and Cyprus c.1050–1310* (London, 1967), p. 356; Annibale Ilari, *Il Granpriorato Giovannita di Roma: Ricerche storiche ed ipotesi* (Taranto, 1998), pp. 76–7; Roberto Greci, 'Prime presenze Gerosolomitane nell'Emilia occidentale e nella bassa Lombardia', in Josepha Costa Restagno (ed.), *Riviera di Levante tra Emilia e Toscana: Un crocevia per l'ordine di San Giovanni* (Genoa, 2001), pp. 405–19, here p. 410. On the basis of the above-mentioned charter, as well as in the light of recent research, the duration of Engherrand's tenure of office can now be revised: he served from 1261 until 1294; see Marina Gazzini, 'L'insediamento Gerosolomitano a Parma nel basso medieoevo: Attività ospedaliera e gestione del culto civico', in Costa Restagno (ed.), *Riviera di Levante tra Emilia e Toscana*, pp. 421–41, here p. 429. Engherrand also acted as prior of Lombardy between 1263 and 1273; see Renato Bordone, 'I cavalieri de San Giovanni ad Asti e nel Monferrato durante il medioevo', in Josepha Costa Restagno (ed.), *Cavalieri de San Giovanni e territorio: La Liguria tra Provenza e Lombardia nei secoli XIII–XVII* (Bordighera, 1999), pp. 339–75, here pp. 354–5, 364; Renato Bordone, 'Priori del gran priorato di Lombardia', in Ricardo Tomasi di Netro and Luisa Clotilde Gentile (eds), '*Gentilhuomini Christiani e Religiosi Cavalieri': Nove secoli dell'Ordine di Malta in Piemonte* (Milan, 2000), p. 163. I would like to thank Elena Bellomo for helping me to procure some of the above-mentioned works.

25   For the location of Grignano, which is near Trieste, see map 5 in Miha Kosi, 'The age of the crusades in the south-east of the empire (between the Alps and the Adriatic)', in Hunyadi and Laszlovszky (eds), *The Crusades and the Military Orders*, pp. 123–65, here p. 146.

26   He served as commander of Padua and Barbarano in 1306 (Padua, Archivio di Stato, Commenda di Malta, Filza no. 7; Vicenza, Archivio di Stato, Corporazioni Religiose Soppresse, Buste 3065–94). He appeared in Treviso in 1311; see Giampaolo Cagnin, *Templari e Giovanniti in Territorio Trevigiano (secoli XII–XIV)* (Treviso, 1992), pp. 26, 77, 88. I would like to thank Anthony Luttrell for drawing my attention to the unpublished primary sources of 1306 and for allowing me to use the notes he made in Italy.

27   Pier Carlo Begotti, *Templari e giovanniti in Friuli: La Mason di San Quirino* (Fiume, Veneto, 1991), pp. 53, 57, 115–16; Luttrell, 'The Hospitaller priory of Venice', p. 133; Benvenuto Castellarin, *Ospedali e commende del Sovrano*

Ordine di San Giovanni di Gerusalemme-di Rodi-di Malta a Volta di Ronchis e in Friuli (Latisana, 1998), p. 68. Castellarin identified another Gragnana in the sources, namely Meus de Gragnana, prior of S. Bartolomeo de Volta in 1367 (ibid., pp. 100–2).

28 Df. 257974; Df. 258481.

29 *Subcriptas baiulias capituli generalis retinuit dominus magistri auctoritate dicti capituli ad manum suam ordinandas per ipsum sup. Videlicet: . . . Priorem Ungarie . . . et prioratus ipsorum.* National Library of Malta, Archives of the Order of Malta (AOM) 280, fol. 21r; edition: Charles L. Tipton, 'The 1330 chapter general of the Knights Hospitallers at Montpellier', *Traditio*, 24 (1968), 293–308, here 308.

30 AOM 280, fol. 33v; edition: Pál Engel, '14. századi magyar vonatkozású iratok a johannita lovagrend máltai levéltárából' (Fourteenth-century documents from the archives of the order of St John in Malta with reference to the history of Hungary), *Történelmi Szemle*, 39 (1997), 111–18, here 115–16; see also Fejér, *Codex diplomaticus*, vol. 8, pt. 4, pp. 204, 465, 530; ibid., vol. 9, pt. 1, pp. 515–18; ibid., vol. 9, pt. 4, p. 614; AOM 317, fol. 211r; Smičiklas, *Codex diplomaticus*, vol. 10, p. 555; ibid., vol. 11, p. 438.

31 See AOM 280, fols 45r–46v.

32 Benoît Beaucage, *Visites générales des commanderies de l'Ordre des Hospitaliers dépendantes du Grand Prieuré de Saint-Gilles, 1338* (Aix-en-Provence, 1982), p. 382; see Luttrell, 'The Hospitallers in Hungary', p. 273.

33 Beaucage, *Visites générales*, p. 369; AOM 280, fol. 34r. There is evidence for another Cornuti (not counting Baudon and Gérard Cornuti) from this region, namely Raymond Cornuti (Manosque): 1389/90, AOM 324, fol. 122r.

34 Beaucage, *Visites générales*, p. 382; Smičiklas, *Codex diplomaticus*, vol. 10, pp. 555–7.

35 Smičiklas, *Codex diplomaticus*, vol. 11, pp. 566–7.

36 AOM 317, fol. 211r–v. It is not certain that Pierre Cornuti was still alive at that time; the last charter that (indirectly) reports him as acting was issued on 10 February 1348: Smičiklas, *Codex diplomaticus*, vol. 11, pp. 438–41.

37 Pierre Furoni was commander of Trinquetaille: AOM 317, fol. 15r; Beaucage, *Visites générales*, pp. 2, 426, 588; see also Anthony Luttrell, 'Le origini della precettoria capitolare di Santo Stefano di Monopoli', in Cosimo D'Angela and Angelo Sante Trisciuzzi (eds), *Fasano nella storia dei Cavalieri di Malta in Puglia*, Atti del Convegno internazionale di studi, Fasano, 14–16 maggio 1998 (Bari, 2001), pp. 89–100, here 98.

38 Reiszig, *A jeruzsálemi*, vol. 1, pp. 100–2; Raybaud, *Histoire des Grands Prieurs*, vol. 1, pp. 311–15.

39 Reiszig, *A jeruzsálemi*, vol. 1, pp. 100–12; see Leone Gessi, 'Fra Moriale', *Rivista del Sovrano Ordine Militare di Malta*, 2, 3 (1938), 13–23.

40 Smičiklas, *Codex diplomaticus*, vol. 12, pp. 165–7.

41 Smičiklas, *Codex diplomaticus*, vol. 11, pp. 444–5; Samu Barabás (ed.), *A római szent birodalmi széki Teleki család oklevéltára* (Charters of the Teleki family) (Budapest, 1895), pp. 84–7.

[42] Dl. 106127 (Fejér, *Codex diplomaticus*, vol. 9, pt. 7, p. 153); Dl. 106134.

[43] Fejér, *Codex diplomaticus*, vol. 9, pt. 4, pp. 523–4.

[44] Theiner, *Vetera monumenta*, vol. 2, pp. 153–4; Joseph Delaville le Roulx, *Les Hospitaliers à Rhodes, 1310–1421* (Paris, 1913), pp. 174, 197; see Anthony Luttrell, 'Change and conflict within the Hospitaller province of Italy after 1291', in Sarnowsky (ed.), *Mendicants, Military Orders and Regionalism*, pp. 185–99, here p. 198; Luttrell, 'The Hospitallers in Hungary', pp. 274–5.

[45] Theiner, *Vetera monumenta*, vol. 2, p. 197; Luttrell, 'The Hospitallers in Hungary', p. 275; Dl. 6203; Dl. 6204; Fejér, *Codex diplomaticus*, vol. 9, pt. 7, pp. 347–56.

[46] 22 November 1373 (1427): AOM 347, fol. 51r–v. It seems that – with the exception of the period of the schism – this agreement remained in place well into the fifteenth century; see AOM 348, fol. 128; R. Valentini, 'Un capitolo generale degli Ospitalieri di S. Giovanni tenuto in Vaticano nel 1446', *Archivio Storico di Malta*, 7 (1936), 133–49, here 134–5.

[47] Theiner, *Vetera monumenta*, vol. 2, p. 197; Delaville, *Les Hospitaliers à Rhodes*, p. 198.

[48] Fejér, *Codex diplomaticus*, vol. 10, pt. 2, p. 179 (Dl. 7111).

[49] Between 1384 and 1386, i.e. during the schism, a third Cornuti (Gérard) played an important role in the Hungarian-Slavonian priory. He followed the Roman obedience and, in addition to serving as commander of Gora and Dubica, became *procurator* of the priory in 1386: AOM 281, fols 92v, 93v.

[50] See for example Fejér, *Codex diplomaticus*, vol. 9, pt. 5, pp. 68–9, vol. 9, pt. 7, pp. 374–6; Dl. 6363; Df. 233327.

[51] Zsolt Hunyadi, 'The Hospitallers in the kingdom of Hungary: commanderies, personnel, and a particular activity up to *c.*1400', in Hunyadi and Laszlovszky (eds), *The Crusades and the Military Orders*, pp. 253–68, here p. 262.

[52] AOM 322, fol. 251r; edition: Zsolt Hunyadi, 'Adalékok a johannita magyarszlavón (vránai) perjelségre kirótt rendi adók kérdéséhez' (Contributions to the question of the taxes levied on the Hungarian-Slavonian Hospitaller priory), *Acta Universitatis Szegediensis, Acta Historica*, 116 (2002), 31–49, here 42–3.

[53] AOM 322, fols 251v–252r.

[54] AOM 322, fol. 253r; Lelja Dobronić, *Viteški redovi: Templari i Ivanovci u Hrvatskoj*, (Knightly orders: Templars and Hospitallers in Croatia) (Zagreb, 1984), pp. 170–1.

[55] AOM 322, fol. 253r; edition (with misreadings): Dobronić, *Viteški redovi*, pp. 170–1.

[56] AOM 323, fol. 192v.

[57] AOM 281, fol. 37v.

[58] AOM 322, fol. 222r.

[59] Lajos Thallóczy and Sándor Horváth (eds), *Codex diplomaticus partium regno Hungariae adnexarum (Comitatuum Dubicza, Orbász et Szana) 1244–1718* (Budapest, 1912), pp. 109, 111; Dl. 35274.

[60] AOM 281, fol. 93v.

[61] Fejér, *Codex diplomaticus*, vol. 10, pt. 1, p. 135.

[62] Within a year, a certain Lucas, a follower of Palisna, had been appointed
      commander of Dubica; he may have been identical with Lucas, the
      Hospitallers' lieutenant prior since 1379: Fejér, *Codex diplomaticus*, vol. 10,
      pt. 1, pp. 130–1; Imre Nagy et al. (eds), *Zala vármegye története: Oklevéltár,
      1024–1490* (A history of Zala county: charters), 2 vols (Budapest, 1886–90),
      vol. 2, pp. 208–9.

[63] Thallóczy and Horváth, *Codex diplomaticus*, p. 111; Béla Radvánszky and
      Levente Závodszky (eds), *A Héderváry család oklevéltára* (Charters of the
      Héderváry family), 2 vols (Budapest, 1909–22), vol. 1, p. 97; Smičiklas,
      Codex diplomaticus, vol. 16, pp. 518–19.

[64] AOM 281, fol. 92v.

[65] AOM 281, fol. 86r–v. In Hungarian sources, Palisna does not resurface as
      prior until 28 January 1387: Fejér, *Codex diplomaticus*, vol. 10, pt. 1, p. 375.

[66] Pál Engel (ed.), *Magyarország világi archontológiája, 1301–1457* (A secular
      archontology of Hungary, 1301–1457), 2 vols (Budapest, 1996), vol. 1, p. 81;
      Neven Budak, 'John of Palisna, the Hospitaller prior of Vrana', in Hunyadi
      and Laszlovszky (eds), *The Crusades and the Military Orders*, pp. 283–90,
      here p. 286.

[67] Zsolt Hunyadi, 'The *Locus Credibilis* in Hungarian Hospitaller commanderies',
      in Anthony Luttrell and Léon Pressouyre (eds), *La Commanderie: Institution
      des ordres militaires dans l'Occident médiéval* (Paris, 2002), pp. 285–96.

[68] Hunyadi, 'Hospitallers in the kingdom of Hungary', pp. 263–4.

[69] For example: William (Bela, Čiče, Csurgó, Hresno, Székesfehérvár, Újudvar);
      Hugh (Csurgó, Pakrac, Székesfehérvár, Újudvar); Giacomo da Siena (Gora);
      Lorenzo de Perugia (Sopron); *Argellin*, John *Gallicus* (Székesfehérvár); Peter
      Ymberthus (Szirák, Szomolya, Tolmács); Marco de Bologna (Vrana). In
      some cases (for example in Sopron), locals can be found among the
      personnel: Rudewan (1274), Theoderic (1276), or Detric (1276) might have
      been local townsmen of German origin.

[70] Jenö Házi (ed.), *Sopron szabad királyi város története: Oklevelek* (A history
      of the royal exempt town of Sopron: charters), 2 vols (Sopron, 1921–43),
      vol. 1, pt. 1, pp. 34–5; Hans Wagner and Irmtraut Lindeck-Pozza (eds),
      *Urkundenbuch des Burgenlandes und der angrenzenden Gebiete der Komitate
      Wieselburg, Ödenburg und Eisenburg*, 4 vols (Graz, Cologne and Vienna,
      1955–85), vol. 3, pp. 129–30.

[71] Zsolt Hunyadi, 'The Knights of St. John and the Hungarian private legal
      literacy up to the mid-fourteenth century', in Marcell Sebök and Balázs Nagy
      (eds), . . . *The Man of Many Devices, Who Wandered Full Many Ways:
      Festschrift in honor of János M. Bak* (Budapest, 1999), pp. 507–19, here p. 514.

[72] Hunyadi, 'The *Locus Credibilis* in Hungarian Hospitaller commanderies',
      p. 291.

[73] Nagy, *Codex diplomaticus*, vol. 1, pp. 389–90; Dl. 2337.

14

Catalan Hospitallers in Rhodes in the First Half of the Fifteenth Century

PIERRE BONNEAUD

Until 1153 the patrimony of the Hospitallers in Aragon and Catalonia was controlled by the Provençal priory of St Gilles; after that it became a separate priory, the so-called castellany of Amposta. By the end of the fourteenth century, the castellany had considerably grown in size as it had been given property, mostly by the kings of Aragon, in the territories of south-western Catalonia, Valencia and Majorca – territories which had been reconquered from the Moors during the twelfth and thirteenth centuries. After the dissolution of the Order of the Temple and lengthy negotiations concluded in 1317, King James II of Aragon obtained permission from the pope to create a new 'national' order, the Order of Montesa, which received all former Templar as well as Hospitaller commanderies in the kingdom of Valencia. The Hospitaller castellany of Amposta was granted the remaining Templar property in Aragon, Catalonia and Majorca (an independent kingdom at the time). The Templar patrimony in these territories was so extensive that the castellany alone was unable to control and properly manage its former and new commanderies. Consequently, in 1319, the Hospital decided to create a new priory. Thirty commanderies in the principality of Catalonia and the kingdom of Majorca were taken from the castellany's supervision in order to form the priory of Catalonia, although the castellany kept four important commanderies in southern Catalonia (in addition to those that it held in Aragon).[1]

The Catalan priory was not one of the most important priories among the order's twenty-three western priories. It controlled only thirty commanderies, while St Gilles, for example, controlled ninety. The prior held four prosperous commanderies as his personal *camerae* (houses from which he drew income for his personal expenses), and about twenty-five commanders and thirty other brother-knights reported to him directly. Despite these rather modest figures, in 1373/5 the priory ranked third among the western priories with regard to the transfer of income of Rhodes in the form of *responsiones, mortuaria* (income from offices whose holders had recently died) and *spolia* (the property of deceased brothers).[2] Majorca, Mas-Deu, Barbera, Gardeny, Barcelona, Bajoles and a few other commanderies were receiving very attractive incomes.

The priories in the west were not only required to send subsidies to the convent at Rhodes, they were also expected to participate in the defence of this Christian stronghold by sending some of their commanders and knights to the convent. The journey to Rhodes increased the brothers' chances to launch their careers – either in their own priory or at the convent. By the beginning of the fifteenth century, the Catalan Hospitallers in Rhodes were almost perfect examples of the critical statement by Philippe de Mézières that the few brothers who journeyed to the island stayed just the length of time necessary to obtain a commandery in the west and then left.[3] No more than ten Catalans must have resided at the convent at any one time.[4] Three of them, Pere de Vilafranca, Pere Despomer and Gracià de Mahissens, were appointed priors of Catalonia by the grand master (or his lieutenant) and his council in 1396, 1404 and 1409 respectively, after they had resided at the convent intermittently and after they had become *drapier*, the highest-ranking office in the *langue* of Spain. Others, like Brother Berenguer Battle, obtained their first commandery after several years of staying in Rhodes.[5] However, Antoni de Fluvià, a Catalan from the castellany of Amposta, stayed at the convent for over thirty years before he received his first commandery in Aragon, namely Huesca (*c*.1420),[6] and in 1408, King Martin I of Aragon issued a recommendation to the grand master of the Hospital in favour of Joan de Mur who, after twenty-five years of residence in Rhodes, had yet to receive his first commandery.[7] These last two examples suggest that a journey to the convent did not guarantee that one would obtain a commandery.

In fact, until the end of the Great Schism in 1417, the 'Avignonese' Pope Benedict XIII, who had found refuge in the territories of the Aragonese crown, handed out commanderies at will in the priory of Catalonia and the castellany of Amposta, disregarding the regulations and interests of the convent. In 1411, the brothers at the convent declared to Pope John XXIII that the brothers of the *langue* of Spain were unwilling to come to Rhodes because Benedict XIII was granting the order's offices, commanderies and properties in Spain to brothers of his choice, although it was the prerogative of the grand master and the convent to do so.[8]

However, after the end of the Great Schism had been declared at the Council of Constance (1417), the Catalan Hospitallers began to visit the convent in unusually high numbers. In 1418, Grand Master Philibert de Naillac granted permits to the prior of Catalonia and several of his commanders to admit twenty-four new knights who were summoned to Rhodes with horses and armour. He also ordered ten commanders and seven brothers-at-arms to journey to the island.[9] During the next thirty years, the grand master issued many further convocations to Rhodes. Between 1415 and 1447, fifty-one knights of the Catalan priory can be identified with certainty as present at the convent, but this number would increase to seventy-seven if one were to take into account those twenty-six who were instructed to come but whose presence in Rhodes is not recorded in the archives of the order (which are, unfortunately, missing for several of these years).

An unusually large number of brother-knights from the priories of the *langue* of Spain, including the priory of Catalonia, was admitted into the order and summoned to Rhodes. In 1418–19, the knights of the Iberian peninsula represented 59 per cent of the total number of admissions into the order and, among them, 32 per cent came from the Catalan priory.[10] The order was probably ready to revitalize – with 'fresh blood' – the ranks of its Spanish priories, whose administration and recruitment had been subject to Pope Benedict's will for many years. Undoubtedly, the increasing number of Spanish brothers was also related to the declining influence of the French *langues* within the order, after years of domination. In the French priories, many commanderies had fallen into complete decay because of the destruction, devastation and depopulation of the Hundred Years War and private armed conflicts.[11]

A passage to Rhodes with arms and a horse was an expensive affair, and the commanders were authorized to farm out their commanderies and use the rents, paid in advance by farmers, to finance their journey, while the newly admitted knights were expected to receive money from their families until they would be granted a commandery. The peaceful situation in Catalonia and the prosperity of several of its commanderies distinguished the priory of Catalonia from many other western priories.

Catalonia, as well as Aragon, may have appeared – at that time – to be reservoirs from which commanders and knights could be summoned to Rhodes. Furthermore, during the first half of the fifteenth century, the Catalan trade in the Mediterranean had developed considerably, and the merchants of Barcelona were using the port of Rhodes as a base or a relay for their activities in the east. Rhodes occupied the first place among the destinations of Catalan shipments to the eastern Mediter-ranean, and these shipments amounted to 46 per cent of their trade volume.[12] These circumstances boded well for the development of Catalan influence at the headquarters of the Hospital.

At the convent, the need to protect the island against the increasingly threatening Ottomans and Mamelukes was very strongly felt, although no real attack or skirmish against Rhodes occurred between 1402 and 1440. The loss of the castle of Smyrna in 1402 was still a vivid memory, and even more so the invasion of Cyprus by the Mamelukes in 1426, when King Janus had been taken to Cairo as a prisoner. In 1434, rumours of an impending attack by the sultan of Egypt prompted the grand master to order seven commanders and three brothers who were still in Catalonia to make their passage to the island,[13] but it was not until 1440 that a real attack against the Hospitaller possessions took place. The siege of Rhodes in 1444 by an army from Egypt, which had succeeded in landing on the island, lasted forty days before it could be repelled. During the first half of the fifteenth century, defending their islands rather than preparing military expeditions had become an absolute priority for the Hospitallers of Rhodes.

Possibly in order to encourage more frequent and longer stays in Rhodes, the grand masters of the order and their council made a long residence in the eastern Mediterranean a condition for acquiring seniority rights (*ancianitas*). These seniority rights became necessary in order to gain access to a first commandery and, later on, to better commanderies as well as to higher offices. The statutes issued by the general chapters of 1410, 1420, 1428 and 1440 strongly complemented former rules of the fourteenth century that were aimed at giving more advancement rights to brothers residing at the convent.[14] Grand Master Juan Fernández de Heredia's fourteen-year-long absence from Rhodes until 1396, followed by his successor Naillac's personal involvement in the west in the lengthy and contentious final solution of the Great Schism – both of which caused the convent to be governed by lieutenants for prolonged periods of time – had not been favourable to an enforcement of the rights of *ancianitas*. After the end of the Council of Constance in 1417 and the return of the grand master to Rhodes in 1420, the time had come to restore the convent as the unique and legitimate centre of decision-making with regard to the order's affairs and careers, and to encourage more knights of the western priories to come to Rhodes.

Following the death of Naillac, Antoni de Fluvià, a Catalan, was elected grand master in 1421. Fluvià had been residing in Rhodes for over thirty years, a very unusual length of time for a Catalan. Only at a late stage had he gained access to significant offices, namely in 1411 to that of *drapier*, the highest office in the *langue* of Spain, and in 1420 to the commanderies of Huesca and Cyprus; in 1419, he had been designated as the grand master's lieutenant. There is something mysterious about Fluvià's election to the grand mastership, because many previous grand masters had held significant offices in the west. In his case, it seemed as if the rights and ranks of the most ancient brothers of the convent took precedence over any other possible choice.

Fluvià, the son of a modest family of *milites* from central Catalonia, remained grand master for sixteen years, until his death in 1437. He certainly favoured Catalan Hospitallers who stayed in Rhodes. The major offices of his *domus* and of the town of Rhodes, which he had the personal right to fill according to his own discretion, were given to brothers from the Catalan priory or the castellany of Amposta – for example, the offices of seneschal, chamberlain, castellan of Rhodes, bailiff of the *commercium* (who presided over the mercantile court) and bailiff of the town. Fluvià also made several donations to the brothers of the *langue* of Spain, such as the grant of a vineyard, the rents of which had to be used to repair or rebuild the *auberge* (or 'inn') of Spain and to improve the lodgings of the Spanish brothers.[15]

Not all the achievements of his successful government can be listed here, but his actions are probably best characterized as those of a 'frenetic legislator' – an expression used by Jürgen Sarnowsky.[16] The seventy-seven statutes adopted by the two general chapters he convened in 1428 and 1433 regulated practically every aspect of the order's organization and daily affairs. He enforced and completed Naillac's regulations on *ancianitas* and made residence on Rhodes mandatory for any career in the order. He also revived the old condition that one had to be born into a knightly lineage in order to become a brother-knight, and he required proof of origin as well as of physical and moral aptitude which had to be presented at a provincial chapter prior to one's admission as a knight.

Fluvià's legacy is also engraved on the walls of Rhodes where many
of his arms can still be seen today, along the defensive walls and towers
that he had built on the west and south flanks of the town, as well as on
many civilian buildings, including the *auberge* of Spain. Architects have
emphasized how the Catalan architectural style of the later Middle
Ages is present in the old town of Rhodes. On his deathbed, Fluvià made
a donation for the construction of a new hospital, which was inaugur-
ated in 1484.[17]

A remarkable Catalan grand master, a Catalan-style town and active
business links between Barcelona and Rhodes were good incentives for
brothers of the Catalan priory to journey to the east. Even more so was
the obligation to stay at the convent to obtain a commandery and make
a successful career in the order.

Between 1415 and 1447, thirty-five Hospitallers who are known to
have held a commandery in the priory (including the priors themselves)
visited Rhodes; this represents 69 per cent of the fifty-one commanders
of the priory documented for this same period. Of the sixty-one brother-
knights who did not receive a commandery during this same time, only
sixteen, that is 26 per cent, are known to have journeyed to the convent.
However, another twenty-six were requested by the grand master to
come – at the time of their admission or later – but their presence in
Rhodes is not documented. Because of the small number of commanderies in the priory, it was normal that a newly admitted knight had
to wait ten years – if not fifteen or eighteen or even thirty (in one case) –
before he received a first commandery. The *ancianitas* rules led many of
the Catalan Hospitallers to stay at the convent for long periods of time,
often over ten years, and, in order to obtain higher offices, sometimes
up to thirty years.

While the priors of Catalonia had previously made use of their right
to hand out commanderies with the agreement of their provincial
chapter, between 1420 and 1450 all appointments to Catalan commanderies appear to have originated or been ratified in Rhodes. A stiff
competition developed among the Catalan Hospitallers residing at the
convent in their quest for a first and then better commanderies and,
later on, for higher conventual offices, which provided access to the
oligarchic council of the grand master and might eventually lead to an
appointment as prior of Catalonia or castellan of Amposta. Within the
auberge of Spain, many conflicts occurred between brothers who
claimed to have more *ancianitas* rights than their colleagues and
competed for access to the best commanderies or to higher functions. In

one of these disputes, Brother Guillem de Sagaró even questioned the right of Brother Gracià de Ripoll to receive the commandery of St Llorenç, stating that Ripoll was not from a knightly lineage, until a meeting of the *esgart* court (where the brothers debated and decided certain internal complaints) recognized the legitimacy of Ripoll's claim.[18] Access to the office of *drapier*, the highest in the *langue* of Spain, caused much discord. In 1434, Joan de Vilafranca, castellan of Rhodes, claimed that he had more seniority rights than Rafel Saplana, who had been preferred over him as the new *drapier*, and requested that his disagreement be recorded in the chancery registers. Saplana replied that he had been recognized as *benemerens et ancianor* (well deserving and older) in front of three other candidates, including Vilafranca, by the assembly of the *langue* of Spain.[19] When Saplana became prior of Catalonia in 1439, a Catalan of the castellany of Amposta, Pere Ramón Sacosta (Raymond Zacosta), was at first chosen as the new *drapier*, but his appointment was opposed by a group of Catalan and Aragonese brothers led by Felip d'Hortal, a commander from the priory who was recognized as *drapier* by the grand master, Jean de Lastic. However, Sacosta presented his claim successfully at the Roman Curia and was back in the office in 1442.

Many brothers were merely concerned with receiving their first commandery and later exchanging it for a better one. Every vacancy started a 'game of musical chairs' causing continual changes in the commanderies' leadership. In a period of ten years, six different commanders held St Llorenç, a typical first commandery. In 1442, the Catalan brothers, who were allowed to hold assemblies, claimed and obtained from Fluvià's successor, Jean de Lastic, the right to declare the ranking of seniority among them to regulate access to the commanderies, except for those reserved to the choice of the grand master and his council and the prior's *camerae*.[20]

Between 1415 and 1447, twelve Hospitallers from the Catalan priory obtained high offices at the convent, and some embarked on remarkable careers.[21] Two Catalans from the castellany of Amposta, Joan de Vilagut (castellan of Amposta in 1433 and lieutenant of the grand master in 1445) and Ramón Sacosta (*drapier* in 1442 and grand master of the order in 1462), also played an important role in the convent where they spent most of their careers. Conventual bailiffs (that is to say the *drapier* in the case of the *langue* of Spain), capitulary bailiffs and the seneschal (the first of the officers of the grand master's *domus*) were members of the grand master's council. Ten out of the twelve mentioned earlier gained access to this exclusive circle after having been granted one or several of these offices. Being preferred to members of other priories of the *langue* of Spain, seven became *drapiers*, an office that often led to an appointment as prior of Catalonia. Three Catalan *drapiers*, Gualbes, Saplana and Hortal, became priors of Catalonia while Xetmar and Sacosta became castellans of Amposta. Rafel Saplana's life provides a good example of the different steps in a successful career in Rhodes: he arrived on Rhodes in 1421, received his first Catalan commandery in 1428, changed to four better ones within six years and further acceded to the capitular bailiwick of Athens and Negroponte as well as to the office of bailiff of Rhodes. In 1434 he was elected *drapier* and finally, in 1439, he was appointed prior of Catalonia at the death of Gualbes.

The majority of the Catalan commanders and brothers known to have been in Rhodes in the thirty-year period between 1418 and 1448 belonged to noble and knightly families (60 per cent). Many of them were born into very obscure and impoverished lineages of *milites*, but they fulfilled the renewed demand for knightly origin according to the statutes. However, another 33 per cent came from Catalonia's urban society and the remaining 7 per cent are difficult to identify. The influential Barcelonese patricians claimed to have the same rights as members of the knighthood to be admitted into the order, and many merchants and lawyers were close to the highest circles of power in Catalonia. Many of the non-noble Catalans in Rhodes had been made knights before Naillac and Fluvià insisted on a knightly origin, but even after the statute on knightly origin had been strongly reaffirmed, sons of influential urban families continued to be admitted, although with caution. Examples of nepotism are mostly found among brothers of urban origin. Four commanders in Rhodes were members of the prestigious and aristocratic family of the Gualbes, among them prior Lluís de Gualbes, while four others, including Gualbes's successor, belonged to the Saplana family, which descended from a rich notary.

The important gathering of Catalan Hospitallers in Rhodes in the first half of the fifteenth century can be considered the prelude to the strong Spanish influence in the order in the following centuries. Twenty-five years after the death of Fluvià, another Catalan, the castellan of Amposta, Ramón Sacosta, was elected grand master of the order. The connections between Rhodes and Catalonia, which were so closely linked to the activities of Barcelona merchants in the Mediterranean, were reinforced by the presence (at the convent in Rhodes) of numerous brothers from the priory or the castellany, whose families were often influential in Catalonia. The interest of the Catalans in the Hospitallers of Rhodes appears in the legendary descriptions of the siege of Rhodes (1440) in two contemporary literary works: Francesc Ferrer's *Romans de la armada del Soldà contra Rodes* and Joanot Martorell's *Tirant lo Blanc*.[22]

However, several disturbing consequences resulted from the new situation. There were simply too many Catalan brothers in Rhodes. In 1445, the grand master Jean de Lastic, complaining about the *copiositas* of brothers from the priories of Catalonia and Auvergne and from the castellany of Amposta in the convent, as well as about the cost of feeding them, ordered the priors to stop making use of any admission permits they might still be holding. In Catalonia, many commanderies, left without their commanders, were farmed under the control of family members who received their rents in cash. The priory was no longer governed by a collective leadership because it became impossible to bring together more than three or four commanders for the provincial chapters, although these continued to be held as the statutes ordered.

Last but not least, because the rents of the commanderies were easy to obtain and the commanders could 'escape' from their commanderies easily, the Aragonese kings managed to secure – for their own affairs – various Catalan Hospitallers, who, against the will of the grand master, stopped going to Rhodes. The Aragonese monarchs had always been eager to exercise some control over the resources and the personnel of the Hospital, up to the point that they had, at times, tried to stop all departures of knights and all sending of subsidies from the Aragonese and Catalan priories to Rhodes.[23] The fifteenth century was marked by the long reign of Alfonso V, the 'Magnanimous' (1416–58), whose ambitious project to conquer the kingdom of Naples met with the opposition of the pope and the reservations of his Catalan subjects. Alfonso attempted to enforce the dispensing of Catalan commanderies to his protégés and succeeded in building up a group of ten Hospitallers in his service, who fought in Italy at his side and used the rents of their commanderies to finance their equipment and expenses. For this reason and because of his unsuccessful endeavour to impose priors of his choice in his kingdoms, against the rules of the convent, he initially faced strong opposition from the Hospitallers' grand master Antoni de Fluvià. But after the 'Magnanimous' had gained access to the throne of Naples in 1442, Fluvià's successor, Jean de Lastic, who had to face two attacks from the Mamelukes in 1440 and 1444, received pledges of protection from Alfonso, who carried out an active policy of presence in the Balkans and the eastern Mediterranean. Consequently, the influence of the king of Aragon in the affairs of the Hospital, in Spain as well as in Rhodes, increased without meeting much further resistance from the grand master.[24]

Notes

[1]　Joaquin Miret y Sans, *Les Cases dels Templers i Hospitalers en Catalunya* (Barcelona, 1910), is still a major source of information for the history of these orders in Aragon and Catalonia. Maria Luisa Ledesma Rubio, *Templarios y Hospitalarios en el Reino de Aragón* (Zaragoza, 1982), essentially deals with Aragon and the castellany of Amposta. The relations between Rhodes and the Aragonese and Catalan priories are not really addressed in any of these two works. Valuable and abundant information on the western priories and their links to the convent can be found in Anthony Luttrell, *The Hospitallers in Cyprus, Rhodes, Greece and the West, 1291–1440* (London 1978); Anthony Luttrell, *Latin Greece, the Hospitallers and the Crusades, 1291–1440* (London, 1982); Anthony Luttrell, *The Hospitallers of Rhodes and their Mediterranean World* (Aldershot, 1992); Anthony Luttrell, *The Hospitaller State on Rhodes and its Western Provinces, 1306–1462* (Aldershot 1999). Maria Bonet Donato, *La Orden del Hospital en la Corona de Aragón: Poder y Gobierno en la Castellania de Amposta (ss. XII–XV)* (Madrid, 1994), is also important because of the author's use of the Hospitaller archives on Malta, even though it deals with the castellany of Amposta and not the priory of Catalonia. Most of our information about Catalan Hospitallers in Rhodes in the fifteenth century comes from archival sources: in Barcelona from the Archivio de la Corona de Aragón (ACA) with its Archivio de Gran Priorado (ACA, AGP) and its archives of the royal chancery (ACA, RC); and in Malta, from the Archives of the Hospital at the National Library of Malta (NLM).

[2]　Anthony Luttrell, 'The Hospitallers' western accounts, 1373/4 and 1374/5', in Luttrell, *Hospitaller State on Rhodes*, no. XI, pp. 8–9.

[3]　Anthony Luttrell, 'Rhodes: base militaire, colonie, métropole de 1306 à 1440', in Luttrell, *Hospitaller State on Rhodes*, no. VII, p. 238.

[4]　Anthony Luttrell, 'The Hospitaller priory of Catalunya in the 14th century', in Luttrell, *Hospitaller State on Rhodes*, no. XVI.

[5]　In 1385, Battle had received the commandery of Tortosa from the lieutenant of the master, after eight years of residence in Rhodes: ACA, RC 1374, fol. 104.

[6]　ACA, RC 2171, fol. 77v and NLM 345, fols 193v and 210v.

[7]　ACA, RC 2184, fol. 107v.

[8]　NLM 339, fol. 223. John XXIII was the successor of Alexander V appointed by the Council of Pisa and recognized by the order.

[9]　NLM 342, fols 104–9.

[10] A total of forty-four brother-knights of the *langue* of Spain were admitted in 1418–19, namely twenty-four in the priory of Catalonia, nine in the castellany of Amposta and eleven in the priories of Castile and Portugal; meanwhile only thirty-one knights were admitted in the other western priories: NLM 342.

[11] Benoît Beaucage, 'L'effondrement de la gestion du patrimoine de l'Hôpital en France du sud-est (1373–1429)', *Provence historique*, 45, 179 (1995), 119–43, has clearly shown this for Provence and emphasized that the priory of St Gilles was no longer able to send knights to Rhodes.

[12] Mario Del Treppo, *I mercanti catalani e l'espansione della Corona d'Aragona nel secolo XV* (Naples, 1972).

[13] NLM 351, fol. 79v.

[14] The statutes of these general chapters are at Archives départementales de la Haute-Garonne (ADHG) in Toulouse. The following deal with the rights of *ancianitas*: statutes 23 and 24 of 1410 (ADHG, H 13, fol. 74r–v), statute 33 of 1420 (ADHG, H 13, fol. 67), statute 28 of 1428 (ADHG, H 13, fol. 101) and an unnumbered statute of 1440 (ADHG, H 14, fol. 136).

[15] NLM 347, fol. 92r–v.

[16] Jürgen Sarnowsky, *Macht und Herrschaft im Johanniterorden des 15. Jahrhunderts: Verfassung und Verwaltung der Johanniter auf Rhodos (1421–1522)* (Münster, 2001), p. 137.

[17] The architectural legacy of Fluvià in Rhodes has been emphasized at length by Albert Gabriel, *La cité de Rhodes, MCCCX–MDXXII: Architecture civile et religieuse* (Paris, 1923), Fotini Karassava-Tsilingiri, 'Antoni Fluvià i l'arquitectura de Rodes al segle XV', *L'Avenç*, 179 (1994), 34–8, as well as Ana-Maria Kasdagli and Katerina Manoussou-Della, 'The defences of Rhodes and the Tower of Saint-John', *Fort: The International Journal of Fortification and Military Architecture*, 24 (1996), 15–35.

[18] NLM 352, fol. 78r–v.

[19] NLM 350, fols 143v–144 and NLM 351, fols 79v, 80.

[20] NLM 355, fols 107v–109.

[21] They were Dalmau Ramon Xetmar (*drapier* 1421), Lluís de Gualbes (*drapier* 1423–8, seneschal 1422–6), Ramón Roger d'Erill (*drapier* 1428–32, bailiff of Athens and Negroponte 1423–8), Gabriel de Gualbes (*drapier* 1432–3), Gispert de Miralpeix (*drapier* 1434, lieutenant of the master for the island of Cos 1428–33), Rafel Saplana (*drapier* 1434–9, bailiff of Athens and Negroponte 1434, bailiff of Rhodes 1434), Felip d'Hortal (*drapier* 1441–4, grand commander of Cyprus 1444–7), Lluís de Mur (seneschal 1428–37, bailiff of Athens and Negroponte 1434–44), Garcia de Torres (bailiff of Athens and Negroponte 1428, bailiff of *commerch* 1428, ambassador to the Roman Curia 1428), Joan de Vilafranca (castellan of Rhodes 1428–39), Albert Ermengol (bailiff of Rhodes 1428), Jaume de la Geltrú (captain of St Peter's Castle 1433 and 1446, lieutenant of the *drapier* 1446).

[22] Francesc Ferrer, *Obra completa*, ed. Jaume Auferil (Barcelona, 1983), pp. 254–68; Joanot Martorell, *Tirant lo Blanc i altres escrits de Joannot Martorell*, ed. Martín de Riquer (Barcelona, 1990), pp. 295–334.

[23] See Anthony Luttrell, 'The Aragonese Crown and the Knights Hospitallers of Rhodes: 1291–1350', in Luttrell, *Hospitallers in Cyprus, Rhodes, Greece and the West*, no. XI; Anthony Luttrell, 'La Corona de Aragón y las Ordenes Militares durante el siglo XIV', in Luttrell, *Hospitallers in Cyprus, Rhodes, Greece and the West*, no. XII.

[24] For the general outlines of the complex reign of Alfonso V, see Alan Ryder, *Alfonso the Magnanimous, King of Aragon, Naples and Sicily (1396–1458)* (Oxford, 1990). For the king's policy in the eastern Mediterranean and his relations with Rhodes, see Constantin Marinescu, *La politique orientale d'Alphonse V d'Aragon, roi de Naples (1416–1458)* (Barcelona, 1994). For the conflicts between the king and the Hospitaller master Antoni de Fluvià, see Pierre Bonneaud, 'Diferencias y conflictos entre Alfonso el Magnánimo, el Maestre de Rodas y los Hospitalarios catalanes (1426–36)', in Ricardo Izquierdo Benito and Francisco Ruiz Gómez (eds), *Las Órdenes militares en la Península iberica*, vol. 1, *Edad Media* (Cuenca, 2000), pp. 457–71.

15

Secure Base and Constraints of Mobility: The Rheno-Flemish Bailiwick of the Teutonic Knights between Regional Bonds and Service to the Grand Master in the Later Middle Ages

KLAUS VAN EICKELS

When studying mobility in the military orders, one must carefully distinguish between two forms. On the one hand, there was 'mobility by transfer': brothers were transferred from one house to another – be it within the same region, between regions or to and from the order's main areas of activity (i.e. the Holy Land or whatever was substituted for it after the loss of the kingdom of Jerusalem). On the other hand, there was 'secure base mobility': brothers were travelling in the service of the order while remaining attached to their house of origin. Constant affiliation to one house of the order over a long period of time must therefore not be mistaken for immobility. Neither was the appointment to a new office always indicative of real mobility, since officials were sometimes appointed without taking residence in their respective new commanderies.

These aspects of mobility can be studied on a small scale in the Rheno-Flemish bailiwick of the Teutonic Knights. Traditional historiography has argued that the Teutonic Order – after a dynamic period of expansion – began to ossify because of the increasing immobility of brothers who considered their commanderies as personal benefices rather than as offices to be held on behalf of the order.[1] Yet, this development was not as linear as it may seem. From the very beginning, there was a marked tension between the individual brothers' attachment to certain regions or houses and the unrestricted mobility required by the order's central administration. The order's houses could only exist and thrive as long as the brothers maintained local networks and social bonds; at the same time, the order as a whole could only function as long as the brothers remained available for tasks outside their region of origin.

Brothers who remained attached to their original houses were not necessarily immobile; in fact, they were often prepared to travel rather extensively. Examples of this kind of local attachment can be found at a very early date: Giles Berthout the Bearded, lord of Oudenburg, entered the order in 1227/8 at a fairly advanced age. He had been lord of Oudenburg for twenty years by virtue of his marriage to the heiress of the lordship, but after his eldest stepson had reached adult age he could no longer claim the title. Instead of accepting this loss of status, Giles renounced his marriage and entered the Teutonic Order.[2]

It seems that he did not make any substantial donations to the order at that time, since his own rather mediocre inheritance was passed on to his own sons. Rather, the order accepted him because of his involvement in local networks of power and friendship and because of his close relationship to the English court. In 1216, he had fought, together with other Flemish knights, for King John of England against the invasion of the Lord Louis (later King Louis VIII of France) who was then claiming the English crown.[3] In 1235, Giles the Bearded negotiated the marriage between the sister of the English king (Isabella) and Emperor Frederick II, and in the following years he repeatedly travelled to London to receive the payments agreed upon as the bride's marriage portion.[4] During his fourteen years as a brother-knight Giles probably resided at Oudenburg, for in 1219, when he and his wife had been sick during the Fifth Crusade's siege of Damietta, they had founded a hospital there.[5]

Giles the Bearded probably insisted on staying on the Flemish possessions that he and his relatives had given to the order. He had entered the order to avoid the loss of social status. Moving to a distant house of the order would have made him a subordinate member of that house because of his late entry into the order. As long as he resided at Oudenburg, however, he remained independent. At the same time, he was more than willing to undertake long journeys, especially those that added to his honour – such as the embassy to the English court on behalf of the emperor. However, he also voyaged to fulfil administrative tasks, as in 1237 when he received in person the first documented payment of the annual rent that King Henry III had granted to the Teutonic Knights during Giles's stay at his court two years earlier.[6]

The willingness of brothers and commanders to travel on behalf of the order did not disappear during the fifteenth and sixteenth centuries.

In 1419, the commander of Koblenz led 200 knightly mercenaries to Prussia (and it is of no concern here that his journey ended somewhere in the middle of Germany when he was informed that a truce had been concluded and that the knights were no longer needed).[7] Louis of Saunsheim (1501–24) repeatedly served as the grand master's ambassador to the imperial court, the imperial diet and several princely courts of the empire.[8] In 1444, the commander of Althaus came from Prussia to Mechelen, the administrative centre of the Teutonic Knights in Brabant and Flanders, in order to raise 20,000 guilders for the grand master by selling eternal and life annuities.[9]

The conflicts that occurred usually had an economic background. In the fifteenth century, the brothers of Koblenz protested against the annual wine transport they owed to the grand master and his officials. Yet, their protest was not directed against the obligation to have the ship accompanied by a brother down to the North Sea; rather, the conflict stemmed from the question of whether their house or the grand master would have to pay for the travel expenses.[10]

Not all brothers preferred the secure base of their region of origin. Moving to the centre of the order's activities was riskier, but it also offered attractive career opportunities. Much depended on how the socio-economic situation of a brother's region of origin compared to that of his potential area of relocation; the order's military success in the target region was also a significant factor. In the order's early years, the grand master seems to have had no problem recruiting brothers who were ready to serve outside their region of origin. As long as the order expanded, the prospect of advancing in the order's hierarchy provided a strong incentive.

In the fourteenth century, when expansion stagnated, this incentive was counterbalanced by other factors. As access to advancement became more restricted – simply because there were no longer as many vacancies to be filled every year – the brothers insisted more and more on remaining in, or only moving to, an environment where they would fit in. Social background and regional origin became decisive factors. Livonia, for example, was dominated by Westphalians. Brothers from other bailiwicks had almost no chance of being promoted to leading positions in Livonia. In the fifteenth century, the grand master's attempt to take over the Livonian branch of the order by sending Rhenish brothers to Livonia in great numbers failed.[11]

In the bailiwick of Koblenz, social background was equally important. Brothers from the patrician families of the Rhineland's big cities occupied the leading positions in most of the order's houses there.[12]

Outside their region of origin, however, their claim to be of noble descent was often considered doubtful. Thus, the threat to transfer unruly brothers to Prussia against their will became a particularly effective punishment.[13] Yet, service for the grand master remained an attractive option: since the mid-fourteenth century, all commanders of Koblenz were Rhenish brothers who had served in Prussia for some time before being appointed to their position. Obviously, the Rheno-Flemish bailiwick was one of the most attractive positions the grand master could offer to a brother from the Rhineland.[14]

When the order's size decreased significantly in the fifteenth century, the factors impeding mobility increased dramatically. In 1454, when great parts of Prussia were lost at the beginning of the Thirteen Years War, the grand master sent a considerable number of brothers from Prussia to Koblenz with letters requesting to receive them there. In 1456, the commander complained about their insubordination and, specifically, about their excessive funding demands for themselves as well as their friends, squires and servants.[15] Once again competition for resources, not mobility as such, was at stake. The conflict was also fuelled by social disparities and regional networks of power. The brothers from Prussia were knights and found it rather difficult to live in a bailiwick that was almost entirely dominated by priests of the order. Moreover, some of the 'Prussian brothers' originated from families near Koblenz and even tried to invoke the assistance of the archbishop of Trier in their struggle against the commander of the bailiwick who was then residing in Cologne.[16]

The example of Koblenz at the end of the fifteenth century warns us against the misconception that mobility indicates unity and that local ties might be indicative of fragmentation: Werner Spiess of Büllesheim, appointed commander of Koblenz in 1486 and deposed in 1501, found himself in conflict with the brothers of the commanderies under his direct control soon after his appointment. His struggle against losing his attractive position resulted not only in armed conflict, but also in numerous journeys to Prussia where he defended himself against the charges put forward against him by the brothers of the order. At the same time, these same brothers actively sought the support of regional princes, especially the archbishop of Trier who intervened on their behalf. The grand master as well as the archbishop became involved in the conflict. What appears in the sources as a confrontation between a mobile commander and immobile brothers (who relied on local net-working rather than the order's hierarchy), should rather be read as symptoms of inner strife (and not in terms of mobility or immobility).[17]

While 'mobility by transfer' is more easily discerned in the sources, 'secure base mobility' was equally important for the Teutonic Order as a whole. A brother's socio-economic situation largely determined whether he would exchange the security of a position in his region of origin for the chances of advancement by transfer. It seems that conflicts concerning the mobility and transfer of brothers were often conflicts about revenues, expenditure or social selection. Therefore, mobility has to be studied in its broader context.

Notes

[1] Hans Prutz, *Die geistlichen Ritterorden: Ihre Stellung zur kirchlichen, politischen, gesellschaftlichen und wirtschaftlichen Entwicklung des Mittelalters* (Berlin, 1908); Marian Tumler, *Der Deutsche Orden im Werden, Wachsen und Wirken bis 1400 mit einem Abriß der Geschichte des Ordens von 1400 bis zur neuesten Zeit* (Vienna, 1955); Erich Maschke, 'Die inneren Wandlungen des Deutschen Ritterordens', in Waldemar Besson (ed.), *Geschichte und Gegenwartsbewusstsein, historische Betrachtungen und Untersuchungen: Festschrift für Hans Rothfels zum 70. Geburtstag dargebracht von Kollegen, Freunden und Schülern* (Göttingen, 1963), pp. 249–77.

[2] Theo Luykx, *Een typish vertegenwoordiger van den XIIIe eeuwschen adel in onze gewesten: Gilles Berthout met den baard, kamerheer van Vlaanderen en broeder van de Duitsche Orde in Pitsemburg te Mechelen* (Antwerp, 1944); Jean Theodore de Raadt, 'Égide Berthout Ier dit à-la-barbe', *Annales de la société d'archéologie de Bruxelles*, 2 (1888–9), 100–7.

[3] In 1207, he and his brother accepted an English money fief. In May 1213, he is recorded as present at the English court. On 16 July 1216, King John granted him safe-conduct for his return to Flanders; Luykx, *Een typish vertegenwoordiger*, pp. 17–22.

[4] Hans Koeppen, 'Die englische Rente für den Deutschen Orden', in *Festschrift für Hermann Heimpel zum 70. Geburtstag am 19. September 1971* (Göttingen, 1971–2), pp. 402–21, here p. 406.

[5] Klaus van Eickels, *Die Deutschordensballei Koblenz und ihre wirtschaftliche Entwicklung im Spätmittelalter* (Marburg, 1995), pp. 24–8.

[6] Koeppen, 'Die englische Rente', pp. 403, 407; cf. Eickels, *Die Deutschordensballei Koblenz*, p. 30.

[7] Hans Limburg, *Die Hochmeister des Deutschen Ordens und die Ballei Koblenz* (Bad Godesberg, 1969), p. 80.

[8] Ibid., pp. 158–66.

[9] Ibid., pp. 85–6; cf. Eickels, *Die Deutschordensballei Koblenz*, p. 206.

[10] Eickels, *Die Deutschordensballei Koblenz*, pp. 200–3.

[11]   Klaus Militzer, 'Rheinländer im mittelalterlichen Livland', *Rheinische Vierteljahrsblätter*, 61 (1997), 79–95.

[12]   Eickels, *Die Deutschordensballei Koblenz*, pp. 53–6.

[13]   Limburg, *Die Hochmeister des Deutschen Ordens*, p. 69.

[14]   Eickels, *Die Deutschordensballei Koblenz*, p. 203; Limburg, *Die Hochmeister des Deutschen Ordens*, pp. 69ff.

[15]   Heinrich Reimer, 'Verfall der Deutschordensballei Koblenz im 15. Jahrhundert', *Trierisches Archiv*, 11 (1907), 1–42, here doc. X (June 1456), p. 33: the commander of Koblenz complains to the grand master about the insubordination of the 'brothers from Prussia'. Cf. Eickels, *Die Deutschordensballei Koblenz*, pp. 203–5; Limburg, *Die Hochmeister des Deutschen Ordens*, pp. 110–12.

[16]   Reimer, 'Verfall der Deutschordensballei Koblenz', docs XI (Landeshauptarchiv Koblenz, Abteilung 1 C 17044, fols 35v–41; 7 April 1460) and XI (Landeshauptarchiv Koblenz, Abteilung 1 C 17044, fol. 35r; 31 May 1460). The Prussian brothers in Koblenz (archdiocese of Trier) jointly complain to the archbishop of Trier as their local bishop about their commander who is from Bonn (archdiocese of Cologne); cf. Limburg, *Die Hochmeister des Deutschen Ordens*, p. 110. The brothers from Prussia insisted that the commander was discriminating against them (i.e. he did not respect the prerogatives they claimed by virtue of their local origin). Moreover, they pointed out that the priests of the order were so overcharged with administrative duties that they could not even celebrate mass at the commandery regularly. Here again, mobility is at stake: claiming that priests of the order should celebrate mass in person (rather than employ vicars) meant, in fact, that they should resign from their offices, since their duties as office-holders required that they be able to travel freely, unbound by regular duties of divine service.

[17]   Limburg, *Die Hochmeister des Deutschen Ordens*, pp. 126–57.

16

Lepers, Land and Loyalty: The Order of St Lazarus of Jerusalem in England and the Holy Land, *c*.1150–1300

DAVID MARCOMBE

This chapter examines the history of the Order of St Lazarus in its early years when the English province was still part of a wider, international venture. Its principal focus is the question of the inter- action of personnel, resources and ideology between England and the Holy Land. As with much crusader history, the main problem in writing it has been the relative lack of documentation. This is sometimes bad enough for major orders, such as the Templars and Hospitallers, but it is even worse for a small operation such as St Lazarus. For the history of the order in the Holy Land we have only a fragment of a cartulary to fall back upon, and certainly nothing akin to a set of statutes which might have spelt out working relationships within the order and explained how vital tasks were supposed to be carried out. The most comprehensive statutes to exist date from the thirteenth century and relate to the commandery at Seedorf in Switzerland, but even these fail to explain the important chain of command between the centre and the periphery.[1] This unfortunate situation must be due partly to the destruction of records following the fall of Acre in 1291 and partly to the privileges of the order which meant that it was exempt from many of the archive-generating activities that usually bring such institutions to the attention of historians. The history of the Order of St Lazarus is therefore likely to remain a relatively dark corner of the crusading world with only a little light to shed on the nature and scope of its activities.[2] Nevertheless, there are occasional bright spots – some- times to be found in unlikely places – which allow questions of mobility at least to be addressed. Beyond that, the chapter assesses the importance of the order's landholdings in England, questions the extent to which its connection with leprosy provided an overarching cohesive force and measures the loyalty due to the general master against the shifting importance of these two key influences.

Much has been written in the past about the ancient origins of the order and it is beyond dispute that a leper hospital, dedicated to St Lazarus, existed outside the walls of Jerusalem long before the First Crusade. However, it is only in the 1130s that clear evidence emerges that this institution had reorganized itself under a master and chapter. The form of organization was unusual. The master, who was himself supposed to be a leper, supervised a community made up of leper brothers, healthy brothers to support them and chaplains to provide the spiritual services required by both. The first recorded master, Bartholomew, who appears in 1153, may have been a Templar who left his order to minister to the sick.[3] The newly organized hospital soon won the support of the aristocracy of the Latin kingdom and of patrons in western Europe, and from the 1140s onwards grants of lands, tithes and privileges began to proliferate. The Templars also offered their support and from the late twelfth century, at least, it began to be accepted that the hospital of St Lazarus provided an appropriate retreat for lepers from the knightly class and, indeed, those from the Order of the Temple in particular. This development and the need of the crusader states for ever-increasing supplies of soldiers caused the hospital of St Lazarus to become militarized to some extent, a development which was certainly well under way by the early thirteenth century.[4] The gestation of leprosy is such that for about seven years after diagnosis a sufferer can fulfil a useful role as a fighting man, a point well borne out by the military exploits of the leper king, Baldwin IV.[5] Thus, there was no reason why knightly, leprous inmates of the Jerusalem hospital should not, for a time, continue their fighting role and in this way the unique and novel concept of the 'leper knight' was born.

By the middle of the thirteenth century, by which time the order had re-established itself at Acre, this pristine ideology was already under some pressure. Military setbacks meant that the early generations of leper knights were all but wiped out and those same reverses put a strain on the landed endowment in the Holy Land.[6] Compromises with the founding ideology were therefore inevitable. In 1253, for example, Pope Innocent IV decreed that the master need not be a leper, and at about the same time the order began to place increasing emphasis on the recruitment of healthy knights, in just the same way as the Templars and Hospitallers. Loss of land in the Latin kingdom caused the order to rely more heavily on its western European estates and also on a series of papal privileges – particularly in respect of rights to indulgences and alms-gathering – which were being granted in the thirteenth century.[7] By the time of the fall of Acre in 1291 the Order of St Lazarus had changed and developed substantially since its early years. Moreover, the public perception of leprosy was also shifting. From the positive view that lepers were sharers in Christ's suffering, which was popular in the twelfth century, a very different perception was emerging in the harsh economic climate of the early fourteenth century when lepers (alongside Muslims and Jews) were seen as scapegoats for all of the ills besetting humankind.[8]

The Order of St Lazarus gained its first foothold in England with a grant of land near Wymondham, Norfolk, by William of Aubigny some time before 1146.[9] Although England was thus one of the first western kingdoms in which the order picked up land, it was not until a much larger grant was made at Burton, Leicestershire, by Roger of Mowbray in about 1157 that it put down permanent roots. Burton, or Burton Lazars as it was soon to be called, became the location of a commandery which came to control an extensive estate in the immediate vicinity and offshoots in other parts of the country.[10] By 1200 the English estate comprised lands as far afield as Sussex, Northumberland, Derbyshire and Norfolk, many of them administered from satellite commanderies such as Choseley, Norfolk or Harehope, Northumberland (Figure 7). Most of these appear to have fallen under the direct jurisdiction of the master of Burton Lazars, with the one possible exception of Locko, Derbyshire, which may have had some direct accounting role to Jerusalem and remained out of the orbit of Burton Lazars.[11] Some of the principal early patrons of the order in England were crusaders who had been to Jerusalem and witnessed the work of the hospital there at first hand. Roger of Mowbray made three visits to the Holy Land, and William of Ferrers, Henry de Lacy and William Burdet all had impeccable crusading credentials.[12] Nigel of Amundeville, in giving land to the order at Carlton-le-Moorland, Lincolnshire, summed up well the motivation of such men, acknowledging 'the great honours done to him by the brothers of St Lazarus in parts across the sea'.[13] Although in terms of the totality of benefactors crusaders were to make up only about 5 per cent of the whole, they did tend to give the most important estates, particularly in places such as Burton Lazars and Spondon, Derbyshire, which were always cornerstones of the order's wealth.

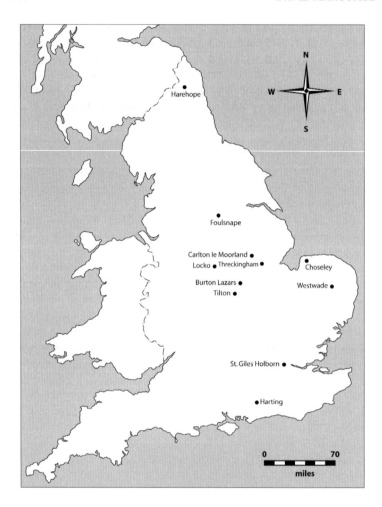

Figure 7 Map of England, showing commanderies and hospitals
of the Order of St Lazarus before 1300

How was the order in England connected with its masters overseas?
First, there can be no doubt that the link existed, because the earliest
land grants in England were not made to the English order, but
specifically and unambiguously to the 'lepers of Jerusalem'.[14] It was up
to the master of the Jerusalem hospital, or the general master as he was
beginning to be called in the thirteenth century, to determine the
administrative and organizational processes which would be put in

place to ensure efficient transfer of funds and manpower from western Europe to the Holy Land. We know very little about these processes, but there are one or two clues which are suggestive of the nature of this critical relationship. By the thirteenth century, for example, it is clear that the order was divided up into provinces and that England and Germany enjoyed provincial status.[15] The master of Burton Lazars, after having been described in a variety of ways in the twelfth century, by the thirteenth century was generally accepted as 'commander and custodian of all the alms of St Lazarus on this side of the sea' or 'perpetual and provincial general of the said order in England' which, in practical terms, also included the Lazarite estate in Scotland.[16]

His mode of appointment might have remained a mystery, had it not been for the chance survival of a document generated by the master Nicholas of Dover in about 1390. According to Dover, when a new master was required representatives were summoned from all the English commanderies (about ten in all) to a general chapter held at Burton Lazars. A new master would then be elected and his name sent to the general master who was only expected to provide verbal confirmation of the election.[17] Dover suggests that the appointment was for life, but other evidence implies that some masters, at least, were appointed for a term of years and then moved on to other jobs.[18] Once appointed, the master of Burton Lazars enjoyed some important prerogatives which gave him considerable freedom of action. He alone had the right to admit new brothers to the English branch of the order; he was responsible for presenting clerks to benefices, prosecuting lawsuits and exercising discipline in his province – and, most important, returning an annual contribution, or *apportum*, to the mother house in the Holy Land.[19] It also fell within his remit to see that sufficient masters were appointed to the subsidiary commanderies, and the fortuitous survival of a contract between Sir Adam Veau, master of Burton Lazars, and Robert of Robeby, commander of Harehope, dated 1308, outlines how this relationship worked. Robeby was granted the supervision of Harehope for life, though, it seems, under a series of five-year contracts which bound him to specific financial arrangements with the master. Each year he was to make the trek south from Northumberland to Leicestershire, a journey of about 200 miles, where he was to attend a general chapter at Burton Lazars, where 'advice and help' would be given with regard to his charge.[20]

It is less clear what prerogatives the general master enjoyed in England. He could short-circuit the provincial administration of the master of Burton Lazars, for example, by appointing his own commissioners to carry out specific tasks or visitations, which he did in the early fourteenth century when Richard of Leighton and Thomas of Sutton were made 'general attorneys' in the matter of alms-gathering.[21] However, on other occasions the chain of command seems less clearly defined, with a measure of doubt about who actually spoke for the order in England. When an important royal pension failed to be paid after 1260 the Crown was bombarded with petitions, from both the English Lazarites and those 'over the sea', to have it restored.[22] Now, of course, this could have been a deliberate tactic, subjecting the king to a two-pronged attack in the hope of breaking him down sooner. However, it could just as well be an example of one hand not knowing precisely what the other was doing. If the relationship between the general master and the master of Burton Lazars seems somewhat ill defined (certainly on the basis of surviving documentation) the English province appears to have been pulled together much more tightly by legally binding contracts and the need to report back continually to its Leicestershire headquarters. Constitutionally it could be that in the relationship between the centre and the periphery, the periphery had certain significant advantages.

It was accepted from the earliest days that the basic function of the English province was to support the activities of the order in the Holy Land, in other words to provide money for the upkeep of the Jerusalem and Acre hospitals and, latterly, to support an increasingly expensive military role. How was this fundamental goal achieved? The order in England drew finances from its landed endowment and the exercise of its papal privileges, and both of these areas must be considered in terms of the 'horizontal' movement of resources between England and the east. With regard to land, estates of varying size were administered from most of the English commanderies of the order. The largest, Burton Lazars, had a consolidated and ever-expanding *demesne* (domain) based on an area of prosperous arable and livestock farming (Figure 8). The *taxatio* (tax assessment) of 1291 valued this Leicestershire and Rutland estate at £46 10s 2d, including the proceeds of the appropriated rectory of Lowesby.[23] At Locko, the *taxatio* provides a more detailed account and we are able to calculate both the extent of the property administered from the commandery and the contribution sent overseas as an *apportum*. The commander there administered enclosed manors at Spondon and Locko, rented land, stock and a windmill. He was also responsible for the collection of assize rents and the management of a court. All of this brought in £5 6s 10d, much less than the Burton Lazars estate in terms of land. However, the commander of Locko probably also collected the

lucrative appropriated tithes of Spondon – valued at £33 6s 8d – and if
the temporalities and spiritualities of this estate are added together we
arrive at a grand total of £38 13s 6d, very close to the total income of
Burton Lazars, which may have been one of the reasons for Locko
retaining a measure of independence within the province, not to
mention any conditions which may have been set down by its probable
founder, William of Ferrers, earl of Derby.[24]

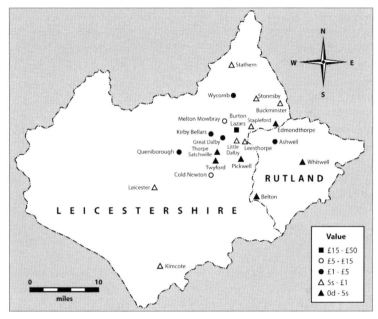

Figure 8 Map of Leicestershire and Rutland, showing estates of the Order of
St Lazarus with the values given in the *Valor Ecclesiasticus* of 1535

It is possible that the figures noted in the *taxatio* represent an
'underestimate' of the real income of both Burton Lazars and Locko,
and in the latter case there is independent evidence to support an
annual gross income, from both temporalities and spiritualities, in the
region of £80.[25] Out of this the commandery was probably capable of
yielding a net return of about £60 per annum in the thirteenth century,
once running costs were deducted. This fits well with a statement in
1347 that Locko owed an annual *apportum* of £20 to the principal house
of the order (at that time at Boigny in France).[26] In other words, about
a third of its net income was going overseas each year, a practice similar

to that followed by both the Templars and Hospitallers. If these
calculations are extended to the entire holdings of the order in the
southern province, as noted in the *taxatio*, temporalities come out at
£63 3s 6¾d and spiritualities at £70 6s 8d per annum.[27] Allowing for
underassessment, this might reflect a 'real' income of about £267 on
which an annual *apportum* of £66 may not have been an unreasonable
expectation – considerably more, perhaps, if the income of the northern
province, Scotland and miscellaneous receipts are also taken into
account. The English province could have been raising £100, or more,
per annum for the hospital at Acre during the prosperous years of the
thirteenth century, much of it coming from the valuable concentrations
of land and tithe around Burton Lazars and Locko. In the context of
the somewhat disparate European landholdings of the order this was a
considerable achievement, and it helps to explain why, after the fall of
Acre, England became the centre of a power struggle between English
and French factions within the order, each anxious to hang on to these
rich pickings.[28]

Income from landed estates, however, only provides a partial picture
of the resources the English province was capable of sending to the
Holy Land. Their papal privileges empowered the Lazarites to traffic in
indulgences and to solicit for alms, and nowhere is the income from
these sources, which may have been quite considerable, set down.[29] Some
of the properties of the order were deliberately selected to facilitate
alms-gathering from travellers and other casual visitors. At Westwade,
Norfolk, the order maintained a bridge chapel over the River Tiffey on
the road from Wymondham to Dereham. It was difficult for travellers
to pass by without making a contribution.[30] At Threckingham, Lincolnshire, a short-lived establishment grew up very close to the site of Stow
Green Fair, a major social and commercial centre in the county in the
thirteenth century.[31] More important than either of these, under a grant
from Pope Innocent III representatives of the order were allowed into
parish churches once a year to collect alms 'for the maintenance of the
standard of St Lazarus against the enemies of the Cross'.[32]

The effectiveness of these diverse methods of income generation,
certainly during the period of enthusiasm for the crusade in the thirteenth
century, is confirmed by a charter of John, patriarch of Jerusalem,
dated 1323. In it he paints a picture of representatives of the order
targeting almost any large gathering of clergy and laity: synods, courts,
markets, fairs – anything would do. There they exhorted local people to
contribute whatever they could – horses, weapons, jewellery and even

their own persons – to help fight the 'infidel', promising eternal life to those volunteers who had the misfortune to be killed or captured. In the same charter, interestingly, Patriarch John acknowledges that brothers of St Lazarus were not quite the same as others living under the Augustinian rule. Because of their continual comings and goings – administering their far-flung estates and soliciting for alms and contributions – he recites an indulgence to those 'diligently administering matters who will have carelessly omitted the divine office'.[33]

This neglect of the *opus Dei*, not to mention the potential drawing away of tithes and other contributions to the parish clergy, was not designed to endear the Lazarites to local bishops and secular clerks of all complexions. Though the order seems to have been held in high regard by the laity because of its heroic fight against the 'infidel', many of the clergy had a very different view. In 1265, when Pope Clement IV issued a comprehensive confirmation of the privileges of the order, he was obliged to rebuke its clerical detractors and in particular urge them to 'receive them kindly and treat them honourably' in their alms-gathering activities.[34] After 1271 the king weighed in with similar support of the order with a series of protections enrolled on the Patent Rolls but, by then, the heyday of income generation from such sources was drawing to a close and was certainly seriously damaged by the fall of Acre and the non-participation of the Lazarites in the crusade following that event.[35] The interests of the order were further impaired by the activities of impostors, competition from other institutions with similar privileges and their own internal rivalries – all taking place against the backdrop of a deteriorating economic profile in the early fourteenth century. The last royal protection for alms-gathering was noted on the Patent Rolls in 1356, and in the late Middle Ages the order was to devise other means of supplementing the income from its landed endowment.[36]

In the thirteenth century, these peripatetic brothers of St Lazarus must have travelled about the country in possession of quite considerable sums of money and sometimes, as might be expected, they came to grief, as did John Paris when he was robbed of £3 by Eustace and Laurence de Folville, notorious Leicestershire brigands, in 1332/3.[37] We must assume, however, that more often than not resources reached their target in the Holy Land either in kind or (before 1307) by exploiting the credit networks of the Templars with whom the order had a close association. Looked at on a map, the estates of the order seem to form a pair of straggling, extended lines through France and Germany towards Barletta which was an important port of embarkation for the Holy Land and which Rafaël Hyacinthe suggests may have been favoured by the Order of St Lazarus (Figure 9).[38] If such a long overland route was not desirable, the order also owned a tenement in King's Lynn, known as Lazar Hill, as early as 1271.[39] This was the only English seaport in which the Lazarites had a foothold before 1299 (when they obtained a base in London) and it was ideally situated for the distribution of resources from the east Midlands and East Anglian estates. However, the only hard evidence we have of transhipment comes in 1256 soon after the order had suffered one of its periodic military disasters at Ramla. In that year the general master, Milo, was in England and along with one William of Hereford was given free passage out of Dover by the king 'with their brothers, men, horses and equipment'.[40] This provides clear evidence of a recruiting drive in England led by no less a person than the general master himself. How common such initiatives were is impossible to say and we can only speculate as to the routes and mechanisms that took English resources to the Holy Land under more normal circumstances.

Figure 9   Map of Europe, showing estates of the Order of St Lazarus (marked as •) in relation to Barletta

The only recorded instance of a general master being in England raises the question of how common it was for the personnel of this international order to serve outside their native provinces. The best evidence we have here is prosopographical, though this is notoriously slippery in the thirteenth century, a transitional period for English surnames when Anglo-Norman nomenclature could be suggestive of origins on either side of the Channel. Indeed, many brothers of St Lazarus, named in charters, have no surnames at all and are simply described as John, Roger or William.[41] Where locative surnames do appear they suggest a recruitment based very firmly in the East Midlands where the estates of the order were strongest – for example, John of Horbling (Lincolnshire), Robert of Dalby (Leicestershire), Geoffrey of Chaddesden (Derbyshire) and Nicholas of Flore (Northamptonshire).[42] Many of these villages, indeed – Dalby and Chaddesden, for example – were places where the Lazarites owned lands or tithes, indicating that local boys were subjected to their influence from an early age. There are, however, one or two examples which may point to wider horizons. *Tirricus Alemannus* (master of Burton Lazars in 1235) was possibly German, and the thirteenth-century brother John *de Rotomago* has the Latinized form of Rouen as his surname.[43] In the early fourteenth century there is a cluster of masters of Burton Lazars whose surnames may also be French – Veau, Aumenyl and Michel, for example – and this may provide further evidence of the power struggle, noted previously, between English and French factions at about that time.[44]

The most interesting cases, however, are those brothers connected with the English province whose names appear to provide an overlap with individuals who became general masters – though, as we shall see, none provides clear-cut evidence of migration between England and the centre or vice versa. Walter *de Novo Castro* was master of Harehope in 1189 and later (late twelfth/early thirteenth century) master of Burton Lazars. A man of the same name appears as general master between 1228 and 1234.[45] The surname and connection with Harehope suggest he may have come from Newcastle-upon-Tyne, about thirty miles away from the Northumberland commandery. However, Barber believes him to have been a member of the aristocracy of the Latin kingdom, and certainly an *émigré* French family of the name of *Chastel Neuf* (Château-neuf) was well established there.[46] Was Walter an Englishman who ended up in the Holy Land with the top job or did he travel from Jerusalem to take up his first post in the cold wastes of the Cheviot Hills? We may, of course, be dealing here with two different people with the same name, especially since forty years (a long time by medieval standards) divides the mastership at Harehope and the general mastership of the order. However, it is just possible: Walter could have been master of Harehope in his twenties and general master in his sixties, though, if he was a leper, as the statutes suggest he should have been as general master, a long life may perhaps seem less likely. Yet there is no way we can be sure.

Similar uncertainty shrouds the case of Sir Richard of Sulegrave who occurs in a deed concerning King's Lynn dated 1271/2 and is described as 'master of the whole order of St Lazarus of Jerusalem'.[47] This sounds rather like the description of a general master and Sulegrave is more clearly English than *Novo Castro* since he takes his name from a village in Northamptonshire and there was no requirement at this date that the general master should be a leper. The theory is all the more compelling because Sulegrave fits neatly into a gap in the list of known general masters.[48] The problem in this case is that we are reliant for our information on a printed early nineteenth-century transcription of the charter, the original having defied all attempts to locate it. Another man, Sir Adam Veau, was master of Burton Lazars in 1308 and general master of the order in 1327.[49] Here we have a definite case of progression based, moreover, on a man with a very distinctive name. The difficulty is that 'Veau' could either be English or French, so it is impossible to say with certainty if Adam was a Frenchman who served for a while in England (which fits well with the theory of French 'infiltration' in the early fourteenth century) or an Englishman (possibly a member of the well-established Vaux family) who transferred to France. Similarly with John Paris, the brother of Locko robbed by the notorious Folvilles in 1332/3: is he the same man as John de Paris, general master in 1357, and, if so, is he, like Veau, English or French?[50] Ambiguity of surname origin lets us down once again. Thus, with regard to the interchange of personnel at the highest level, we are left with some non-proven cases. Veau at least makes it clear that such high-level interaction was possible, though the details of movement must remain hazy. With regard to the rank-and-file brothers of St Lazarus and most of the masters of Burton Lazars, local and regional recruitment appears to have been the dominant force. The balance of evidence, once more, suggests that the English province enjoyed a fair degree of independence and autonomy, though with the possibility of intervention from headquarters if the need arose.

So far this chapter has dwelt on the practicalities of horizontal mobility in terms of administrative procedures, personnel and the transfer of funds. However, the importation from the Holy Land which caused the most concern and helped to split the order apart in the fourteenth century was its ideology, which, as already stated, was unusual and also fundamentally flawed because of its ambiguity. The institution responsible for this ideology was a leper hospital at Jerusalem which, during the twelfth century, undoubtedly did sterling work for those suffering from this terrible disease. Indeed, it seems clear that its example stirred the likes of Roger of Mowbray to offer practical support. However, what exactly were they supporting? What did they expect to get for their money? Apart from the usual *quid pro quo* of prayers for the souls of founders and benefactors, there is evidence to suggest that Mowbray and others anticipated that the authorities in Jerusalem would offer support to lepers by establishing in England and elsewhere institutions which were the mirror image of the Jerusalem hospital – communities of leper brothers, healthy brothers and chaplains living together in quasi-monastic style. It seems that Burton Lazars itself was selected as the headquarters of the English province because, in terms of its topography, it represented an ideal spot for a leper hospital to be located.[51] However, the master in Jerusalem viewed things differently. What he was interested in was financial support for his own institution and the expanding military role that the order in the Holy Land was taking on. What was needed in this context was not so much leper hospitals – costly to run and manage – but commanderies, after the fashion of the Templars, to return a measure of their income to central funds.

Though there may have been leper brothers at Burton Lazars in the first years, this did not last long, and in 1184 William Burdet granted nearby Tilton Hospital to the 'infirm' (i.e. leprous) brothers of St Lazarus, a move which had the advantage of freeing up Burton Lazars to develop its preferred role as a money-raising commandery.[52] Though the Lazarites promised to conduct Tilton according to the rules of the house, by 1290 it was already being run down and was probably abandoned soon after.[53] No doubt the managers of the order cited the decline of leprosy and consequent reduction in the number of leper brothers as sufficient cause for this, but the abandonment of Tilton also had the effect of making available yet more resources for the other activities of the order. The Burdets, who had given the institution in good faith under clearly agreed terms, were not at all pleased with this and a series of bitter disputes centred around the two Leicestershire livings with which Tilton had been endowed, Gaulby and Lowesby. At Gaulby the quarrel was over the advowson (i.e. the right to name the holder of a church benefice), well-meaningly given to the order by Pope Alexander IV in

1255 because of reverses suffered in the crusade, but also claimed by the
Burdets.[54] At Lowesby the question of the advowson was also in dispute,
but the main bone of contention here was the appropriation of tithes by
the Lazarites. Riots broke out in the 1290s culminating in an act of
bloodshed perpetrated by Sir William Burdet in the churchyard causing
it to require reconsecration – an obligation which the surly Burdets had
still not carried out by 1311.[55]

This breakdown of relations between the Lazarites and the descendants of one of their principal English patrons was an unedifying
spectacle, yet it summed up the crisis of confidence which was beginning to surround the order by the late thirteenth century. With Acre in
the hands of the 'infidel' and leprosy in headlong retreat across Europe,
this was not quite the same order patronized by Mowbray, Ferrers and
the first Burdet, and the only way in which the Lazarites could attempt
to keep their supporters on board was by diversification of the services
they offered and an increasing exploitation of the powerful mythology
associated with the leper knights. The problem had begun because of
misconceptions surrounding the unusual and ill-defined aims and
objectives of the order and had become gradually worse because of the
military failures of the crusaders in the thirteenth century. An ideology
which had been uncritically accepted on the crest of a wave of enthusiasm in the twelfth century had, in time, worked as a canker at the very
heart of the Order of St Lazarus, breeding misunderstanding, resent-
ment and, finally, threatening to destroy the order altogether.

In the absence of much evidence to the contrary it must be assumed
that the Order of St Lazarus functioned reasonably efficiently in the
twelfth and thirteenth centuries as a machine to shift resources of money
and men from England to the Holy Land. However, the order was
significantly smaller and less well-off than the Templars and Hospitallers,
and its central administration may well have been much less clearly
defined, giving more authority to the periphery and less to the centre.
This would help to explain why things broke down so cataclysmically in
the fourteenth century. Lepers, land and loyalty were integral to that
collapse. Though fundamental to the 'image' of the order, leprosy was
in decline by 1300 and the degree of provision for lepers had always
been a controversial issue between the brothers in the east (where they
were integral) and those in the west (where they were not). When push
came to shove, the order's European landholdings, especially the wealthy
and consolidated estates in England, were the real prize at stake: coveted
by the general master because of their important contribution to central

funds and by the English Lazarites in anticipation of the reorganization and independence they might make possible. In all of this traditional loyalties were tested to the extreme and eventually to breaking point – not only the loyalty owed by the province to its general master, but also loyalties within the English province between the master of Burton Lazars and the descendants of some of the order's earliest patrons. Because of these deep fissures, the fall of Acre in 1291 effectively signalled the death of the Order of St Lazarus as an international force and the end of an age when its brothers tramped the highways of western Europe collecting up the gifts of the faithful for a noble and heroic cause.

Notes

[1] Kay Peter Jankrift, *Leprose als Streiter Gottes: Institutionalisierung und Organisation des Ordens vom Heiligen Lazarus von seinen Anfängen bis zum Jahr 1350* (Münster, 1996), pp. 102–11, 132–50.

[2] The best modern study of the order outside England is Rafaël Hyacinthe, *L'ordre de Saint-Lazare de Jérusalem au Moyen Âge* (Millau, 2003). For England see David Marcombe, *Leper Knights: The Order of St Lazarus of Jerusalem in England, c.1150–1544* (Woodbridge, 2003).

[3] Marcombe, *Leper Knights*, pp. 6–9; Malcolm Barber, 'The Order of St Lazarus and the Crusades', *The Catholic Historical Review*, 80 (1994), 439–56, here 450.

[4] Marcombe, *Leper Knights*, pp. 10–13. For the landed endowments in the Holy Land see Alexandre de Marsy (ed.), 'Fragment d'un cartulaire de l'ordre de Saint-Lazare en Terre Sainte', *Archives de l'Orient Latin*, 2 (1884), documents, 121–57.

[5] Bernard Hamilton, *The Leper King and his Heirs: Baldwin IV and the Crusader Kingdom of Jerusalem* (Cambridge, 2000), pp. 132–58.

[6] Marcombe, *Leper Knights*, pp. 13–15.

[7] Ibid., pp. 14–16.

[8] See, for example, Malcolm Barber, 'Lepers, Jews and Moslems: the plot to overthrow Christendom in 1321', *History*, 66 (1981), 1–17.

[9] Francis Blomefield, *History of Norfolk*, vol. 2 (1732; second edition London, 1805), pp. 504–5. There may have been an earlier grant of property in Scotland by David I. See Marcombe, *Leper Knights*, p. 34.

[10] Marcombe, *Leper Knights*, p. 35.

[11] Ibid., pp. 103–9.

[12] For a study of the patronage of the Order of St Lazarus, see John Walker, 'The patronage of the Templars and the order of St Lazarus in England in the twelfth and thirteenth centuries' (unpublished Ph.D. thesis, University of St Andrews, 1990); Marcombe, *Leper Knights*, pp. 45–6.

13 London, British Library (BL), Cotton MS, Nero C xii, fol. 249.
14 For example ibid., fol. 1a.
15 Marcombe, *Leper Knights*, pp. 19, 66–7.
16 BL, Cotton MS, Nero C xii, fol. 91; The National Archives of the UK: Public Record Office (TNA: PRO), Special Collections (SC) 8/302/15081.
17 TNA: PRO, SC 8/302/15081.
18 Marcombe, *Leper Knights*, p. 68.
19 Ibid., pp. 69–73.
20 Gloucestershire Record Office (GRO), Berkeley Castle Muniments, J7/67/ 02/001/00/00 (MF 1354).
21 Marcombe, *Leper Knights*, p. 70.
22 TNA: PRO, SC 8/54/2654; 8/219/10908; 8/163/8103.
23 Marcombe, *Leper Knights*, pp. 48–9, 55–7, 109–10, 203.
24 Thomas Astle, Samuel Ayscough and John Caley (eds), *Taxatio ecclesiastica Angliae et Walliae, auctoritate P. Nicholai IV, circa A.D. 1291* (London, 1802), pp. 246, 264.
25 Marcombe, *Leper Knights*, p. 105.
26 TNA: PRO, SC 8/210/10456.
27 Marcombe, *Leper Knights*, pp. 56, 203.
28 Ibid., pp. 75–7.
29 Ibid., pp. 175–86.
30 Blomefield, *History of Norfolk*, vol. 2, pp. 504–5. For an illustration of this institution see Marcombe, *Leper Knights*, p. 179.
31 Marcombe, *Leper Knights*, pp. 179–80.
32 *Calendar of the Patent Rolls Preserved in the Public Record Office, Prepared under the Superintendence of the Deputy Keeper of the Records* (London, 1891–1939) (*CPR*), *Edward I, 1281–1292*, p. 137.
33 GRO, Berkeley Castle Muniments, J7/67/02/002/00/00 (MF 1297).
34 Luigi Tomassetti et al. (eds), *Bullarium, diplomatum et privilegiorum sanctorum Romanorum pontificum Taurinensis editio*, vol. 3 (Turin, 1858), pp. 727–9.
35 *CPR, Henry III, 1266–1272*, p. 526; ibid., *Edward I, 1281–1292*, pp. 113, 137, 431; ibid., *Edward II, 1307–1313*, p. 344; ibid., *1313–1317*, pp. 1, 214, 394; ibid., *1317–1321*, pp. 131, 571; ibid., *1324–1327*, p. 126; ibid., *Edward III, 1327–1330*, pp. 238, 412; ibid., *1330–1334*, p. 242; ibid., *1345–1348*, p. 284; ibid., *1348–1350*, pp. 108, 203; ibid., *1354–1358*, p. 284.
36 *CPR, Edward III, 1354–1358*, p. 352.
37 William Henry Stevenson (ed.), *Report on the Manuscripts of Lord Middleton*, Historical Manuscripts Commission (London, 1911), p. 278.
38 Hyacinthe, *L'ordre de Saint-Lazare*, pp. 78–82.
39 Charles Parkin, *History of Norfolk*, vol. 8 (London, 1808), pp. 493–4; Elizabeth and Paul Rutledge, 'King's Lynn and Great Yarmouth: Two Thirteenth-Century Surveys', *Norfolk Archaeology*, 37, pt. 1 (1978), 92–114, here 94, 108; Dorothy Mary Owen, *The Making of King's Lynn* (Oxford, 1984), pp. 186–7.
40 *Close Rolls of the Reign of Henry III Preserved in the Public Record Office,*

Printed under the Superintendence of the Deputy Keeper of the Records (London, 1902–38), *1254–1256*, p. 419; the master is mentioned again but unnamed at *Close Rolls of the Reign of Henry III, 1256–1259*, p. 130.

[41] See, for example, TNA: PRO, King's Bench (*coram rege* rolls) 27/33 m. 7 which lists Osbert, Reyner, Geoffrey, John, William, Roger, Ralph and John (1277/8).

[42] Marcombe, *Leper Knights*, p. 73.

[43] Ibid.; for *Tirricus Alemannus* see *The Chartulary of St John of Pontefract*, ed. R. Holmes, vol. 1, Yorkshire Archaeological Society, Record Series, 25 (1899), pp. 199–200.

[44] Marcombe, *Leper Knights*, p. 253.

[45] Douglas Samuel Boutflower, *Fasti Dunelmenses* (Durham, 1926), p. 195; BL, Cotton MS, Nero C xii, fols 5, 67; Paris, Archives Nationales (AN), S 4841/B, doc. 16; Marsy, 'Fragment d'un cartulaire', nos 34, 35.

[46] Barber, 'The Order of St Lazarus and the Crusades', 443.

[47] Parkin, *History of Norfolk*, vol. 8, pp. 493–4.

[48] No general master is noted between Miles (1256) and Thomas de Sainville (1277). Marcombe, *Leper Knights*, p. 251.

[49] GRO, Berkeley Castle Muniments, J7/67/02/001/00/00 (MF 1354); AN, S 4884, doc. 9.

[50] Jankrift, *Leprose als Streiter Gottes*, p. 206; AN, S 4884, doc. 9.

[51] Marcombe, *Leper Knights*, pp. 35, 146.

[52] BL, Cotton MS, Nero C xii, fol. 203.

[53] *Calendar of the Close Rolls Preserved in the Public Record Office, Prepared under the Superintendence of the Deputy Keeper of the Records* (London, 1892–1963), *Edward III, 1343–1346*, p. 631; BL, Cotton MS, Nero C xii, fols 209–11.

[54] Charles Bourel de la Roncière et al. (eds), *Les Registres d'Alexandre IV* (Paris, 1902), p. 122 no. 404; Marcombe, *Leper Knights*, p. 200.

[55] Marcombe, *Leper Knights*, p. 202.

17

Internal Mobility in the Order of Avis (Twelfth to Fourteenth Centuries)

MARIA CRISTINA CUNHA

The reflections presented in this chapter are merely a small segment of a more extensive ongoing study on the Order of Saint Benedict (San Benito) of Avis from its beginnings around 1176 until the late fourteenth century. Recent research pertaining to Avis allows us a better understanding of the origins and development of the order and its property,[1] as well as its relationship with the Portuguese monarchy during this period.[2] Yet as a result of this research based on the order's documents, it has become apparent that in some aspects these documents have not been examined in a systematic fashion. One such aspect is the mobility of the members of the order: even though in the cartulary of Avis (now in the archive of Torre do Tombo)[3] there are only very few documents that refer explicitly to the brothers' mobility within and outside the country, this mobility must have had a much larger dimension than a superficial analysis of the documents would seem to suggest. Thus, if one takes the information available not only in the order's own documents, but also in the chronicles of the Portuguese kings and in royal and other charters, one finds a number of indirect references that indicate the presence of the master or the knights of Avis in different parts of the kingdom. These references seem to suggest three 'key' aspects pertaining to mobility in the Order of Avis: the order's relations with the Portuguese monarchy, the order's territorial expansion and the order's filial connection to the Order of Calatrava. It is to these 'key' aspects that we now turn.

The *militia* of the brothers of Évora – known as the Order (of Saint Benedict) of Avis from 1211, when Alfonso II donated a place named

Avis to the brothers, – was established between March 1175 and April 1176 in response to Almohad invasions and in light of the Templars' obvious inability to secure effectively a number of fortresses which had been entrusted to them by Alfonso Henriques (1137–85).[4] Whether or not he was a co-founder of the *militia* (it is not known whether the idea to found this *militia* came from the king himself or whether he only proposed the name of their first master), in early April 1176 Alfonso Henriques gave the brothers the castle of Coruche and some houses and vineyards in the old *alcázar* (fortress) of Évora, as well as some houses in Santarém.[5] The alleged reasons for these first donations on the part of Alfonso were *utilitatem christianis et defensionem regni* (the benefit to the Christians and the defence of the realm), which pointed to a future collaboration between the knights of Évora and the royal troops, especially when it came to the defence of castles on the Moorish frontier. It is possible that the knights of Évora were entrusted, in addition to the defence of Coruche, with garrisoning the castle of that same city. However, it was not until 1187 that the *militia* of Évora received the castles of Alcanede and Juromenha (once conquered), as well as the village of Alpedriz.[6] The holding of these places indicates that during the first years of its existence this monastic-military institution developed (in terms of its membership) sufficiently not only to secure the holding of these regions, but also to participate effectively in the *reconquista*. These responsibilities continued after the death of the first Portuguese king, which occurred in December 1185. As a compensation for services rendered, Sancho I (1185–1211) gave them the castle of Mafra.[7] At the same time, the knights collaborated with the king to repopulate the kingdom by granting charters to settlers (*forais*).[8]

During the reign of Alfonso II (1211–23), the prestige gained by the brothers of Évora was already so considerable that individuals made donations to them, and their holdings were so extensive that they generated sufficient income to enable the knights to purchase various properties.[9] It was Alfonso II who, in 1211, presented the *militia* with the location of Avis,[10] where a castle would be constructed and where the main convent of the order, which from then on would be known as the Order of Avis, took residence. As the order continued to serve the king at a military level,[11] Alfonso not only confirmed all former royal donations; he also granted them, in 1217, a charter of protection.[12]

It is not known what the position of the Order of Avis was during the conflicts which characterized the reign of Sancho II and which were the reason for his deposition. That does not mean that the order's military activities were abandoned, as can clearly be seen from the participation of the knights of Avis in the conquest of the Algarve in the middle of the thirteenth century and their participation alongside King Ferdinand III of Castile in the conquest of Seville in 1248.[13]

Once the *reconquista* of the Portuguese territories was completed, the Order of Avis continued to be actively involved in the defence of the realm, as well as in the construction and upkeep of various fortifications. At the same time, the monarchy tried to control the *militia*, more or less successfully. This royal attitude can be understood, on the one hand, as one of the measures of centralization which some kings from Alfonso II onwards were trying to enforce, and on the other hand, in a more 'international' sense, as with the establishment of a border between the kingdoms of Portugal and Castile. The presence and the mobility of brothers in territories which had been entrusted to them in regions bordering neighbouring kingdoms were clearly linked to their military activities. At the end of the thirteenth century, this presence became absolutely necessary. The chronicle of King Denis (*Diniz*) relates an incident which occurred in 1295 and which illustrates this point. After Denis had entered Castile through the marks of Ciudad Rodrigo and Ledesma,

> certain leaders and lords of Castile, among them Don Alfonso Pires de Gusmão, got together not only to attack King Denis, but also to enter [his territory]; as they entered with many people from Andalusia and its border region, many men and women from Portugal were killed and captured in this attack . . . When they encountered the master of Avis with as many people as he could muster, both sides engaged in a fierce battle in which many were killed and damage was done to both sides; but at the end the master was defeated because he had fewer troops and many of them had been killed and 900 captured . . .[14]

As one can see from what has just been related, Denis ensured that the order remained in his service, much as his royal predecessors had done. The motives expressed in the donation charters issued to the order during his reign show this clearly: *polo muito serviço* (for much service),[15] *en galardom do serviço que miz fez* (as a reward for service rendered to me),[16] *por muyto serviço que . . . a dicta ordim e convento fezestes a mim e aaqueles onde eu venho* (for much service that the said order and convent has rendered to me and those that were before me).[17] However, it was the royal involvement in the election of one of the order's masters (Garcia Perez) which caused some of the order's commanders to go to court. In 1311, the master who had been elected by the electoral commission of the 'thirteen' (*treze*) was not to the liking of all brothers, and those who suspected that they might lose their commanderies and benefices appealed to the king. The king guaranteed, together with the master, that the knights would keep the ranks and positions that they had held before, and permitted – thus breaking one of the stipulations in the rule of this military order – that any brother who felt that he had been wronged could now take his complaints directly to the king.[18]

The close relationship between the monarchy and the military order, while it was tainted by occasional confrontations of various natures and origins, can also be seen in the presence of the master (and probably of several knights) at the royal court and in his involvement in the general politics of the kingdom.[19] While, compared to other military orders, the order's presence at court and its participation in the kingdom's foreign policy may have been minimal and quite discreet, it must have existed nevertheless, because the order was linked to another military order whose headquarters were based in the kingdom of Castile. This phenomenon has been discussed elsewhere, namely in the context of the occupation of the Algarve by Alfonso III of Portugal in the middle of the thirteenth century:[20] in the conflict that took place between the Portuguese and the Castilian kings over the jurisdiction of the Algarve, the Order of Avis played a major role, as it accepted the donation of the castle of Albufeira both from Alfonso III of Portugal (in 1250)[21] and from Alfonso X of Castile (in 1257).[22] Thus the Order of Avis demonstrated that the solutions proposed to the Castilian monarchy were viable, consequently resolving what was, at the time, the key point of dispute in the diplomatic relations between the two kingdoms (that is, to whom the recently conquered kingdom of the Algarve should belong).

While its link to a Castilian military order could turn the Order of Avis into an essential factor for the relationship between the monarchs of both kingdoms, this link can apparently also explain the reduction in the order's diplomatic activities on behalf of the kings of Portugal. It is possible that the pro-Castilian sensitivity which is noticeable in the Order of Avis from its early days contributed to a climate of some royal distrust of the order. However, one cannot ignore the hypothesis that this same sensitivity may have actually enhanced the order's usefulness. The question of the Algarve has already been addressed. Another example, about one hundred years later, would be the participation of Gonçalo

Vaz, master of Avis, in a solemn embassy to Castile (in 1335) with the objective of asking Juan Manuel of Castile to give his daughter Constance in marriage to the son of the Portuguese king.[23]

With regard to the mobility of the members of the Order of Avis, it has to be emphasized that the relationship between the monarchy and the order must have especially contributed to the knights' mobility within the kingdom, even though there are only very few concrete examples, particularly after the end of the *reconquista*, to prove this. The end of the custom of listing witnesses and corroborators in the royal diplomas, as well as the very complex organization of the central administration which is evident for the entire duration of the fourteenth century (and is visible in the diplomatic language used for legal trans-actions), prevents us from asserting the presence of the masters of Avis or their representatives at court.

In light of the origin and development of the Order of Avis and its possessions, one can easily understand that its members must always have known some internal mobility: the donation of castles and places to the order by the first Portuguese kings as a result of the order's military involvement in the *reconquista* certainly required mobility on the part of the brothers. In fact, the defence of their possessions made it necessary for contingents of the order's knights to be present at various places, and for this purpose brothers had been sent from the central convent since the order's beginnings. On the other hand, the need to organize the possessions that the order was acquiring in the course of the thirteenth and fourteenth centuries (through royal and private donations as well as through purchase), led to the creation of com-manderies located from the north to the south of the country. The head of each of these territories was a commander who, according to the rule, had to be in residence.

Situated in areas that were very different geographically, the revenue of the commanderies varied greatly. Therefore, some of them probably appeared more attractive to the knights than others. This raises a question: could the commandery of Oriz, the only one situated north of the River Douro, for example, have served as a place of 'punishment' for those knights who had violated the rule or could it have been a springboard to other commanderies with larger revenue? It was the responsibility of each commander to see to the upkeep of the property under penalty of forfeiting his post, as well as to welcome any brother of the order when he passed by,[24] whether it was an official visit[25] or not. The mobility of the commanders within the territory of their actual commanderies, letting out certain properties to tenants and collecting various revenues, can be traced in documents which show them intervening on behalf of their order.[26] Following the order's rule, the commanders, at least once a year, had to travel to the order's central convent in order to participate in the general chapter. It is not known whether this annual obligation was always met. There are, however, some instances of commanders issuing legal documents together with the master in the convent of Avis,[27] probably because they had met there to resolve specific problems and not because they had been convened for the great meeting of the order. The highest frequency of attendance can be shown for those commanders whose commanderies were situated in close proximity to Avis (such as Benavila, Cabeço and Pedroso).[28] However, there were cases where the commanders of Albufeira or Oriz, to mention only the ones that are known to have resided the furthest away, were present when documents were drawn up in the chapter of the order by the scribe of the convent or the local notary.

Like the commanders, the master was occasionally absent from the convent in Avis. His presence at court and his military involvement on the frontier have already been mentioned. During times of stability, he probably travelled on circuit in the territory that belonged to the master's domain in order to resolve problems pertaining to the organization of these possessions (for example, in 1321, the master appeared as a grantor in three documents issued in different places).[29] In 1296, a problem of territorial boundaries had to be postponed because, according to the representatives of the order, it could only be decided in the presence of the master, who, at that point, was unable to appear in person.[30]

Those brothers of the order who were not of any particular rank or position were certainly mobile on some local level, however not always with positive results. Accordingly, the definitions (*definições*) issued in the middle of the fourteenth century provided for penalties to be applied to those who visited the convent of Avis in groups,[31] who talked to lay people or who abandoned their houses as fugitives.[32]

Above all, the mobility of the brothers of Avis was connected to the filial relationship of this military order to the Castilian order of Calatrava. That is at least the impression one gathers from the documents that have come down to us. At an unspecified date, but soon after the foundation of the *militia* of Évora (the immediate predecessor of the Order of Avis), this affiliation required visits from the master of Calatrava or one of his representatives to the Portuguese branch of the order, accompanied by a Cistercian abbot, to confirm the master (if an election had just taken place) and to check the lifestyle and spirituality of the Portuguese brothers as well as the correct management of their possessions.[33] With regard to the brothers of Avis, this affiliation not only allowed them to participate in the election of the Castilian master but also to attend the chapters convened by that master. Even though it is not known whether the master of Avis was ever present at the election of his Castilian superior, there is no doubt that, in 1342, João Rodrigues Pimentel was elected master of Avis in the presence of representatives of the master of Calatrava, in a meeting expressly assembled for this purpose, and that his election was afterwards confirmed by them.[34] Approximately one hundred years earlier, in 1238, the master of Calatrava, Don Martim, accompanied by the Cistercian abbot of Sotos Albos, had visited the convent of Avis where he confirmed Martim Fernandes, who had been elected earlier at an unknown date, as master of the Portuguese *militia*.[35]

There is evidence of further visits of brothers from Calatrava to the Portuguese convent: for example, Don Gomes (the master of Calatrava) was present in 1241 when an agreement was signed between the master of Avis and the commander of the Order of Santiago (Don Paio Peres Correia).[36] However, we only know of two trips that Portuguese knights took to the convent of the Order of Calatrava in the territory of Castile. These trips have to be seen in the context of the jurisdiction that Calatrava had over its Portuguese branch, and it is to them that we now turn. In May of 1346 in the chapter of Calatrava, João Rodrigues Gouveia (the former grand commander of Avis) and Rodrigo Aires (the former cellarer of Avis) presented to João Rodrigues (the master of Calatrava) complaints regarding the behaviour of the Portuguese master, Don João Rodrigues Pimentel, who had been elected four years earlier (see above). Accordingly, they requested that he (the master of Calatrava), 'like a father abbot of the house of Avis' (*como padre abad de la casa de Avis*), would come to visit and to correct (*visitar e correger*). Since the master of Calatrava was unable to travel to the Portuguese convent, he authorized his grand commander, Don Pero Estevez, to make the trip. Upon his return to Calatrava, the grand commander presented an account of his findings.[37] However, João Rodrigues Gouveia, who was also present in the chapter at Calatrava, said that he had been offended in the course of this visitation as brother João (the Portuguese master) had issued a verdict against him for rebellion and had excommunicated him in the presence of the grand commander (of Calatrava).[38] The former Portuguese commander (João Rodrigues Gouveia) justified his absence in the chapter of the convent of Avis, which had been gathered during the visit of the representatives of the master of Calatrava, by saying that while he was staying in Estremoz he had received a letter from Don Pero Estevez suggesting that he should not be present at the said visitation because he would not be able to correct the damage that he had done.[39] In light of this and other arguments, which were confirmed by the actual *visitator* (Pero Estevez), the master of Calatrava instructed the prior of his convent to lift the excommunication which had been imposed on the Portuguese brother at the chapter of Avis.

What is significant about this incident is the presence of Portuguese brothers in the Castilian order. The second appearance of João Rodrigues Gouveia in Calatrava had to do with his attempt to explain his attitude during the visitation, but the precise reasons for his first trip to Calatrava remain unknown. It is certain that there had been, within the Order of Avis, some complaints against the master, Don João Rodrigues Pimentel. This is confirmed by a document which informs us about some part of the chapter held in Avis in the presence of the *visitator* from Calatrava (Pero Estevez), which pertained to a question that had brought the commander of Cabeço de Vide (Fernão Rodrigues) and the master Rodrigues Pimentel into conflict.[40] The outcome of this confrontation, which reveals a certain internal instability in the Order of Avis, remains unknown, but we do know that the master remained in office and that the discontented brothers are not referred to in any subsequent documents of the *militia*.[41]

This being a unique case, it cannot be confirmed that the Portuguese brothers appealed to their Castilian superiors at other times. Since we are not aware of any other document in the archive of the Order of Avis that would allow us to make the case for a more or less frequent recourse to the mother-house (Calatrava), the confirmation of this hypothesis will have to wait until a systematic comparison of all the witnesses who appear in the documents of Calatrava with all the known brothers of Avis can provide concrete proof of this Portuguese presence in the Castilian convent.

In light of what has been said so far, it seems only logical that, since the Order of Avis was a religious institution of military character, the knights did leave the convent of Avis, or the houses that the order owned, to aid the king in fighting the Muslims (in the context of the *reconquista*) or to defend the borders of the kingdom – especially after

1249, the year the *reconquista* ended in the territory of Portugal. The extent of the brothers' mobility remains unknown and largely has to be guessed. It has, however, been possible to verify that the commanders were frequently mobile within the areas entrusted to them and that they did travel to the convent in Avis. They travelled when there were problems in the order or when they felt that they had been wronged, and then they turned to the king, as in 1311[42] and 1346,[43] or to the master of Calatrava (also in 1346, as shown previously).

With regard to the assigning of commanderies, which required the central convent to send out brothers, several questions remain. The existence of commanders in the internal organization of the Order of Avis since at least 1222[44] makes one wonder what criteria the master employed to distribute the different commanderies among the knights. For example, since these commanders could not have been novices, it would be interesting to know what role *ancienitas* may have played when it came to the administration of the order's various possessions. While the documents that have survived do not permit us to establish a *cursus honorum*, it is clear that some commanderies were more important than others, not only because of their revenue but also because of their location. Even though the distance between the central convent of Avis and the order's commanderies was not as great as it was for military orders with headquarters in Palestine, for a 'national' order the north of the country as well as the extreme south can be considered quite remote from the *militia*'s centre of decision-making. However, to what extent were commanders sent to a certain region because that region was their place of origin? Were commanderies that were located further away from the centre desirable or were brothers that were sent there being deliberately 'removed' from the centre?

Assuming that the knights we know about probably did not travel alone, but rather with a greater or smaller company of servants who also belonged to the order, our treatment of the mobility of the brothers of Avis turns out to be more sketchy than we would have desired: of the overall mobility, we are able to note only that of a few, and those few are either some of the more important knights or those whose mobility – for one reason or another – left a record on parchment.

(Translated from the Portuguese by Jochen Burgtorf)

Notes

1   Maria Cristina Almeida e Cunha, 'A Ordem Militar de Avis (das origens a 1329)' (unpublished MA thesis, Faculdade de Letras da Universidade do Porto, 1989).

2   Maria Cristina Cunha, 'A Ordem de Avis e a monarquia portuguesa até ao final do reinado de D. Dinis', *Revista da Faculdade de Letras – História*, second series, 12 (1995), 113–23.

3   The full name of this national archive is *Instituto dos Arquivos Nacionais, Torre do Tombo*. In subsequent notes, I will refer to it as T.T. For the documents contained in the *cartório* of Avis, see Maria Cristina Cunha, 'Chancelarias Particulares, Escrivães e Documentos: algumas notas a propósito da Ordem de Avis nos séc. XIII–XIV', in *As Ordens Militares em Portugal: Actas do 1o Encontro sobre Ordens Militares* (Palmela, 1991), pp. 181–9.

4   Rui de Azevedo, 'Primórdios da Ordem Militar de Évora', *Boletim da Junta Distrital de Évora*, 8 (1967), 45–62.

5   T.T., *Ordem de Avis*, no. 66, and *Gaveta* 4, m. 1, no. 17; published in E. Abiah Reuter, *Chancelarias Medievais Portuguesas*, vol. 1 (Coimbra, 1938), pp. 356–7, and Rui de Azevedo, *Documentos Medievais Portugueses*, vol. 1, part 1 (Lisbon, 1958), p. 427.

6   January 1187 (T.T., *Ordem de Avis*, no. 65, and *Gaveta* 4, m. 1, no. 22; published in Rui de Azevedo, Avelino Jesus da Costa and Marcelino Rodrigues Pereira (eds), *Documentos de D. Sancho I (1174–1211)*, vol. 1 (Coimbra, 1979), p. 29 no. 17.

7   1 May 1193 (T.T., *Ordem de Avis*, no. 64); published in Azevedo, *Documentos de D. Sancho I (1174–1211)*, vol. 1, pp. 101–2 no. 65.

8   On 25 April 1200, the master of Avis granted a charter to the settlers of Benavente: *Portugaliae monumenta historica a seculo octavo post Christum usque ad quintundecimum iussu Academiae Scientiarum Olisponensis edita: Leges* (Lisbon, 1867–88), pp. 512–14.

9   The documents that have survived do not allow us to reconstruct the process of the formation of the order's possessions (or patrimony) in detail. However, a papal bull of 17 May 1201 (*Religiosam vitam eligentibus*) confirmed to the Order of Calatrava, of which Avis was a filiation, the possessions located in Évora, Coruche, Benavente, Santarém, Lisboa, Mafra, Alcanede, Alpedriz, Oriz, Selva Escura and Panóias (T.T., *Ordem de Avis*, no. 2).

10   30 June 1211 (T.T., *Ordem de Avis*, no. 61).

11   According to António Brandão, *Crónica de D. Afonso II* (Porto, 1945), p. 218, the master of Avis, D. Fernando Eanes, defeated the Moors of Serpa and Moura in 1220.

12   23 September 1217 (T.T., *Ordem de Avis*, no. 68).

13   On 15 January 1248, Ferdinand III gave the Order of Avis the sum of 2,000 small *morabitinos*, on condition that it conquered Seville, with a promise to

convert this amount into farms and places of equivalent value (T.T., *Ordem de Avis*, no. 100); published in Aurea Javierre Mur, 'La Orden de Calatrava en Portugal', *Boletim de la Real Academia de la Historia*, 130 (1952), 323–76, here 371–4.

14 *Crónica de D. Dinis*, ed. Carlos da Silva Tarouca (Coimbra, 1947), chapter 8: *alguns capitães e senhores de Castela, dos quais era D. Afonso Pires de Gusmão, se ajuntaram, não para dar batalha a el-Rei D. Dinis, mas para entrar, como entraram com muitas gentes da Andaluzia e da sua frontaria, da qual entrada mataram e cativaram de Portugal muitos homens e mulheres . . . Ao encontro do qual saiu o Mestre de Avis, com as gentes que pôde, e houveram ambos dura peleja, em que houve muitas mortes e danos de ambas as partes, no fim da qual foi o mestre vencido por as menos gentes que tinha, e muitos dos seus foram mortos, e novecentos cativos.*

15 2 May 1297 (T.T., *Gaveta* 4, m. 1, no. 3, and *Chancelaria Dinis*, 1. 2, fols 135v–136).

16 22 November 1299 (T.T., *Ordem de Avis*, no. 82).

17 2 January 1305 (T.T., *Ordem de Avis*, no. 363, and *Chancelaria Dinis*, 1. 3, fol. 36v).

18 Maria Cristina Almeida e Cunha, 'A eleição do Mestre de Avis nos séculos XIII–XV', *Revista da Faculdade de Letras – História*, second series, 13 (1996), 103–122, here 107–8.

19 For example, on 8 December 1273 the master of Avis (Don Simão Soares) witnessed a donation charter of the king of Portugal; published in *Archivo Historico Portuguez*, 6 (1908), 231–2.

20 Maria Cristina Cunha and Maria Cristina Pimenta, 'Algumas considerações sobre as relações entre os monarcas castelhanos e a Ordem de Avis no século XIII', *Boletim do Arquivo Distrital do Porto*, 2 (1985), 47–57.

21 1 March 1250 (T.T., *Ordem de Avis*, nos 69 and 70).

22 8 May 1257 (T.T., *Ordem de Avis*, no. 110).

23 Manuel Francisco de Barros e Sousa Visconde de Santarém, *Quadro elementar das relações politicas e diplomaticas de Portugal com as diversas potencias do mundo*, vol. 1 (sec. XV) (Paris, 1842), p. 160, and Frei Bernardo de Brito, *Monarquia Lusitana* (Lisbon, 1985), pt. 7, book 8, chapter 1, p. 345.

24 According to the rule, the chapter would have determined who would visit the commanderies. The commanderies had to receive the *visitatores*, who were soon also moved around within the order.

25 The definitions (*definições*) promulgated on 4 March 1342 in Avis stipulate with regard to the *visitator* from Calatrava (the commander of Maqueda) that the brothers of the *militia* must always be well received in the houses of the order when they approached them (*bem recebudos nas casas da Ordem quando hi acaecerem*).

26 For example, the commander of Oriz was present in Cabeceiras de Basto on 5 April 1308 (T.T., *Ordem de Avis*, no. 296) and in Guimarães on 11 April 1308 (T.T., *Ordem de Avis*, no. 297).

[27] 18 April 1334 (T.T., *Ordem de Avis*, nos 428 and 484) and 21 April 1334 (T.T., *Ordem de Avis*, no. 492).

[28] 15 August 1349 (T.T., *Ordem de Avis*, no. 382), 4 June 1352 (T.T., *Ordem de Avis*, no. 705, fol. 1r–v), 27 December 1363 (T.T., *Ordem de Avis*, no. 572), 2 May 1376 (T.T., *Ordem de Avis*, no. 479).

[29] 18 June 1321 – Fronteira (T.T., *Ordem de Avis*, no. 281), 5 July 1321 – Veiros (T.T., *Mosteiro de S. Pedro de Arouca, Gaveta* 4, m. 5, no. 3), 1 November 1321 – Avis (T.T., *Ordem de Avis*, no. 321).

[30] 26 February 1296 (T.T., *Ordem de Avis*, no. 208).

[31] Derek W. Lomax, 'Algunos estatutos primitivos de la Orden de Calatrava', *Hispania*, 21 (1961), 483–93, here 493.

[32] Paragraph 18 of the definitions (*definições*) of 1342; published in Javierre Mur, 'La Orden de Calatrava en Portugal', 345.

[33] Miguel de Oliveira, 'A milícia de Évora e a Ordem de Calatrava', *Lusitania Sacra*, 1 (1956), 51–64, seems to suggest that the supremacy of Calatrava was only honorific, but presents acts of jurisdiction that show the authority of the Castilian master with regard to the *militia* and the brothers of Avis.

[34] 3 March 1342 (T.T., *Ordem de Avis*, no. 1001); published in Cunha, 'A eleição do Mestre de Avis', 103–22.

[35] 22 August 1238; published in *Bulario de la Orden de Calatrava* (Barcelona, 1981), fol. 69, and Javierre Mur, 'La Orden de Calatrava en Portugal', doc. 1.

[36] 14 October 1241 (T.T., *Ordem de Avis*, no. 116); published in Javierre Mur, 'La Orden de Calatrava en Portugal', doc. 2.

[37] T.T., *Ordem de Avis*, no. 388.

[38] Ibid.: *recibiera agravio en la dicha visitacion por una sentencia que dizia que diera don frey Johan . . . contra el en que lo judgara por rebelde e pusiera en el sentencia de escomunion presente el dicho comendador mayor*.

[39] Ibid.: *el non fuesse a la dicha visitacion ca el non poderia correger los agravios que le ficieram*.

[40] 9 June 1346 (T.T., *Ordem de Avis*, no. 387).

[41] On 7 November 1351, the master Don João Rodrigues Pimentel was dead and a new election was under way (T.T., *Ordem de Avis*, no. 536).

[42] Cunha, 'A eleição do Mestre de Avis', 107–8.

[43] It is known that before August of 1346, Master Don João Rodrigues Pimentel gave orders to strip the commander of Cabeço de Vide of the properties with which he had been entrusted. The commander appealed to the king, who ordered that the properties had to be returned to the commander, because they had not been confiscated in the proper form (the document is inserted in T.T., *Ordem de Avis*, no. 387).

[44] The first reference that we have for a commander in the Order of Avis (namely that of Coruche) dates from 1222 (T.T., *Ordem de Avis*, no. 174).

18

Conclusion

JOCHEN BURGTORF, ALAN FOREY
AND HELEN NICHOLSON

Some of the masters in the past have summoned and dispatched some of
our brothers in a disorderly fashion and without need.

Letter of the Hospitallers' central convent to Master William of
Villaret, 3 April 1296 (Delaville, *Cartulaire*, vol. 3, no. 4310)

The chapters of this volume have considered many aspects of the
subject of international mobility in the military religious orders, but
it is clear that this is only a starting-point. The majority of the chapters
here have dealt with the twelfth and thirteenth centuries, the period on
which the bulk of recent research has been centred. Some chapters go
down to the end of the fourteenth century, but only a few have considered the fifteenth century. This concentration of research does not
reflect the existing evidence: far more survives for the fifteenth century,
and rather more for the fourteenth century, than for the twelfth and
thirteenth. However, as the quantity of evidence increases, so does the
amount of work required to consolidate it and to draw conclusions. We
hope that the research published here will act as a spur to further work
on the later period. Most of the chapters focus on the Temple and
the Hospital; only one considers a military order based in the Iberian
peninsula. Mobility within the Spanish orders merits more extensive
examination.

There are obviously other themes which could be examined more
fully. The importance of language differences has been touched upon in

the chapters here, but there is scope for further investigation of the problems which were created by the mobility of brothers who would have had difficulty in communicating with those of other regions and tongues. This would have been particularly true of the situation at the headquarters of the Temple and the Hospital, as these orders drew members from all parts of western Christendom.

A comparison between the studies presented here reveals considerable variations between theory and practice as well as changes during the period. For example, although in theory there might have been a 'standard' level of responsion (usually cited by historians as one-third of income), in fact the level of responsion varied considerably. Furthermore, although in the twelfth and thirteenth centuries the primary function of the leading orders was the defence of the Holy Land, the local and regional studies here indicate that even before 1291 the majority of brothers in the military religious orders did not travel outside their home area. We may surmise that those receiving them into the order made a decision on whether a newly admitted brother would be more useful in the local area or on the military front in the east. Alternatively, despite the orders' stated expectation that brothers might be sent anywhere, some brothers may have demanded to be allowed to remain in their local area. If they had important family connections in the region it would have been difficult for the order to transfer them overseas without losing local patronage. But it is clear that a distinction in this context is to be made between various groups in an order. In the Temple sergeants were likely to spend their whole careers in western provinces. The majority of the Templars questioned in Cyprus in the early fourteenth century were knights, even though at that time in the order as a whole knights were heavily outnumbered by sergeants. Templar officials who travelled to or from the east for administrative purposes were also usually of considerable standing and likely to be knights. Although not all military orders had exactly the same distinctions of rank, the situation was probably similar in other orders, with those of lesser rank being more sedentary.

Yet the most sedentary members of military orders were probably not the brothers of any rank, but the sisters. All the military religious orders had female members, either as full sisters or at various levels of association, who would normally live segregated from the brothers. The lack of references to the movement of women would be understandable if the only reason for moving personnel was to move fighting men to the military front and to send brothers who could no longer fight into retirement away from the front. While women may have been involved in the care of the sick (although this role has been little explored for the military religious orders), their primary role in the military religious orders was prayer; they played no active military part. However, the studies in this volume have shown that military need was not the sole reason for movement: brothers were also moved within provinces to take up administrative posts. It appears that sisters did not have to move within provinces for administrative reasons. The differing situation of the various groups within an order is a subject for further research.

The studies here have referred to some of the means by which the orders controlled and directed mobility, such as the need for the master to obtain the permission of the convent before dispatching or summoning a brother, and the need for a brother to obtain a licence from the master before coming to the convent or leaving it. The extract from the letter of the Hospitallers' central convent to Master William of Villaret quoted at the beginning of this conclusion suggests that significant violations of the proper protocol with regard to the brothers' mobility did occur. Nevertheless, as many of the letters granting licence to travel survive from the fourteenth and fifteenth centuries, much more research can be done on this subject. It should also be asked whether mobility always fulfilled the intended objectives. The effectiveness of the summoning of provincial officials to headquarters and of the dispatch of visitors as a means of maintaining control within an order merits fuller consideration. Distance and the slowness of communications often meant that it was difficult for central authorities to ensure that their wishes were fully implemented. Prolonged absences of heads of provinces while visiting their orders' headquarters must also have had repercussions on provincial administration.

The problems of the practicalities of travel offer further scope for research. Articles in this volume have considered some of the logistical problems, but there is scope for fuller investigation. The modes and costs of transport require more consideration. Travel was also beset with dangers: it would be interesting to know whether the foundering of ships or the perils of land travel had any significant effect on the functioning of military orders. Yet another aspect relates to the use of space within the military orders' houses. How did individual houses of the military orders in the west lodge members of their own orders who were visiting from other houses? Did visiting brothers have to share the brothers' dormitory or were they assigned a separate room? Travelling brothers obviously brought to their hosts the expense of lodging and feeding them. How far was this a burden on individual houses in the west? Did travelling brothers also bring problems of discipline to the houses of their order where they lodged?

How far did brothers join a military religious order specifically in order to travel? It is difficult to point to certain instances, although John Malkaw is one example discussed here. Certainly some pilgrims went to the Holy Land partly out of curiosity and the desire to see new places. The evidence considered in this volume indicates that any brother who did join a military religious order hoping to travel might well be disappointed. At times of crisis on the military frontier the orders would be anxious to recruit as many suitable fighters as possible, but not all who came forward to fight would be suitable material.

As has been shown, however, the extent of mobility was not determined solely by the orders themselves. The ever-changing political constellations in Europe and the east – for example the relations between pope and emperor, between England and France as well as between western merchant cities and their eastern colonies – could serve as catalysts as well as hindrances for mobility. Some of the studies presented here suggest that the travel that occurred in the military religious orders needs to be interpreted in a much broader context: all these brothers were travelling 'on Christ's business', yet they were obviously conducting the business of others as well. This aspect of mobility could well be examined more fully from the surviving sources.

A related, but distinct, area for future research concerns the journeys of outsiders who had links with military orders, such as pilgrims, particularly in the west. The care which pilgrims received in the Holy Land from some orders has received much scholarly attention, but the military orders' activities in relation to pilgrims and other travellers in the west has been largely overlooked. Another related but distinct area for consideration is the question of national interests within the orders. The studies in this volume highlight that at different periods different national interests predominated at the orders' central headquarters. Originally founded by merchants from the Italian city of Amalfi, from the late twelfth to the fourteenth century the Hospital of St John was dominated by the French; in the fifteenth century and later it was dominated by the Spanish. From the 1530s Italian influence again became important. Historians of the Hospitallers have tended to assume that because the French were predominant in the order's central convents in the thirteenth century they were also predominant in the twelfth, but in fact this was not the case; nor was it the case for the Templars. Careful distinctions must be made between the centre and the very diverse periphery, and further prosopographical studies – especially for the orders' provinces – are needed to obtain a more complete picture with regard to the various national interests prevalent in the orders at different times.

The studies in this volume do not conclude research in the area of international mobility within the military religious orders, but – we hope – will serve to open it up and reveal possibilities for future research. Although not all of the orders considered here survived beyond the fifteenth century, many of the themes here could be profitably considered for the later history of the military religious orders, into the Counter-Reformation and beyond.

Indices

Key to Indices

Av. = Order of Avis
cast. = castellan
com. = commander
drap. = *drapier*
gr. = grand
H = Hospitaller
Laz. = Order of St Lazarus

m. = master (or grand master)
mar. = marshal
T = Templar
TK = Teutonic Order
turc. = *turcopolier*
vis. = visitor

Index of Subjects

Index of Places

Index of Persons

Montreal du Bar (Frà Moriale), Provençal
condotierre; H prior of Hungary 145–6
Niccolò Debaro, H prior of St Catherine's 53
Nicholas, H chaplain; representative of the
prior of Hungary 149
Nicholas IV, pope 13, 105
Nicholas V, pope 40–2
Nicholas Böckler, Dominican inquisitor 77
Nicholas of Dover, Laz. m. 177
Nicholas of Flore, Laz. 183
Nicholas of Hales, H 97
Nicholas Lorgne, H mar.; gr. com. 22
Nicholas of Montecucco (*Nicola
Lombardus*), T 103, 109
Nicholas *Peccia* (de Peche), T 100
Nicole de Giresme, H prior of France 50, 56
Nigel of Amundeville, patron of Laz. 175

O., H gr. com. 21
O. of Vend., T gr. com. 21
Odo, T gr. com. 21
Ogerius, H gr. com. 21
Onofrio Solanes, H 51, 57
Orsini (Ursini), H m. 43, 52
Osbert, Laz. 189
Otto of St George, T 103
Otto of Wittelsbach, Bavarian noble 104

P., H proctor of Hungary 142
Paio Peres Correia, com. of the Order of
Santiago 196
Paul II, pope 42–3
Pere Despomer, H prior of Catalonia 156
Pere de Vilafranca, H prior of Catalonia 156
Pero Estevez, com. of the Order of
Calatrava; vis. of Av. 196–7
Perseus, mythological hero 133
Peter, H com. of Sopron 148
Peter I, king of Cyprus I 90
Peter III, king of Aragon 106–7
Peter *Aicardi*, T 116
Peter Astruc, T 116
Peter of Beaune, H mar. 22
Peter *Boneti*, T 128
Peter *Cadelli* of *Castro Gyra*, T 103
Peter of Camphaet, T com. of Alfambra,
Villel, Gardeny, St Eulalie, Pézenas,
Espalion 122–3
Peter of *Castillon*, T 72
Peter *de Castronovo*, T 115
Peter *de Claustro*, T 135
Peter *de Conders*, T 136
Peter *de Deo*, T com. of St Gilles, Horta, Miravet,
Zaragoza, Toulouse 120, 123, 127
Peter Ferendi, H com. (vis. of England) 90
Peter *de Gavaretto*, T com. of Gimbrède,
Montsaunès, Bordères, Toulouse 123–4

Peter of Hagham, H hospitaller 12, 23
Peter Holt, H prior of Ireland; turc. 90
Peter of Limoges, T 138
Peter of Madic, T m. of Auvergne-Limousin
137, 140–1
Peter of Malon, T com. of Peyrens,
St Gilles, Mas-Deu 123
Peter of *Manaia/Mone(t)a*, T gr. com. 21
Peter of Mirmande, cast. of Krak des
Chevaliers; H gr. com. 22, 29, 32–3
Peter *de Mosterio*, T 116
Peter of Noblat, T 132, 136, 139
Peter of St Just, T com. of Corbins 66–7, 73
Peter of St Roman, T gr. com. 21
Peter of St Tiberias, T sub-com. of St Gilles 127
Peter of Sevrey, T mar. 20, 22
Peter of Sombrun, T com. of Montsaunès,
Bordères, Argenteins 123
Peter of Thous, T vice-m. Aragon 68, 73
Peter *de Tolosa*, T com. of Toulouse 115
Peter of Vares, T gr. com. 21
Peter (I) of Vieillebride, H gr. com. 22
Peter Visianus, T com. of the ship *St Anna* 108
Peter *Ymberthus*, H official at Szirák,
Szomolya, Tolmács 154
Philibert de Naillac, H m. 57, 157–9, 162
Philip IV, king of France 12
Philip, count of Alsace 28
Philip, duke of Burgundy 42
Philip Ewyas, H 93
Philip de Thame, H prior of England 92–3, 98
Philippe de Mézières, 14th-/15th-c. French
crusader and author 156
Pierre (*Peyre*) Cornuti, H prior of Hungary
145, 152
Pierre d'Aubusson, H ambassador 42, 57
Pierre Furoni, H com. of Trinquetaille 152
Pierre Lamand, H proctor general 39–41
Pietro de Gragnana, H com. (in Hungary) 144
Pius II, pope 42
Pons, H mar. 22
Pons Blan, H gr. com. 21
Pons of Cuers, H com. of Orange, Beaulieu 26
Pons of Fay, H com. of Hungary 143–4
Pons of Gusans, T turc. 11, 20
Pons *Rufus*, T 116, 125

R. (or B.), H proctor Hungary 142–3
Rafel Saplana, H bailiff of Athens,
Negroponte, Rhodes; drap.; prior of
Catalonia 161–2, 165
Raimbald, H mar. 17, 22
Raimbald (II) of Caromb, T gr. com. 17, 21
Raimund Motet, H gr. com. 22
Rainald of Vichiers, T com. of the palace at
Acre; m. of France; mar.; m. 22, 118
Ralph, Laz. 189